National Statecraft and European Integration

National Statecraft and European Integration

The Conservative Government and the European Union,
1979–1997

Jim Buller

PINTER

London and New York

Pinter
A Continuum Imprint
Wellington House, 125 Strand, London WC2R 0BB
370 Lexington Avenue, New York, NY 10017–6503

First published 2000

British Library Cataloguing in Publication Data

A catalogue record for this book is available from the British Library.

ISBN 1–85567–588–9 (hardback)

Library of Congress Cataloging-in-Publication Data

Buller Jim.
    National statecraft and European integration: the conservative government and the European Union, 1979–97 / Jim Buller.
      p. cm.
    Includes bibliographical references and index.
    ISBN 1–85567–588–9 (hardback)
    1. European Union–Great Britain. 2. Conservative Party (Great Britain) 3. Great Britain–Politics and government–1979-1997. I. Title.

HC240.25.G7 B85 2000
337.1'42–dc21
                                      00-021790

Typeset by YH*t*, London
Printed and bound in Great Britain by The Cromwell Press, Trowbridge

Contents LIBRARY SERVICES

Abbreviations   vi

Acknowledgements   viii

1   The Europeanization of British Policy: A Statecraft Approach   1

2   Domestic Economic Problems and External Market Solutions: Britain's Relations with the European Union in Historical Perspective   22

3   Resurrecting the Old Autonomy Code: 'Monetarism in One Country' and the Challenge of International Economic Forces   48

4   The Europeanization of Conservative Statecraft   68

5   The Negotiation of the Single European Act: Institutional Legacies and the Problem of Foreign Policy Implementation   88

6   European Integration and the Challenge to Conservative Statecraft   119

7   Falling Apart over the 'Heart of Europe': Euro-scepticism and the Electoral Decline of the Conservative Party   140

8   Conclusions   165

Bibliography   173

Index   185

Abbreviations

BL	British Leyland
CAP	Common Agricultural Policy
CBI	Confederation of British Industry
CFSP	Common Foreign and Security Policy
COLA	Cabinet Office Legal Advisers
DEA	Department of Economic Affairs
ECB	European Central Bank
ECJ	European Court of Justice
ECOFIN	Council of Economic and Finance Ministers
ECU	European Currency Unit
EDC	Economic Development Council
EMS	European Monetary System
EMU	Economic and Monetary Union
EPC	European Political Cooperation
ERM	Exchange Rate Mechanism
ETUC	European Trade Union Confederation
EU	European Union
GATT	General Agreement on Tariffs and Trade

GDP	Gross Domestic Product
HMG	Her Majesty's Government
IGC	Intergovernmental Conference
IoD	Institute of Directors
IRC	Industrial Reorganisation Council
JHA	Justice and Home Affairs
MAFF	Ministry of Agriculture, Fisheries and Food
MEP	Member of the European Parliament
MTFS	Medium Term Financial Strategy
NATO	North Atlantic Treaty Organization
NEB	National Enterprise Board
NEC	National Executive Committee
NEDC	National Economic Development Council
NIRC	National Industrial Relations Court
OPEC	Organization of Petroleum Exporting Countries
OSA	Overseas Sterling Area
PAD	Political Actor Designation
PSBR	Public Sector Borrowing Requirement
SEA	Single European Act
SNP	Scottish National Party
TEU	Treaty on European Union
TUC	Trades Union Congress
UK REP	UK Permanent Representative
UNICE	Union des Confederations de l'Industrie et des Employeurs d'Europe
WEU	Western European Union

Acknowledgements

A number of academic and personal debts have been incurred in the writing of this book. Special thanks must go to Martin Smith and Andrew Gamble. They supervised my PhD at Sheffield, out of which this book emerged, and continued to give important advice and support long after the thesis was finished. Stephen George, Rod Rhodes, Michael Smith and Dave Marsh also provided valuable insights on earlier drafts. Indeed, Dave's comments were memorably (characteristically?) covered in dirt after being dropped all over the floor at a Bristol Rovers game.

It would be impossible to finish a book like this without mentioning the importance of Jim Bulpitt. Jim was a source of inspiration in a number of ways. The influence of his work on the arguments that follow is, of course, self-evident. Less obvious perhaps is the imprint of his personality and style. In applying his theoretical approach, I have tried, above all, to say *something different* about the subject of Britain's relations with the European Union. Unfortunately, I will never know if Jim would have approved. What I do know is that I will miss him greatly – more, I suspect, than he would have realized.

Most importantly, I would like to thank my family. Without their constant and unquestioning support, this book would never have been started, let alone completed. They have suffered years of neglect, despaired endlessly about the prospects of me getting a 'proper job', yet never wavered in their loyalty. Finally, a massive thank you must go out to all the friends, both within and beyond university life, who have kept me going throughout this project. There are too many to list individually. They know who they are.

To Lucy

CHAPTER ONE

The Europeanization of British Policy: A Statecraft Approach

This book is concerned with the policy of successive Conservative govern-ments towards the European Union in the 1980s and the 1990s.[1] During this period, it has been popular to view Britain as an 'awkward' or 'semi-detached' partner, consistently 'out on a limb' within this regional organization because of its 'offshore' mentality (see, for example, Radice 1992; George 1992, 1994; H. Wallace 1996, 1997; Denman 1996). Some debate has taken place in the literature concerning the precise definition of 'awkwardness' and the analytical focus of those concerned with exploring this phenomenon (see Buller 1995; George 1995; Wilks 1996). Consequently, it was suggested that the term referred to Britain's persistently clumsy negotiating style in relation to its EU partners. British policy-makers were difficult to deal with because they found it hard to accept the EU's methods of doing business. These practices included the acceptance of 'linkages' between different policy issues and the construc-tion of alliances or coalitions around policy packages. Cooperation, concession and compromise were not words in the lexicon of British negotiators. Instead, obstructionism and bloody-mindedness was the order of the day. There seemed no better epitaph to Conservative policy towards the EU at this time than the often mentioned power and influence of Mrs Thatcher's (in)famous 'handbag'.

However, during this period, it became increasingly clear that a gap existed between this negotiating style and the substance of policy. Despite such 'awkward' diplomacy, Conservative leaders signed two major amendments to the Treaty of Rome and were negotiating a third before they left office in 1997. At the day-to-day level, they accepted and implemented the vast majority of EU legislation which resulted from these agreements. Of course, there were exceptions, most notably the opt-outs on the Single Currency and the Social Chapter. However, as we shall see in Chapter 7, reservations existed concerning whether these *legal* exemptions could 'protect' British business

1

from the *economic* consequences of these policies being followed elsewhere in the EU. Put in different terms, eighteen years of Conservative rule had witnessed the gradual 'Europeanization' of British policy, especially in the area of economic management. The main preoccupation of this book is to explain this process and, more particularly, to delineate the contribution that Conservative Party leaders have made to encouraging or hindering it.[2]

Before beginning, it is essential to clarify what we mean by Europeanization. On the one hand, the term has been used to describe an external process, which has impacted relatively autonomously on British politics. In a recent discussion, Bulmer and Burch (1998) have unpacked Europeanization and, have highlighted two areas where its imprint can be witnessed in Whitehall. The first concerns the content of public policy, perhaps the most manifest example of this trend. Of course, the impact of Europeanization is not uniform: some policy areas are more 'Europeanized' than others. For example, in the area of trade policy, Articles 110–116 of the EEC Treaty endow the Union with exclusive competence to conduct external trade relations on behalf of member states. Moreover, the Council of Ministers remain closely involved in the process. The influence of French negotiators on the Union's response to the GATT talks in the early 1990s is testimony to this fact (Dinan 1994: 437–51). However, it is the Commission which is responsible for presenting and defending an agreed line in negotiations with third countries, as the recent trade disputes with the USA have shown. Conversely, in the area of foreign and defence policy, the impact of Europeanization has been less as member states have traditionally been unwilling to cede sovereignty on issues perceived to be crucial to the national interest. Increasingly, some progress seems to have been made in this area in the 1990s. Indeed, the present Blair government is presently leading the way with proposals to fold the Western European Union into the EU. In a similar vein, it has suggested that all member states adopt EU-wide EMU style convergence criteria in an effort to encourage defence consolidation (*The Times* 21 October 1998; *Financial Times* 10 March 1999; 13 May 1999; Buller 2000b).

Second, Bulmer and Burch highlight the impact of European integration on Britain's domestic institutions. Here the definition of institutions must be clarified, as institutional analysis has become a real growth area in the social sciences in recent years (for example, see March and Olson 1989; Steinmo *et al.* 1992; Rhodes 1995; Hall and Taylor 1996). According to 'New Institutionalism', analysis of institutions encompasses more than dry, old constitutional studies of the various organs of the state under review. Instead, this approach has increasingly called for the study of: 'informal procedures, routines, norms and conventions embedded in the organizational structure of the polity or political economy' (Hall and Taylor 1996: 938). Similarly, Bulmer and Burch provide a fourfold classification of institutions, stretching from the formal institutional structure of a polity, its processes and procedures, the codes and guidelines underpinning those processes, through to the cultural context of decision-making (Bulmer and Burch 1998: 604; see also George 1995: 45–6).

If Europeanization has increasingly affected British policy in significant, yet variable, ways, Bulmer and Burch are clear that this process has not affected the formal machinery of government in Whitehall. This is not to deny that there has been no institutional change at all. A European Secretariat was created within the Cabinet Office to cope with the task of greater policy coordination across Whitehall (Edwards 1992: 76–7). This change included the setting up of a team of Cabinet Office Legal Advisers (COLA) to counsel on all legal aspects of membership as they developed. Moreover, ministers established UK Permanent Representative (UK REP), a cadre of Brussels-based officials to provide the government with a more direct presence in, and better source of, information about EU affairs. That said, as Bulmer and Burch have argued, the overwhelming majority of European business has been absorbed into the Whitehall machinery with little institutional change or disruption. The early dismissal of proposals for a Minister for Europe after membership was achieved provides a nice illustration of this point (Bulmer and Burch 1998: 612).

If Europeanization represents an external process, which impacts on the British Polity, the role of domestic politics in understanding this phenomenon remains unclear (Jordan 1999). In this context, the paradox that emerges from Bulmer and Burch's discussion is the apparent dissonance between the stasis of Britain's formal institutional set-up and the changing nature of policy that is emanating from it. This problem is heightened if we consider some of the more general literature on Britain's relations with the EU. A common theme of this work is the assertion that Whitehall's adjustment to the process of European integration has been hindered by the legacy of Britain's evolutionary and unbroken constitutional development over the past three centuries (Bulmer 1992: 28; Armstrong and Bulmer 1996: 254). As a result, a more cooperative approach has been frustrated by at least three factors: a continued attachment to the myth of national sovereignty (W. Wallace 1986: 380); the persistence of an adversarial political culture at Westminster (Ashford 1992: 119); and long-standing divisions within the two main political parties over the European issue (Ashford 1992: 120; H. Wallace 1996). It would be foolish to deny the general validity of these arguments. However, if they are taken at face value, it would be difficult to see how the Europeanization of British policy could have taken place at all.

It should be noted that a more complex theoretical discussion of the relationship between domestic institutions and policy outcomes is contained in the work of Armstrong and Bulmer (1996). These two authors are clear that institutions merely shape policy outcomes in a variety of ways. More particularly, the authors identify two 'routes' down which policy can be channelled. 'Route One' refers to EU policy matters which quickly and publicly enter the parliamentary arena for debate and can be 'vetoed' by substantial or symbolic concerns about sovereignty. 'Route Two' applies to policy conducted in informal and relatively closed groups or networks. These proposals are vulnerable to the possibility of veto by interest groups or other parties with specialist resources or sanctions (Armstrong and Bulmer 1996: 262–3). Although this account demonstrates that institutions may provide varied policy outcomes, the discussion of veto points still implies an institutional bias against change. In short, then, more attention needs to be given to understanding the domestic sources of Europeanization. We need to explore in more detail whether this process of policy change might be partly explained by the goals and strategies of domestic actors working within these institutions.

In the context of the discussion above, this book is driven by a number of more specific empirical questions concerning the policy of successive Conservative governments towards the EU. These can be stated as follows:

- Why, in signing the Single European Act (SEA), were the Conservatives content to give away partial control over many aspects of supply-side policy, by agreeing to the inclusion of qualified majority voting in the Council of Ministers on issues pertaining to the completion of the Single Market? This measure raised the future prospect that ministers might be outvoted on a number of issues, including: the abolition of frontier controls; the harmonization of technical standards covering EU goods and services; the removal of any existing state aids to industry; and the opening up of public procurement procedures. It should be added that the SEA also provided for an extension of the European Parliament's 'cooperation procedure' in this area. This gave MEPs the right to a 'second reading' of all the Commission's legislative proposals on a restricted number of subjects.

- Second, in 'shadowing' the Deutschmark and then joining the Exchange Rate Mechanism in 1990, why was the Conservative government content to place further external constraints on its conduct of economic management? Indeed, why after the disaster of 'Black Wednesday' did the Major government ratify the Treaty on European Union (TEU), including a commitment to complete Stages One and Two of the Single Currency? Moreover, why was the Conservative leadership not willing to rule out membership of the 'first wave' in 1999?

- Third, why did the Conservatives accept the increased Europeanization of economic policy when the merits of the ideas behind this process were largely hypothetical and essentially contested? As we shall see throughout the book, the economic case for joining and strengthening membership of the EU is something that has divided academics and policy-makers alike. Just as one could find 'experts' who argued that the completion of the

Single Market and entry into the ERM would lead to low and stable inflation, increased investment opportunities, growth and jobs, plausible arguments could be found to counter these conclusions. The question remains: if policy 'wonks' were so split over their prognostications, why did Conservative leaders accept the advice of some over others? Whatever the answer, one point seems clear: we need to consider more than the role of advisers and the 'objective' quality of their ideas when it comes to understanding policy outcomes.

- Fourth, how did the Conservatives attempt to implement their objectives at the EU level during this period? What constraints and opportunities did they face? Bearing in mind Britain's 'bloody-minded' diplomacy over the issue of EU budgetary contributions, how can we explain the apparent success of British negotiators in ensuring that the Single Market project was placed at the heart of the SEA, especially when, as we shall see, other member states were preoccupied with suggestions for institutional reform? Moreover, how can we account for the rapid decline of that apparent influence in the late 1980s?

- Finally, why did the Conservative Party, electorally one of the most successful political parties in the twentieth century, eventually tear itself apart over the European question? At the start of the 1990s, Major and his advisers could plausibly argue that the Maastricht Treaty represented the 'high water mark' of the 'integrationist tide'. As Chapter 7 shows, during the Maastricht negotiations, the British team replaced the phrase 'federal vocation' with 'ever closer union among the peoples of Europe'. In addition, the concept of subsidiarity was explicitly inserted into the main body of EU law for the first time. It was true that EMU remained a persistent and unsettling prospect for British policy-makers. However, it is important to remember that the process had been plagued by constant uncertainty. A year after 'Black Wednesday', the ERM collapsed altogether, only to be resurrected by widening the fluctuation bands from 2.5 to 15 per cent. At the same time, repeated doubts existed concerning whether certain member states would meet the convergence criteria by 1999. And, of course, Britain had an opt-out from the whole project should it develop in ways not welcomed by Whitehall. While Euro-sceptical concerns were understandable, it is difficult to explain why they eventually brought the Conservative Party down on this issue.

In the light of these questions, the theoretical approach to be adopted is Statecraft. A fuller justification for what some might consider to be an old-fashioned choice will be detailed below. However, two initial points are worth making. While Statecraft has been adapted to apply to the study of British foreign policy, it gives analytical priority to the domestic level. More particularly, it has been concerned with the role of party leaders and how they manage the linkage between the national and international levels (Bulpitt 1988: 182). For a book concerned in part to investigate the Conservative Party's response to Europeanization, Statecraft would appear to be theoretically relevant to this subject matter. At the same time, to this author's knowledge, Bulpitt's work has never been explicitly applied to a detailed study of Britain's relations with the EU. There is the added possibility that this approach might throw up fresh insights into this topic, thus generating new lines of inquiry.

These comments aside, Statecraft has three principle advantages for our examination of the Europeanization of British economic policy. First, it is sensitive to a number of theoretical issues involved in confronting this broad analytical focus. Second, when it comes to exploring the domestic sources of Europeanization, Statecraft provides a rich and sophisticated account of the interests of one particular group highlighted above: the Conservative Party in office. This issue is the main concern of the first half of the book. Finally, Statecraft is underpinned by an ontological position which allows it to examine how the Conservatives appeared to lose control of the EU policy-making process, with such disastrous consequences for the party in the 1990s. This subject provides the principle focus of the second half of the book. Before we discuss these advantages in more depth, a working definition of Statecraft is required.

The Statecraft perspective is most explicitly associated with the work of Jim Bulpitt (see, for example, Bulpitt 1982, 1983, 1986, 1988, 1995). As already noted, Bulpitt gave analytical priority to the study of how party leaders in Britain govern over time. More specifically, Bulpitt was preoccupied with the behaviour of what he called 'the Court': 'the formal Chief Executive plus his/her political friends and advisers' (Bulpitt 1995: 518). According to this approach, this elite group will possess three things when practising statecraft. The first is a set of governing objectives. These will include the achievement of a necessary degree of governing competence to ensure the party wins the next general election (Bulpitt 1986: 21). The second is a governing code containing a reasonably coherent set of principles, methods and practices through which these objectives would be realized. Finally, the Court will operate a set of 'political support mechanisms' designed to facilitate polity management and assist the governing code. These will include such functions as party management and the achievement of Political Argument Hegemony (see also Bulpitt 1995: 520).

1.   Perhaps the first advantage of Statecraft is its appreciation of some of the theoretical issues involved in researching a subject with a broad analytical focus. Bulpitt's main concern throughout his career was to provide a macro-picture of the way the British Polity operated over time. One immediate problem was that this type of analysis required a little knowledge about a lot. At the same time, it demanded some conception of how the various parts of

this system were related and how these relations changed over time. When it is remembered that macro-analysis also necessitated that attention be paid to the external dimension, the need for theoretical parsimony became self-evident. In this context, the Court seemed a reasonable focus for the analysis, if only because it sat at the intersection between foreign and domestic policy. To put the point more strongly, such a top-down perspective was the only way of constructing a macro-picture. Bottom-up approaches appeared to generate an unmanageable mass of complex and contradictory material (Bulpitt 1995: 511–12, 515). Although this study is not concerned with fully fledged macro-analysis, these arguments were deemed relevant to the wide analytical terrain of this book.

However, there is more to Bulpitt's preoccupation with the Court than mere methodological convenience. His choice of the Court reflected a concern with a more fundamental question facing the practice of all social science. This has been termed the problem of 'political actor designation' and refers to the issue of who or what is to be prioritized when it comes to making sense of the empirical material under consideration. As Frey (1985) has argued, choosing the individual, group or class that is to be the principle object of study is a key choice facing all analysts, yet it is a decision which is rarely given explicit consideration. Unfortunately, such neglect is likely to lead to unsatisfactory research findings for two main reasons. First, it is impossible to provide a detailed analysis of the objectives and behaviour of every actor associated with the policy area under study. Hence, the analyst must decide to focus principally on one, or a limited number of actors. Second, if no explicit decision is made concerning the question of actor designation, the analyst runs the risk of implicitly employing a number of different actors at different stages of the analysis. Lack of attention to the first problem is likely to produce work which amounts to little more than description. Lack of concern for the second runs the risk of generating conclusions which are confused, especially when it comes to locating where power lies in the policy area or political system under study.

Bulpitt's conception of the Court owes a lot to the work of Frey, who provides some criteria to assist the analyst when designating a political actor. Two in particular are worth noting in this context. The first is Frey's stipulation that the actor(s) chosen should normally demonstrate enough *behavioural cohesion* to be regarded as a unitary entity (Frey 1985: 141–4; Bulpitt 1995: 518). Frey makes it clear that behavioural cohesion refers to more than shared characteristics. Of crucial importance is some notion of meaningful interaction among the membership of the collectivity which has been selected. Of course, exceptions to this cohesion will occur: absolute unitary behaviour is an impractical criterion in this context. However, in the complete absence of such features, the actor under study is nothing more than an 'aggregate' of its component parts. It follows that, in order to fulfil this standard of cohesiveness, the smaller and more exclusive the group the better.

7

It is because of this stipulation that the concept of the Court was preferred to 'the State' or 'government'.

The second criterion relevant to this study is that the actor designated should be a temporal constant: it should resemble largely the same form for the entire period under consideration (Bulpitt 1995: 518). Of course, the longer the historical perspective, the more abstract the PAD must become in order to accommodate the wide variety of changes that this entity may experience. It is in this context that any form of methodological individualism was ruled out. While the argument below accepts that history is vital to understanding contemporary responses to the EU, it considers the Court's management of the intersection of domestic and external policy over a 75-year period. The narrative begins in 1925, the year that sterling returned to the gold standard. It finishes in 1997, a time where the future policy towards the Euro was an issue that was splitting the Conservative leadership apart. Clearly, no one individual was influential in British politics throughout the entirety of this period.

In short, what follows is not a total explanation of Britain's relations with the EU. Instead, it is intended to be a theoretically informed account of the rather schizophrenic relationship between the Conservative leadership in office and the Europeanization of British economic policy after 1979. However, while analytical priority is given to this actor, the argument below does not neglect or ignore the impact of other groups or structures. As we shall see, Britain's system of industrial relations and changes in the international economy, as well as other European states and EU institutions, were all important in understanding Conservative responses in this policy area. More generally, the intention is to add to our understanding of this topic by looking at familiar material in a new light.

2.   If the focus of this book is the relationship between the Conservative leadership and Europeanization, a second advantage of Statecraft is that it provides a sophisticated and rich account of the interests of this elite group. There is more to Statecraft than the rather banal comment that politicians in office will attempt to win elections and achieve an image of governing competence. The interesting question is how they go about doing this within the institutional confines of the British Polity. In this context, the terms 'governing code' and 'Political Argument Hegemony' require further elucidation.

As already noted, a governing code can be defined as a reasonably coherent set of principles, methods and practices through which the Court will attempt to achieve its governing objectives. That said, the concept needs to be unpacked to show more specifically how the elements of this code are related. In an article published in 1969, Alexander George argued that an important distinction can be made between the philosophical core of the code and the instrumental beliefs which exist on its periphery. Philosophical beliefs are derived from answers to fundamental questions about the essential nature of political life facing the actor under study. Is this political existence primarily one of harmony or conflict? As a result, what are the actor's prospects for the eventual realization of its goals within this environment? Answers to the questions will, in turn, have a decisive influence on a number of instrumental beliefs at the periphery of the code. These beliefs will be concerned with questions such as the selection and implementation of objectives for political action (A. George 1969: 201–15).

How does this general discussion relate to Bulpitt's work on this subject? What are the implications for our understanding of any governing code in the area of British policy towards the EU. Clearly, much of the content of this code will only be understood once the detailed empirical work has been undertaken. That said, from his account of how political leaders understand the political game in Britain, Bulpitt does provide a number of signposts concerning what he understands to be the core philosophical beliefs of the Court's governing code. Not surprisingly for an approach designed to resurrect and reformulate an Elite or Statist interpretation of British politics, Bulpitt, like earlier Elitists, emphasizes that politics is largely about the struggle for power (Dunleavy and O'Leary 1987: 148–53). The main theme of his work to date is to chart the Court's endless struggle to secure its interests and objectives in the face of constraints and resistance to societal forces. In particular, British party leaders understand political life in this way because the political system in Britain guarantees them no peace of mind in electoral terms. These leaders have to contest elections every five years under an electoral system that penalizes third parties with nationwide support and rewards only the winners of the resultant two horse race. Even where these leaders successfully make it into office, they are then faced with an adversarial party system that keeps the government under constant pressure throughout its term of office. The result is a political game in Britain which is more physical, is played at a faster pace than on the Continent and where everything hangs on the final result (Bulpitt 1988: 186–8).

If the Court was faced with a frenetic domestic political climate, Britain's external position throughout the twentieth century helped to complicate the conduct of statecraft in significant ways. For Bulpitt, British politicians have historically had to manage an 'Open Polity'. Britain's far-flung imperial interests, accumulated over the centuries, meant that the domestic economy was vulnerable to a number of external shocks. From a military point of view, the problem was accentuated by an increasing gap between Whitehall's strategic commitments and the resources required to meet them (see, for example, Kennedy 1981). This precarious position suggested that substantial amounts of time and energy would have to be devoted to questions of foreign and defence policy, if only to ensure that the rhetoric of Britain's national greatness remained at least partly convincing.

This discussion concerning the essential nature of political life as understood by the Court feeds into Bulpitt's understanding of the governing code in two principal ways. Faced with this structural context, perhaps the core philosophical belief of this code was the desire to preserve autonomy over matters of 'High Politics' (Bulpitt 1983: 2–3). In simple terms, autonomy can be defined as 'the space or freedom to determine one's actions' (*Collins English Dictionary*, 1987). At the same time, Bulpitt explains that High Politics refers simply to those policy issues that the Court perceives to be important at any particular moment. Unsurprisingly, Bulpitt asserts that foreign and defence policy has dominated this agenda, although matters of economic management have become increasingly important since 1945. It follows then that when Bulpitt writes about autonomy, he is referring to freedom and space from *domestic* forces (interest groups, even fellow colleagues and supporters in the party) (see also Nordlinger 1988: 882). Because of the open nature of the British Polity, *external* autonomy has never been realizable.

For Bulpitt, the Court's pursuit of domestic autonomy over High Politics is accompanied by a concern to peripheralize control and responsibility for matters perceived to be 'Low Politics' (Bulpitt 1983: 2–3). If High Politics represents that category of issues considered to be crucial to the electoral fortunes of the party in office, Low Politics refers to those policy areas deemed to be too awkward or time consuming to deal with. In such circumstances, the Court will attempt to hive off responsibility on to a number of bodies, usually at the sub-national level. It is important to note in passing that autonomy is not synonymous with power or control. Just because an individual has the freedom to do something does not necessarily mean that this goal will be achieved. In fact, one can go further and think of examples where a person might self-consciously put limits on his or her power in order to ensure the full implementation of existing tasks. It follows that autonomy is a relative concept: it is a property that can be gained or lost in different temporal or spatial contexts.

Bulpitt's use of the term Political Argument Hegemony also requires further clarification, as it is directly related to one of the central questions driving the analytical focus of this book. To recap, why have successive Conservative governments presided over the Europeanization of economic policy, when the merits of the ideas underpinning this process were essentially contested? Peter A. Hall asserts that we must be careful not to treat the question of explaining why some ideas are accepted by policy-makers, solely in terms of the role and relative influence of academic bodies or think tanks closely associated with these doctrines. Not only is it rare for such 'experts' to be united in the advice that they offer, but this position assumes that these ideas will be able to 'trickle up' to the relevant politicians and officials, who will receive them with a reasonably open and neutral mind (Hall 1989: 8–10). In short, intervening variables will be needed to explain why optimistic assessments of the economic benefits of Europeanization have gradually been accepted, while more sceptical or negative viewpoints have been downplayed.

The strength of the Statecraft approach is that Bulpitt understands that this relationship between economic ideas and policy outcomes is not so straightforward. His exposition of the concept of Political Argument Hegemony demonstrates clearly that ideas are important to governing success. Such hegemony refers to

> a winning rhetoric in a variety of locations, winning because either the framework of the party's arguments becomes generally acceptable, or because its solutions to a particularly important political problem seem more plausible than its opponents. (Bulpitt 1986: 21–2)

However, as already noted, success in this ideological battle is presented as a support function: policy ideas are to be 'used and abused' (Bulpitt 1996: 226) in a way which assists the leadership in the pursuit of its objectives and governing code. The Court will not be neutral in its perception of the advice and various policy prescriptions it may receive from below. In general terms, these ideas are likely to be accepted or rejected according to their commensurability with existing governing principles and practices.

It follows implicitly from this discussion that policy ideas and the Court's governing code will be mutually implicated in a dialectical relationship that unfolds over time. There may be circumstances where forces or shocks expose the contradictions or limitations of existing governing principles and practices, leading to new ideas being pulled in to justify changes and U-turns. At the same time, such ideas can become generally accepted in a way that helps to entrench or legitimize existing governing codes and the state structures they were founded on (Bulpitt 1995: 520). Put in different terms, when it comes to understanding the question of Political Argument Hegemony, analysis of the ideological level is not enough (see the exchange between Jessop *et al.* and Hall in Jessop *et al.* 1988). The achievement of a 'winning rhetoric in a variety of locations' will depend on the ability of party leaders to articulate a discourse whereby the vision of its governing strategy and accompanying policy programmes are perceived to be consistent and plausible within the existing confines of British state structures. This point needs to be borne in mind when it comes to understanding Conservative policy towards the EU after 1979.

In short, faced with the question of why, after 1979, successive Conservative governments acquiesced in, or even encouraged, the Europeanization of economic policy, Statecraft provides a potentially fruitful foundation for our understanding of the motives and behaviour of the leadership in this context. In part, this actor will be concerned to win elections and achieve some semblance of governing competence in office. More importantly, this behaviour will partly be structured by a governing code, which will have developed over time in response to this leadership's perception of the possibilities for action within the institutional context that surrounds it. That said, the central questions driving this book suggest that this understanding of the governing code needs to be developed further. As already noted, foreign policy has historically been perceived by the Court as a difficult issue, whose careful management requires domestic autonomy. So why, in presiding over the Europeanization of public policy, did Conservative leaders increase the openness of the British Polity, thus potentially complicating further the task of Statecraft? Moreover, what were the precise governing attractions of policies such as the Single Market, ERM membership and the present principled advocacy of the Single Currency? These questions will be addressed in the chapters below.

Like all theoretical approaches, Statecraft rests on a number of untestable assumptions. As Bulpitt himself notes, these need to be made explicit before the analysis begins, if only because they might provoke contention. One assumption which is particularly relevant in this context is that of *rationality*. If state actors are capable of reflecting on the world around them and organizing these calculations into semi-structured codes of behaviour, it follows that these actors will normally behave rationally (Bulpitt 1988: 185–6; and 1995: 520). Whenever possible, they will calculate and scheme, employing strategies to pursue their objectives in a relatively consistent fashion. In more academic language, classic rational decision-making can be summarized in the following way: the policy-making process progresses through a number of clearly defined stages; the decision-makers begin by deciding which objectives or values they want to maximize; all the information then needed for making the decision is collected; all alternative options are compared and contrasted in the light of their ability to maximize objectives/values which have been agreed upon; and an option or combination of options is finally chosen which maximizes these values/objectives (for example, see Leach and Stewart 1982, Chapter 1; Ham and Hill 1984, Chapter 5).

As Bulpitt (1988: 185) has himself acknowledged, the rationality assumption has been subjected to a number of criticisms. One key problem is that while it may provide a picture of how decisions *should* be reached in large organizations, it clearly presents an unrealistic view of the way the policy-making process actually works. Decision-makers do not have the resources to collect all relevant information. Nor do they have the time to consider all the possible options before a final decision is reached. Certain options may be overlooked because of incomplete information, whereas others will be considered off-limits because they are impractical (Lindblom 1959, 1979). A second popular criticism of the assumption is that, having formulated policy, the decision-makers under study can then control the environment within which this implementation takes place. However, as other authors have noted, this implementation phase can be a source of many obstacles and constraints, which, in turn, will feed back into calculations during the policy formulation stage (Marsh and Rhodes 1992).

While the obvious conclusion might be to drop the rationality assumption altogether, Bulpitt erects a twofold defence of the position. His first argument is to suggest that, if the study of politics is not rooted in some concept of rationality, the result can be detrimental to the conclusions that we, as political scientists, reach. In the absence of such an assumption, analysis can be reduced to moralizing or 'weary, idle cynicism' about the incoherence of government. Of course, this is an easy safe option. Ultimately, it may actually present an accurate portrayal of the way governments operate. Unfortunately, however, such a position generates dull and unfruitful research findings (Bulpitt 1988: 186).

Second, while the classic model of rationality is obviously flawed, Bulpitt argues that the 'bounded rationality' model allows this assumption to be resurrected and utilized as a plausible foundation for his interpretation. This model accepts that there are limits to the knowledge of decision-makers who, in turn, will not consider all the alternatives when making policy. At the same time, decision-makers will satisfice, not maximize, choosing options that are good enough to help them achieve their objectives. As a result, change is highly likely to be incremental, reflecting those options which deviate least from existing policy-making routines and practices (Bulpitt 1986: 186). Put another way, what is to count for rational behaviour will be related to governing codes, which, as already noted, are themselves partly a product of perceptions of the structural context that surrounds decision-makers. In a world where economic, social and political life is enormously complicated, such codes are essential for allowing actors to make sense of the vast amount of conflicting and *ad hoc* information they have to deal with at any one time. It follows that in some circumstances, it may be rational to do nothing, particularly if the Court is concerned that it lacks the appropriate policy instruments or capacities to successfully implement its objectives.

3. Having examined the domestic sources of Europeanization, the second half of the book turns to the impact of this process on British politics. More particularly, it analyses how and why the Conservatives appeared to lose control of EU institutions at the end of the 1980s, and charts the implications for the party's political fortunes in the 1990s. A third and final advantage of Statecraft is that it is underpinned by a realist ontology which is capable of addressing these questions. It should be admitted at the outset that this philosophical position is not immediately apparent from Bulpitt's work. Indeed, the discussion below will partly be an exercise in teasing out these implicit theoretical foundations. However, once exposed, the argument is that Statecraft can help us to understand the nature of this structural change at the external level and the subsequent repercussions for Conservative Party politics.

In formal theoretical terms, the issue underlying this subject matter is widely known as the agent/structure problem. Historically, the issue has always revolved around whether students should give analytical primacy to actors or structures when it comes to explaining behaviour. Recently, however, a number of authors have suggested that this either/or approach is misguided. Agents are potentially purposive entities whose actions can reproduce and transform the society in which they live. Yet it is also true to say that society is made up of social relations that structure the interactions between actors. In short, both actors and structures are relevant to understanding the formulation and implementation of public policy. They are necessarily interdependent entities, exhibiting a relationship displaying a 'duality', not 'dualism'. Ontologically, agents possess 'relative autonomy' from these structures (Giddens 1979; Wendt 1987; Dessler 1989; Hay 1996).

One potential concern about Statecraft in this context is the charge of ontological reductionism. Among others, Marsh (1995) has made this criticism in a recent survey of Thatcherism. Bulpitt's work may provide a novel understanding of contemporary British Conservatism, but it is placed firmly in the camp designated for 'unilateral' interpretations. At the centre of this critique is Bulpitt's concern with methodology.[3] Although he accepts that agents and structures are necessarily interlinked, the fact that he gives analytical primacy to the way that agents operate within structures leaves him open to the charge that he downplays the importance of the latter. This impression is not helped by the rationality assumption noted above. While Bulpitt does not discount the importance of mistakes, U-turns or general mismanagement in the development of Statecraft regimes over time (witness for example, Bulpitt's (1986) treatment of the first Thatcher government), his work searches for coherent elite behaviour wherever possible and, implies that politicians always get their way in the end. Seen from this perspective, Statecraft would seem unable to accommodate examples where agents misunderstand and lose control of structures in a way which severely constrains their behaviour.

However, the discussion of Statecraft above would appear to suggest that Bulpitt accepts that agents and structures are mutually implicated in a dialectical relationship. To understand the behaviour of the Conservative Party in office, one needs to chart the dialectical relationship between the Court, its objectives and governing code, the policy ideas/rhetoric it utilizes and the institutional context (domestic and external) within which it tries to practise statecraft. For Bulpitt, there will be times where party leaders in office in Britain will be hemmed in, only able to react to a constellation of awkward and unwelcome structural movements. Conversely, there may be moments when such structures provide opportunities for the Court to pursue its objectives with more freedom. They can be appropriated and in some cases reformed, in the light of various interests and concerns. In this context, it has been suggested above that the Europeanization of British economic policy may have been accepted in the 1980s and 1990s because it provided an external route to domestic governing autonomy.

It has been argued elsewhere that Statecraft rests on a realist ontological position which can accommodate instances where structures can exert autonomous power over agents (in this case, the Court) (Buller 2000a). Of course, realism is not an easy approach to define. That said, Sayer's (1992: 4–6) excellent introduction is good enough for the discussion that follows. According to Sayer, realism rests on seven propositions:

- The world exists independent of our knowledge of it.

- Our knowledge of the world is fallible and theory-laden. As a result, concepts of truth and falsity do not provide a coherent representation of the relationship between the world and our knowledge of it. However, this is not to say that our knowledge of the world is immune from empirical check.

- Social phenomena, such as actions, texts or institutions, are concept dependent. The job of social scientists is not just to explain the production of such phenomena and their material effects. Scholarly attention should also be paid to the question of interpreting what these phenomena mean and understanding how other agents interpret the same phenomena.

- The production of any kind of knowledge (including science) is a social practice. The methods we use in the production of such knowledge will influence its content.

- There is necessity in the world. Objects (including structures) have causal powers, which can be explained through the existence of emergent properties. Such properties emerge from the necessary and internal relations between structures (which are activity-dependent in the past tense), but cannot be explained simply by reference to their origins or component parts. These properties can generate change in conjunction with agents and contingent events or shocks, leading to strategic action and institutional reform.

- The world is stratified. That is to say, the interaction of various groups rests on a social (and political) landscape, which is made up of a number of layers. These layers are the product of previous strategic battles between groups, competing to further their interests within the institutional terrain that surrounds them. At any one time, agents will be interacting with one or more of these layers (just as the layers will be interacting with each other), yet as society develops, this interaction may lead to tensions, contradictions and the emergence of structural properties capable of generating institutional change.

- Social science must be critical of the world (see also Archer 1995).

Despite his giving analytical primacy to the behaviour of the Court, a closer inspection of Bulpitt's empirical work confirms that Statecraft is compatible with this realist position. Take, for example, Bulpitt's discussion of the politicization of UK territorial politics in the 1960s and the 1970s. For Bulpitt, understanding the origins of this challenge involves charting the tensions and contradictions that developed within the related aspects of the structure facing the Court in the early 1960s. Perhaps the first point to restate is that foreign and domestic institutions were internally and necessarily related at this time. The structure of British external relations created a support system, protecting the fragile, insulated position of the Court *vis-à-vis* the periphery. However, by the early 1960s, this external support system was beginning to decline, thus creating tensions at the domestic level. In concrete terms, the phenomenon of British (economic) decline created pressure for a more interventionist strategy promoting both economic and political modernization. The whole structure of territorial politics was included in this remit (Bulpitt 1983: 176–8).

At the same time, as Bulpitt notes, the structure of the British state had a number of hidden penalties which faced the Court as it tried to develop a more interventionist strategy. On the one hand, by promoting separation and autonomy from the periphery, the Court had never taken the time to develop resources and policy instruments capable of controlling local and regional groups. On the other hand, because the territorial question had never penetrated domestic politics in a way which caused continual trouble for politicians at the centre, policy-makers lacked any real detailed knowledge and expertise of how to deal with this problem (Bulpitt 1983: 165–6). Not surprisingly, this combination of structural contradictions and tensions, emergent pressure for modernization and a partial understanding of the environment that surrounded it, led the Court into a number of miscalculations and mistaken policy choices. In the area of territorial politics, the Court over-reacted to pressure for change coming from the periphery. To the extent that there was pressure, it only manifested itself in the form of the Scottish National Party (SNP). Indeed, although national political forces developed in a way that favoured the Nationalists in the 1970s, Bulpitt points out that the overwhelming majority of Scottish voters continued to support British or Unionist parties. As a result, when the Court introduced measures for devolution to contain this pressure, these had the counterproductive effect of raising expectations among local and regional groups. The territorial question became politicized, leading to a decline in governing autonomy and competence. Put another way, the Court's misunderstanding of the structural developments facing it led to strategic action which had the unintended consequence of compromising the existing statecraft regime (Bulpitt 1983: 171–94).

Making this realist theoretical position explicit allows Statecraft to provide a more rounded explanation of the Europeanization of British economic policy. While analytical priority will still be given to the behaviour of the Court, Statecraft can accommodate instances where policy change is more than just the product of the actions of this group. At any particular point in history, the Court will be operating on a structural terrain, which is strategically selective. As a product of past conflicts between groups, this terrain will favour some strategies over others, and may preclude some strategies altogether. At the same time, the contours of this terrain will always be moving. As they interact with each other, or come into contact with various groups, structures will develop tensions and contradictions, leading them to evolve in ways unintended by their original designers. This theoretical position will be particularly useful when it comes to tackling the set of questions under-pinning the second part of the book: that is, to explain how the negotiation of the SEA set off a number of unanticipated consequences, which in turn helped to exacerbate tensions and divisions within the Conservative Party in the 1990s.

This discussion brings us finally to the question of foreign policy imple-mentation at the EU level and its relationship to domestic politics. It is on this point that Statecraft is rather underdeveloped. In his later work, Bulpitt certainly displayed an interest in this issue. In the late 1980s, his analytical focus moved towards British foreign policy and was driven by the following organizing question: 'In what ways, and for what reasons did the [Thatcher government] seek to manage the impact of external forces on the domestic political scene such that their general interests were either positively pro-moted or not adversely affected?' (Bulpitt 1988: 181). In general terms, Bulpitt's answer was that the Court, acting rationally and strategically, will attempt to appropriate external structures and create an external support system to support its domestic political objectives (Bulpitt 1983).

Unfortunately, when it comes to the question of how British policy-makers create such a support system at the EU level, Bulpitt's analysis does not progress much beyond crude intergovernmentalism. He accepts that, within EU institutions, negotiators will attempt to construct coalitions of like-minded states around compromises, side-payments or linkages at the margin. Alternatively, they may threaten non-agreement, as was the case during the protracted discussions over Britain's budget rebate in the first half of the 1980s. In fact, Bulpitt was rather pessimistic concerning Britain's chances of alliance building at the EU level. Ultimately, the successful construction of an external support system will depend on the existing power structure of the EU. For Bulpitt, this regional organization was not an association of equal member states. The driving force behind European integration (or its absence) was the Franco-German axis. When this alliance is relatively strong, the possibilities for building a counter-coalition look rather grim on paper. Italy, Belgium, Luxembourg and the Netherlands are all natural satellites of this axis, whereas a British-led coalition, including Greece, Spain, Portugal and Ireland, is always likely to founder on the subject of EU budgetary matters

(Bulpitt 1992: 269; 1996: 219–20; see also Scharpf 1988: 258–9; Moravcsik 1993: 496–507, 508–13). In short, behind this discussion is an implicit suggestion that EU institutions do not provide a passive, neutral institutional environment for the processing of decisions, although this argument remains unexplored. However, by explicitly acknowledging the realist position underlying the Statecraft interpretation, we are in a position to investigate how the Conservatives appeared to lose control of the EU policy-making process in the 1990s.

Recently, a number of authors have expressed interest in applying neo-institutionalism to the study of the EU. Building on the work of regime analysis in international relations (for example, Krasner 1983), Bulmer *et al.* (1996) have pointed to the importance of *indirect institutional power* to explain the way that EU structures may favour the interests of some states over others. This approach argues that theories of Community policy-making need to move beyond intergovernmentalism and its focus on the observable interaction of member states and the way they use their resources to secure their objectives. Instead, the analysis should explore the possibility that states may attempt to alter the design of EU institutions themselves. Having shaped the institutional context within which policy-making takes place, this indirect institutional power will then serve to bias the interests of some member states over others. Bulmer *et al.* go on to argue that Germany has been particularly effective in exercising such power. This factor helps to explain the increasing influence Bonn has acquired over the EU policy-making process in the 1980s and 1990s. Scharpf (1988) provides a similar argument, but asserts that German influence on the design of EU institutions has had a malign effect, leading to decision-making sclerosis.

As Guzzini (1993: 451) has noted, approaches which emphasize indirect institutional power are ultimately compatible with intergovernmentalism. Institutional regimes, in the last resort, are largely a function of the distribution of power and resources among states. Alternatively, other authors have adapted theories of *structural power* to explain the way EU institutions influence the behaviour of member states. Pierson (1996) has attempted to apply notions of structural power to EU policy-making. Structural power can be distinguished from indirect institutional power in one crucial sense. It rejects, or qualifies, the argument that the evolution of institutions embodies and reflects the long-term interests of the original designers. Institutions can 'escape' from the direct influence of the actors working within them. In turn, they become independent, impersonal sources of power which nevertheless confer systemic advantage to certain actors because of their position. As a result, gaps develop in the ability of member states to control the EC policy-making process. In particular, Pierson (1996) highlights three features, which can lead to persistent gaps in government control of EU business.

First, as already intimated, Pierson (1996: 132–4, 142) stresses the partial autonomy and power that EU institutions can acquire as this regional organization develops. Intergovernmentalists may be correct in arguing that national governments originally created EU institutions to serve their own interests. However, this strategy involved a paradox. If these institutions were supposed to monitor and enforce EU-wide agreements, they would have to have *resources*. It followed that, over time, these supranational institutions might gradually acquire interests and power of their own. A second constraint on the behaviour of member states is what Pierson (1996: 142–4) terms *institutional barriers* to reform. As already noted, the ability of member states to reassert control over the policy-making process will be strengthened if they are able to redesign the institutional context that surrounds them. However, Pierson argues that the possibilities for unpicking institutional reform in the EU are more limited than in other organizations. In order to entrench the process of European integration, actors will build institutions to last. These institutions will be designed to be sticky and any suggestions for reform which depart radically from the original blueprints will have difficulty making it to the drawing board. Finally (and following on from this point), the issue of *sink costs* and the *rising price of exit* will serve as a structural constraint on the behaviour of member states. Put simply, initial institutional or policy decisions become self-reinforcing over time. The effort, resources and commitment put into making these decisions work constrain policy-makers from contemplating radical change. Eventually, these institutions become endowed with a 'normative' status: they are considered part of the 'fabric' of decision-making and will alternatively constrain and empower different national actors. In short, future theoretical accounts of Britain's relations with the EU will have to incorporate these insights into their explanation. Statecraft is no exception to this rule. However, its realist ontological position would seem comparable with this stress on institutional power.

Of course, Statecraft has its problems and limitations. Most notable perhaps is the fact that elite governing codes are difficult to research, as Bulpitt himself recognizes: 'What does one do with an inarticulate or silent Centre, which rarely makes public its code of practice?' (1983: 57). Most obviously there is the problem of secrecy; elite interviews are difficult to conduct, particularly when dealing with sensitive matters of foreign policy. This problem can be circumvented to a certain extent through the use of documentary evidence, such as memoirs, diaries, articles in periodicals and newspapers. Of course, such evidence also has a number of limitations. These documents will provide only a partial viewpoint of the event under consideration and are often written for self-justification or because the author has a particular political axe to grind (Madge 1953: Chapter 2).

That said, once it is remembered that governing codes consist of principles, beliefs and practices of political management, it is possible to operationalize the concept for the purposes of empirical research. Interview schedules can be sensitively structured to probe for the existence of such principles and practices. Interviewees can be asked to reflect on the coherence and importance of ideas filtering into the policy-making process. In the event of differences and disputes within the academic community over the supposed impact of such ideas, these policy-makers can be asked to explain their continual attachment to policies based on them. More specifically, they can be asked to consider any political or governing benefits which accrued from employing such ideas. Any perceived advantages can be recorded and cross-checked against other sources. Once substantiated, the researcher can begin to think about defining them as being part of the governing code. That said, this discussion should not allow us to forget the real methodological problems involved in employing such an approach. Governing codes are latent structures; and as with the analysis of all structures, they can only be inferred from the ideas and political behaviour which appear on the surface of the policy area under study. More often than not, the supporting evidence for such claims is likely to be less than perfect, particularly for those of an empiricist, epistemological disposition. In short, what follows is nothing more than an interpretation of British policy towards the EU. It cannot be directly tested or proved.

Having provided this theoretical discussion, the interpretation below proceeds in the following way. Chapter 2 explores the historical origins of this Europeanization strategy. It suggests that in the area of political economy the Court has often sought the solace of domestic autonomy by linking its fortunes to external institutions, although this governing principle was challenged in the 1960s and the 1970s. Chapter 3 begins the discussion of the Thatcher government. It argues that monetarism should be partly understood as an attempt by the Court to rediscover the governing benefits of domestic autonomy. Unfortunately, the design of this strategy paid little attention to the importance of external economic forces, particularly in a small but open economy like Britain's. By 1984, these external forces were increasingly perceived to be undermining monetarism in one country, leading the Court to cast around for alternative policy instruments. In the light of these implementation problems, Chapter 4 documents how the Court gradually came to accept the Europeanization of economic policy as the route to domestic autonomy. The SEA, with its commitment to the completion of the Single Market, would help to entrench the party's free market supply-side strategy. At the same time, an increasing number of senior policy-makers became attracted to the ERM as an external discipline which would insulate the Court from domestic pressure.

Chapter 5 charts the Court's experience of negotiating the SEA in the mid-1980s. Despite the Court's achievement of most of its objectives, the discussion highlights the real constraints facing British diplomats at this time. However, as Chapter 6 notes, such constraints became even tighter in the late 1980s as a number of broader structural movements in the international system touched off significant pressure for further integration at the

EU level. The discussion then turns to the question of why the Conservative Party collapsed over the European issue in the late 1980s and 1990s. It is argued in Chapters 6 and 7 that these divisions reflected a debate which went to the heart of the Conservative Party: what is the most appropriate Statecraft response to this uncertain environment?

Notes

1. Strictly speaking, one should refer to the European Coal and Steel Community (ECSC) from 1951 to 1957, the ECSC plus the European Economic Community (EEC) and the European Atomic Energy Community (EAEC or Eurotom) from 1957 to 1967 and the European Communities (or Community) from 1967 to 1993. The term 'European Union' only became valid after ratification of the Treaty on European Union at Maastricht. However, for purposes of simplicity, European Union will be used throughout this book, even for periods where it is technically incorrect.
2. It should be stated at the outset that the author is a Euro-sceptic. I remain unconvinced that the EU has offered, or will offer any substantive benefits to 'Britain', although it is worth remembering that the whole exercise of conducting such a cost–benefit analysis is fraught with problems. Perhaps the one enduring attraction of Europeanization is that it allows the 'governing classes' to blur their lines of accountability and escape electoral blame. As we shall see, even this potential advantage has been slow to materialize.
3. In the discussion that follows, I use the term 'methodology' to denote the various methods academics use to carry out their research. 'Ontology' refers to the nature of the world which surrounds us and our existence within it. Epistemology is defined as the theory of knowledge (Abercrombie et al. 1994: 147, 292). Some social scientists will find these definitions too narrow. Others will not recognize the threefold distinction that this article employs. However, for the purpose of the argument developed below, I have found this terminology helpful.

CHAPTER TWO

Domestic Economic Problems and External Market Solutions: Britain's Relations with the European Union in Historical Perspective

The main purpose of this chapter is to chart the historical development of the Court's governing code towards the EU. As noted in Chapter 1, this code will not exist in a vacuum. It will be crucially affected by the Court's perception of the structural environment within which it makes policy. This chapter begins by detailing the structural constraints facing the Court in its conduct of economic (particularly supply-side) economic policy. The analysis is then centred on a number of questions. How, historically, have perceptions of this institutional environment fed into a governing code in this area? What was the relationship between this governing code and external policy before 1961? What was the relationship between EU membership and this governing code as the Court understood it? How did this code influence the Court's response to this regional organization in the 1960s and the 1970s?

In response to these questions, this chapter makes three main arguments. Historically, the Court *perceived itself* to be heavily constrained when it came to the question of promoting reform in the supply-side of the British economy. More particularly, the international orientation of British capital, and the tradition of voluntarism in industrial relations, militated against the development of more interventionist policy instruments in this area. This perception was strengthened by the rather low opinion held of politicians during the inter-war period, particularly concerning their ability to manage the economy. Second, as a result of these structural constraints, neo-classical economic ideas remained attractive to the Court. More specifically, the stress on sound money and free markets conferred little responsibility on state actors who, anyway, had little faith in the usefulness of policy action in this area. At the same time, these economic ideas conferred political advantages: they yielded a relatively neutral and automatic economic policy framework which minimized relations with societal groups. As a result, the principles of *limited responsibility*, *neutrality* and *automatism* in economic policy became central to the Court's governing code in this area. Through these principles, the Court was able to preserve its autonomy, authority and governing competence in this area.

Third, understood in this way, the role of external policy before EU membership was to complement or support these domestic governing principles. In general, this meant constantly promoting the link between any problems in the supply side of the British economy and external market solutions. In specific policy terms, the Empire had always represented an external market solution to domestic problems of unemployment. However, on occasions, usually after the impact of shocks from the international system (either real or perceived), the Court found itself having to appropriate external structures to support its domestic concerns. During the inter-war period, it attempted to secure British access to imperial markets by creating the Overseas Sterling Area. Finally, in the 1960s, with the (perceived public) shock of Britain's relative economic decline, and the failure of Tripartite policy solutions, EU membership represented a straight swap – one external support structure for another. In other words, the Common Market became attractive to the Court not just because of its perceived economic benefits (which were contested anyway). From a governing point of view, this organization represented an automatic, neutral invisible hand allowing British politicians to partially absolve themselves from the economic problems they faced. Discretionary economic policy instruments could gradually be abandoned and governing autonomy and competence restored.

Automatism, Neutrality and External Market Supports: The 'Dual Polity', 1925–61

Providing a comprehensive description of the institutional structure of British economic markets could easily take up a chapter in itself. However, what is just as important in the context of this chapter is how the Court perceived these structural constraints and how these perceptions fed into its governing code for managing the relationship between domestic economic policy and external policy. During the inter-war period, two structural features of British economic markets were particularly important. The first feature was the international orientation of the British economy. By 1918 it had become generally accepted that the fate of the British economy had become inherently linked to international economic forces and trends (see, for example, Hobsbawm 1969: Chapter 7; Gamble 1994: Chapter 2). This dependence could be identified in a number of ways. After the repeal of the Corn Laws in 1846, Britain relinquished her self-sufficiency in agricultural products, and became increasingly reliant on regular imports of food and raw materials to feed the population. Moreover, at no time during the nineteenth century could the value of British manufacturing exports match the value of these imports. To maintain a balance of payments surplus, the Court came to rely increasingly on income from so-called 'invisible' exports: earnings from British shipping, the various financial services provided by the City of London, and interest and dividends from the investment of British capital abroad. By 1914, such overseas investment totalled four thousand million pounds in assets, leading to income of two hundred million pounds a year (Hobsbawm 1969: 152; Gamble 1994: 57). The international orientation of the British economy clearly represented a considerable constraint on the policies followed by any government during this period.

Second, the principle of voluntarism in government–industry relations had important consequences for policy at this time. This principle maintained that, wherever possible, the activities of British firms should be free from government intervention. It was only through such economic freedom that British business would flourish, leading to new products and manufacturing techniques. These in turn, would help Britain to maintain its competitive edge in world markets (which, as already noted, was vital to the success of the British economy). More significantly, Britain's system of industrial relations was distinguished by a lack of individual and collective labour law regulating negotiations between business and unions and a system of free collective bargaining. Under the latter, collective agreements over wages were not legally enforceable contracts, but regarded as 'gentleman's agreements' and, in general, each industry developed its own unique institutions and processes for conducting the bargaining (Marsh 1992: 1–4; R. Taylor 1993: Chapter 1). If the Court had any role at all, it was to 'hold the ring', helping unions and employers to solve their own problems with as little disruption to the British economy as possible (A. Taylor 1994: 501–3).

This principle of voluntarism or self-government can be traced more generally to the importance of liberal ideas in the Victorian era, and partly reflected a deep distrust at this time with the role of government and politicians in economic management. For many economists, taking their cue from the writings of Adam Smith, government was perceived to be an inefficient organization for wealth creation. Many economists feared that Whitehall, if encouraged to take a more interventionist role in the affairs of industry, could actually have a detrimental effect on economic growth. What informed opinion particularly feared was that profligate politicians would succumb to pressure from interest groups to raise public expenditure. Such pandering to the masses would set off inflationary pressures and one only had to look at Germany to understand the shocking consequences of what might happen if such inflationary pressures were allowed to get out of hand. This disdain for politicians was nicely summed up by Philip Lloyd Graham, Minister at the Board of Trade, when he commented on the return to financial orthodoxy in Britain in the 1920s: 'The prevailing mood of the day [was] that the nation was no longer prepared "to be buggered about" by politicians with a strong tendency to mix up the glorification of themselves with the glorification of their country' (quoted in Holland 1991: 104; see also Middleton 1985: 83–91; Tomlinson 1994: 9).

This institutional structure affected the conduct of economic policy in the following ways. First, the Court was very slow to develop policy instruments or capacities which were capable of intervening in the supply side of the British economy to remove any constraints or blockages which might be impeding national economic performance. Instead, these so-called 'real' economic issues, such as economic growth, productivity and employment, were considered by Whitehall to be largely the responsibility of peak groups in society. Despite increasing competition in manufacturing industry from Germany and the USA, as well as the fact that over one million were recorded as being out of work in the 1930s, what was notable about this period were the ideas and blueprints that Whitehall avoided or ignored. These included: Keynes's support for a public works scheme which was adopted, to some effect, in Scandinavia at this time (Winch 1969: 118–22, 220–2); Lloyd-George's call for a British New Deal along the lines of similar reforms in the USA under the Roosevelt Administration; and Macmillan's proposals for Whitehall to take up a new strategic role in planning the activities of British industry (Budd 1978: 51–2; Weir 1989: 61). One commentator sympathetic to the view that a 'corporate bias' developed within British economic policy at this time points to the fact that Whitehall did sanction the formation of cartels by leading firms in the sectors of agriculture and iron and steel, while at the same time providing subsidies to the shipbuilding industry. However, he admits that this in no way added up to a coherent interventionist role for the British state (Middlemas 1994: 465).

Instead of developing indigenous state capacities to implement a programme of restructuring in the supply side of the economy, British policy-makers consistently subscribed to a direct link between problems in the supply side of the economy (particularly unemployment) and the fortune of British manufacturers in international markets. Throughout the 1920s the argument ran as follows: British unemployment was heavily concentrated in export industries and many of these difficulties could be accounted for because of the decline in world trade; the reason for this decline could be linked to business uncertainty created by currency instability; what the unemployed in Britain needed was the removal of this instability by putting the pound back on the gold standard; and this would help to reconstruct the pre-war international economy and revive the system of multilateral trade, thus providing a boost to British export activity and hence employment. Winch provides quotes showing that both Conservative and Labour leaders supported this analysis and Neville Chamberlain's rejection of proposals for a public works scheme could as easily have come from the lips of MacDonald or Snowdon: 'the quickest and most effective contribution which any government can make towards an increase in employment is to create conditions which will encourage and facilitate an improvement in ordinary trade' (quoted in Winch 1969: 222; see also pp. 92–3). As we shall see, the parallels with the policy of the Thatcher government half a century later are striking.

Not surprisingly, faced with these perceived structural constraints, the Court defined its responsibilities for economic management in a restricted way. It aimed to provide a sound 'nominal' framework for British industry and agriculture, which in practice meant a policy of sound money and free markets. More specifically, this required the maintenance of a strong and stable currency, most graphically illustrated by sterling's return to the gold standard in 1925. Second, this meant slavish adherence to the doctrine of the balanced budget. Finally, as already suggested, the Court accepted the responsibility for providing markets for British exports, although, as we shall see, after 1932 this increasingly involved a protected trade block organized around the markets of the Sterling Area. In short, the Court's contacts with peak groups in the economy were characterized by a relationship of relative autonomy. This division of labour over economic policy can be described as a 'Dual Polity', an idea developed by Bulpitt to characterize relations between Whitehall and elected local authorities, but just as applicable in this policy area (Bulpitt 1983, 1986). In short, despite being at the heart of an international economic system which still largely reflected British interests in 1918, the domestic position of the Court was, in some ways, peculiarly weak and vulnerable. Paradoxically, the Court not only accepted these constraints, but understood that the Dual Polity conferred a number of opportunities and benefits. More particularly, by defining its policy responsibilities in such narrow and restricted terms, the Court was able to create and nurture some semblance of governing autonomy from domestic forces, with beneficial spin-offs for establishing a reputation of governing competence.

In this context, autonomy was perceived to be linked to the *neutral* qualities of the neo-classical framework. In returning to the gold standard and the doctrine of the balanced budget, the Court hoped that both these policy instruments would serve as a *neutral discipline* which applied to all domestic groups without discrimination. This neutrality would ensure the depoliticization of economic management and the preservation of governing authority. Conversely, one of the arguments against deficit-financing to promote public works programmes in the inter-war period was that it would call into question the neutrality of the state in this era. Having made one interest group a special case for government intervention, the Court realized that it would be difficult to fend off calls for special treatment from other interest groups. As one Treasury document put it, 'But can anyone suppose that, once a precedent of this kind was set, people would remember the special arguments adduced to justify it?' (quoted in Middleton 1985: 87). Deficit-financing would encourage a multitude of demands for public expenditure, making it increasingly difficult for an over-burdened state to stop a rising tide of inflation (see also Holland 1991: 104, 110–12; Tomlinson 1994: 9).

Second, the Court was attracted to this neo-classical framework because of its qualities of *automatism*. For officials, policy could be run almost on automatic pilot by pulling a number of fiscal and monetary levers in the Treasury. If Britain's balance of trade went into deficit, and the domestic economy experienced concomitant problems of growth and employment, Whitehall pointed out that the system would automatically balance itself out. In such circumstances, the pound would fall to the point at which gold would be exported. The resulting loss of revenue would lead to an increase in interest rates, which, in turn, would attract foreign funds. The expected decline in investment activity resulting from higher interest rates would lead to destocking and a fall in the domestic price level. This, in turn, would stimulate exports and curtail imports, and the balance of trade and domestic economic activity would be 'automatically adjusted' (Winch 1969: 83). The attraction for the Court was that, despite the realities, the burden of supply-side adjustments could be made to appear relatively painless. The conduct of economic management could be made to look easy, while politicians would continue to look competent and in authority (Middlemas 1994: 453–4).

In short, the Court came to understand that, at this time, certain benefits were to be gained from accepting it has limited capacity and power over the supply side of the economy. When faced with calls for industrial restructuring in the light of increased foreign competition, the Court could plead impotence, shirk responsibility and preserve its governing autonomy from these domestic pressures. If the main preoccupation of the Court during this period was to maintain some semblance of governing autonomy and competence, the question remains: how, if at all, was the conduct of external policy related to this strategy? The central argument put forward in the paragraphs below is that external policy was developed with the aim of supporting these autonomy concerns. If developed fully, this argument would clearly have a number of dimensions to it. As a number of authors have noted, the policy of appeasement during the inter-war period was maintained to complement the Court's domestic preoccupation with controlling public expenditure and inflation (see, for example, Kennedy 1981). Moreover, after 1945, the newly developed 'special' relationship with the United States helped to resurrect a prestigious global role for British politicians, while allowing them to develop a nuclear capability 'on the cheap' (Buller 1996: 226). However, because of lack of space, the focus of this section is on a different aspect of this external support strategy: policy towards the Empire/Commonwealth.

As already intimated, the Empire had always provided an important supporting role for the Court in the area of economic management. Indeed, the Court took advantage of the connection between the problems of supply-side reform which it faced and the fortunes of British manufacturers in international markets to put off responsibility for developing more interventionist industrial strategies at this time. However, this external support function took on an additional importance for the Court between 1931 and the end of the 1950s. The origins of this increased importance stemmed from the collapse of the gold standard. As already noted, this exchange rate policy was a central pillar of the Court's autonomy strategy at the time. Without the domestic discipline of a fixed exchange rate, the Court feared that politicians would succumb to pressure to increase public expenditure in the face of a recession, thus stoking up an inflationary boom. Their response was to create a Sterling Bloc (which formally became the Overseas Sterling Area (OSA) in 1940), covering most of the Dominions as well as additional European countries. Reinforced by a system of Imperial Preference and a common external tariff, it provided an area in which members traded freely with each other, but little with the outside world.

Faced with the collapse of the gold standard, and with its autonomy strategy under pressure, the Sterling Bloc held a number of attractions for the Centre. Through the Exchange Equalisation Account, the authorities could manipulate the amount of sterling which could be exchanged for another currency, thus protecting the position of British manufacturers and Britain's trade balance (Sanders 1990: 202–3). This would lead to a restoration of confidence in sterling, with important knock-on effects for domestic financial stability. Not surprisingly, the Court turned this argument on its head. It was only by maintaining financial stability at home that London would retain the confidence of other countries in the Sterling Bloc, thus allowing British industry to exploit the substantial commercial business involved. Domestic financial restraint, it was stressed, was essential for export opportunities, growth and jobs (Cain and Hopkins 1993: 72–82). In more theoretical language, the Court was successful in appropriating external structures to bolster or support its domestic autonomy strategy. This external support strategy was to become even more important after 1945, until it began to crumble in the 1950s.

In the light of the subsequent discussion, it is worth noting that the material benefits of Imperial Preference have been questioned. For example, Capie argues that this policy added only 1 per cent to industrial production before 1940, hardly enough to have much of an effect on unemployment at this time (Capie 1983, Chapter 7; see also Holland 1991: 133). Part of the reason for this limited impact was that neither Britain nor the Empire was willing to sanction monopoly access to the other's markets (Holland 1991: 115, 130–1). However, for the Court, this policy conferred additional political benefits. In the words of Holland (1991: 132), the Sterling Bloc

> added, admittedly, to the putative attractions of an imperial refuge from the storms afflicting the world economy. . . . Domestic political factors increased the pressures tending in this direction since Empire trade agreements . . . were one of the few cures which the National Government . . . could be seen diligently applying to the patient.

Put another way, faced with real constraints on the development of domestic industrial policies during this period, Imperial Preference had the advantage

28

of appearing to offer an external solution (or external comfort) to domestic political problems.

Faced with an economy whose institutional structure stressed the international orientation of capital and the importance of voluntarism and self-regulation, we can sum up the Court's governing code in the following way. At the core of the code was a belief in the importance of governing autonomy from domestic forces. This core belief was flanked by a number of instrumental beliefs. These included: a preference for a general, neutral framework of set rules for economic management which applied to all societal groups without discrimination; a desire for policy instruments which allowed macroeconomic policy to be run largely on automatic pilot; and a distaste for discretionary interventionist industrial policies which attempted to discriminate between different industries and firms. The role of external policy was to support these principles. Historically, this had been done by stressing the link between economic problems in the supply side of the economy and external solutions – particularly the importance of access to Empire markets by British industry.

Of course, as this period wore on, a number of qualifications have to be made. It cannot be denied that, after 1940, the Court increasingly experimented with a number of interventionist policy instruments to effect change in the supply side of the economy. After all, there is a general consensus in the literature on British politics that Britain experienced a 'Keynesian revolution' during this period. As a result, the Court: accepted 'as one of its primary aims and responsibilities the maintenance of a high and stable level of employment'; implemented under the Attlee government a programme of nationalization; and experimented with a number of interventionist supply-side policy instruments, particularly planning bodies to organize patterns of production, exports, investment and manpower (Kavanagh 1990: 26–60). However, the argument here is that none of these policies added up to a coherent and sustained interventionist supply-side strategy. Instead, the implementation of these policies was shrouded in uncertainty and ambiguity as ministers demonstrated that they were unprepared to challenge the principles of self-regulation and voluntarism in industry. Put another way, the main beliefs of this governing code, although increasingly called into question, survived largely unaltered during the period 1940–60.

Take, for example, the nationalization programme of the Attlee government. As some critics have noted, public ownership only covered approximately 20 per cent of British industry, with the rest remaining in the private sector. While it was argued at the time that it was only necessary for the government to take control of these commanding heights of the economy to ensure that its objectives were implemented throughout the rest of British industry, in reality many of the industries which were nationalized, such as the coal industry or the railways, had suffered from decades of underfunding and were in serious need of public investment. Of more importance, perhaps, was the actual model of ownership adopted by Labour after 1945. Termed the 'Morrison model' and based on the creation of the London Passenger Transport Board (1931), state control of these strategic industries was to be vested in public boards. These would be composed of experts appointed by a minister and would be charged with the day-to-day running of these industries subject to broad guidelines from Whitehall. The advantage of this model for ministers was that it actually took the issue of nationalization out of politics. Moreover, it should be noted that at the time Labour leaders defined 'experts' largely in terms of the private sector managers already in control of these industries. As a consequence, despite a change in ownership, there was little change in control within the public sector. Indeed, as the 1940s wore on, ministers could be heard complaining about the lack of political control over these boards (Morgan 1984: 95–127; Tomlinson 1994: 188–200).

Uncertainty and ambiguity also plagued the Attlee government's experiment with planning at this time. Labour's intention to stimulate an export drive, to direct industry towards development areas and to plan the utilization of raw materials and manpower was initially reliant on the existing body of physical controls left over from the war. The problem here was that the personnel running these controls remained unaltered after the election. In practice, this meant private sector industrialists continued to manipulate these policy instruments in a way which accorded with their own interests (Tomlinson 1994: 162–3). Of course, there were new planning initiatives. However, as Morgan has argued, ministers remained vague about the exact purpose of the Lord President's Committee, the main planning arm of the Attlee government. This lack of direction was partly responsible for the inability of the Labour government to plan a coherent response to the coal shortage during the winter of 1947, despite the fact that this had been predicted as far back as May 1946 (Morgan 1984: 131). Furthermore, Development Councils, set up to discuss the question of efficiency in production and supply, failed to make much of an impact largely because they were bitterly resisted by employers (Tomlinson 1994: 178–9).

However, Labour's failure to adopt a more directive role in industry can also be put down to the leadership's commitment to parliamentarianism at this time. It is important not to forget the backdrop of the Cold War and the deep impression that Stalinism was making on the Labour leadership. Various documents which were published during these years were at pains to draw a distinction between the totalitarian planning system in Russia and the legitimate democratic planning experiments that the Labour Party was introducing into Britain. To quote the First Economic Survey (1947) on this distinction:

> The former subordinates all individual desires and preferences to the demands of the state. . . . But in normal times, the people of a democratic country will not give up their freedom of choice to their government. A

democratic government must, therefore, conduct its economic planning in a manner which preserves the maximum possible freedom of choice to the individual citizen. (Quoted in Budd 1978: 58–9)

In this context, it should finally be noted that, when the Attlee government began winding down its planning apparatus at the end of the 1940s, part of the reason was that it was perceived by the leadership to be electorally unpopular. Associated with the hardship of war, it is the judgement of one commentator that the electorate could never be persuaded that planning had a positive role (Budd 1978: 79).

In short, when it came to the area of supply-side economic policy, indeed economic policy in general, the Court's capacity to pursue active, interventionist, policies was constrained, or perceived to be constrained, by a number of structural features of the British economy. Although, as this period wore on, and this weakness or vulnerability became an increasing source of concern, the Court made a virtue out of its limited position. It understood that by once again accepting the principles of neo-classical economic theory after 1918, it could define responsibility for policy in a narrow way, thus promoting and protecting its governing autonomy from domestic forces. More particularly, this autonomy was bolstered by the neutral and automatic qualities of this economic framework, which made the whole business of economic management much easier and less time consuming. The role of external policy was to support these domestic concerns, and the Court even demonstrated a willingness and ability to appropriate external structures (the OSA) to bolster this autonomy. When it comes to understanding the Thatcher government's willingness to Europeanize the issue of supply-side policy, this historical connection between domestic and external affairs should be borne in mind.

The Rise of Discretionary Economic Management and the Decline of the Dual Polity, 1961–79

By 1960, this governing code had come under increasing strain, to the point where the Court began to contemplate changes. The crucial event precipitating this upheaval was the fact that evidence of Britain's relative economic decline has now entered the public realm, setting off calls for the structure of the British economy to be modernized. Suddenly, books and pamphlets were awash with statistics showing that, although since 1945 the UK economy had experienced an absolute rise in economic growth and productivity, these rates compared unfavourably with western Europe, the US and Japan. This relatively poor economic performance was especially marked in British manufacturing, and Britain's share of world markets persistently declined during this period (Gamble 1994: 10–18).

Much of this criticism of British economic policy challenged many of the beliefs of the Court's governing code. Although a plethora of explanations for this comparatively poor performance were put forward, more and more critics bemoaned the absence of a coherent state strategy for removing what were perceived to be a number of institutional rigidities in the supply side of the economy. British industry was criticized for the low quality and uncompetitiveness of its goods and its persistent inability to develop an industrial culture or spirit (Weiner 1981). Others blamed the power of the unions, focusing on how the structure of the British labour market, with its voluntary tradition of labour law and the dominance of militant shopfloor workers over national associations, made the British economy more susceptible to strikes than elsewhere. Finally, while the Empire had once provided a valuable source of markets, increasingly the system of Imperial Preference was criticized for insulating British manufacturing from the vigorous winds of international competition (Hall 1986: 26–45; Marquand 1988; Gamble 1994: 18–40).

Not surprisingly, under pressure to preside over reform of the British economy, the Court dropped some of the instrumental beliefs of its governing code. More particularly, it accepted that the external challenge of relative economic decline demanded the adoption of a more coherent interventionist industrial strategy. In the academic literature, these policy changes came to be known by the label Tripartism or Corporatism. In the British context, Tripartism included: the creation of new planning machinery to raise efficiency and investment in British industry and, ultimately, economic growth; various attempts to construct a lasting prices and incomes policy to ensure that this sustained growth effort did not dissipate in the wake of an inflationary boom; and reform of British labour law to encourage more responsibility on the part of trade unions in industrial relations. In other words, this experiment represented the gradual replacement of automatic and neutral policy instruments with a more active, discretionary style of economic management.

While there can be no doubt that these policies demonstrated a significant change in the statecraft of the Court, it is important to note a number of qualifications. While Tripartism undoubtedly represented an attempt to create a coherent interventionist industrial strategy, politicians and civil servants hoped that this policy could be implemented, while at the same time avoiding the need to discriminate between firms. This contradiction caused confusion and ultimately led to the failure of planning in Britain. This result led the Court to become more directive in its approach to the supply side of the economy, particularly in its relations with the trade unions. However, this policy had the deleterious effect of eroding the autonomy and governing competence of the Court. Finally, at the same time, the 'efficient secret' of this period was that the Court continued to hanker after external solutions to its supply-side problems. As the period wore on, a number of politicians and civil servants gradually understood that the EU could play this role, helping to restore the Court's autonomy and governing competence. The discussion below takes each of these points in turn.

When it came to this experiment with Tripartism, the Court initially hoped that planning could be developed in a way which was consistent with the pre-1961 governing code. Despite Macmillan's own interest in this policy, Shanks argues that what originally attracted the Conservative government to the model of French indicative planning was that it seemed to offer the possibility of supply-side restructuring 'by logic and persuasion, without controls or direction'. Put another way, this change could be grafted on to the existing institutional structure of the Dual Polity relatively easily. When the Court realized that the French model did not work in a purely indicative way, policy-makers consciously refrained from adopting the more coercive aspects of the system. Whitehall made no attempt to introduce a new planning instrument, to allow it to assume direct responsibility for the provision of capital to British industry. Moreover, there was no attempt to discriminate between various industrial sectors in the granting of planning permission or government orders. Responsibility for planning was hived off to the National Economic Development Council (NEDC), a purely consultative body, divorced from Whitehall, whose reports had the status only of recommendations (Shanks 1977: 17–30; Hall 1986: 86–7; Smith 1993, Chapter 6).

A similar argument can be constructed in an analysis of the approach of the first Wilson government to planning. Although the process of planning was now integrated into the Whitehall machinery under the auspices of the new Department of Economic Affairs (DEA), as Ponting has argued, ministers failed to resolve the issue of the exact demarcation of responsibilities between the DEA and the Treasury and to question whether George Brown and his colleagues had the necessary powers to implement their recommendations (Ponting 1989: 109–10). Shanks goes further, accusing Brown of conceding important policy instruments to other departments. At the time of drawing up the DEA blueprint, Shanks assumed that he and his colleagues would have control over the level of capital expenditure in the public sector. In his view, the fact that the instrument was traded away by George Brown in a meeting with a Treasury official 'contributed significantly to the subsequent impotence and demise of the DEA' (Shanks 1977: 32).

However, perhaps the most controversial assertion of this lack of commitment to planning is provided by Ponting. He alleges that the Labour leadership signed a number of secret policy agreements with senior members of the Johnson Administration which rendered the objectives of the National Plan redundant. In return for American support for sterling (which had returned to a semi-fixed parity within the new Bretton Woods exchange rate system), Johnson secured commitment from Wilson that there would be no cutting back of defence commitments either in West Germany or east of Suez, no devaluation of the pound and a readiness to introduce deflationary measures in the event of sterling coming under pressure from a balance of payments crisis. The introduction of such deflationary economic packages in July 1965 and July 1966 showed the strength of the leadership's commitment to this

'American Connection' at the expense of the growth objectives of the National Plan (Ponting 1989: 48–58). In many ways, it was this episode, above all else, which highlighted the contradictory nature of the Court's policies at this time. This leads one to question whether a governing code, defined as a relatively coherent and consistent system of beliefs and practices, can be said to have existed at all during this period.

Furthermore, the Court's continued reliance on local Economic Development Councils (EDCs) or 'little Neddies' to implement suggestions for supply-side reform betrayed a continual reluctance to offend the long-established principles of self-government and relative autonomy in its relations with industry. Like their national counterpart, EDCs worked on the basis of consultation and consensus. They had no authority to commit the industries they represented to policy proposals. Furthermore, the effectiveness of EDCs as agents of the state depended on their ability to work through strong trade associations, not a feature common to all sectors of British industry in the 1960s. Not surprisingly, the Court found its efforts to spread the use of discounted cash-flow techniques and better coordination between producers and suppliers in the design of components continually frustrated by its unwillingness to take a more directive role in this area (Shanks 1977: 37; Ponting 1989: 114–15; Middlemas 1994: 472).

If the Court continued to exhibit a reluctance to be more directive and discriminatory in its relations with peak groups in the economy, surely the same could not be said about the experience of the Industrial Reorganization Corporation (IRC)? Here was a body which had an explicit remit to encourage mergers in the name of efficiency, using government funds to push this process along if necessary. Moreover, by 1970, the IRC could point to notable successes, such as ICL, the British computer firm. However, as Tomlinson (1994: 268–70) has noted, the IRC was involved in only 2 per cent of the mergers that took place in the 1960s. Moreover, while it was sensitive to the need to promote rationalization within these new companies, its limited financial resources precluded it from having much financial impact (see also Ponting 1989: 272). In the words of Hall, 'since 1918, industries in Britain have essentially been asked to rationalise themselves' (Hall 1986: 53).

On returning to power in 1974, the Wilson government seemed intent on avoiding these earlier mistakes. The leadership accepted that many of its industrial policies in the 1960s had fallen short of the objectives set by the Cabinet. Once again, party publications stressed the importance of nationalization. The new Labour government would create a National Enterprise Board (NEB), a stateholding company, designed to take a major and continuing equity stake in the top 100 British companies. Complementing this policy would be a new system of planning agreements, where large firms would share information about their company strategies in return for government money. Finally, there would be a new Industry Act giving the government wide-ranging and discretionary powers to intervene in private industry (Tomlinson

1994: 283). It should also be noted that this call for a return to public ownership was partly in response to the Labour leadership's perception of the changing institutional structure of British markets. More particularly, the merger boom of the 1960s had changed fundamentally the structure of British industry in a way which further undermined the capacity of the government to control the private sector. For example, the share of total manufacturing enjoyed by Britain's top 100 companies had increased from 22 per cent in 1948 to 40 per cent in 1970 (Tomlinson 1994: 282). It followed logically that planning as a policy instrument to effect changes in the supply side of the economy was of less use to the Labour leadership. Nothing short of public ownership would now be needed if it wanted to achieve industrial restructuring.

However, despite these manifesto commitments, it remained the case that the Court was unwilling to allow these policy instruments to develop a capacity to intervene directly in the affairs of private industry. Both Holmes (1985: 37) and Tomlinson (1994: 302) argue that Wilson had lost his enthusiasm for nationalization by this time and was quite happy to preside over a watering down of the policy. Party and government publications became increasingly vague about the scope of the NEB role, while at the same time insisting that any planning agreements with industry should be signed on a voluntary basis. As a result, the NEB ended up propping up 'lame ducks' like British Leyland, while only two planning agreements were ever signed.

As the Court gradually lost enthusiasm for planning during this period, it became attracted to a number of other policy instruments in its quest to effect supply-side reform in the British economy. Initially, the Wilson government hoped that a new prices and incomes policy would regulate the growth of wages that would result from the strategy of planned economic expansion (R. Taylor 1993: 135). Moreover, as with the planning experiments noted above, the Court hoped that its new Joint Statement of Intent on prices and wages could be implemented on a voluntary basis, thus not offending the trade unions' traditional freedom to determine its own wage levels free from government interference. However, the gradual slide from a voluntary to a statutory incomes policy became a familiar theme of industrial relations over the next decade. The Wilson government followed up its Joint Statement of Intent with a new National Prices and Incomes Board, which was then given responsibility for monitoring the twelve-month wage freeze imposed after the Seamen's Strike in July 1966 (Shanks 1977: 36–7; Ponting 1989: 80–1). Having watched the National Mineworkers Union destroy the so-called $N - 1$ voluntary pay policy, Heath also moved to a three-stage statutory agreement (Shanks 1977: 64–70; Holmes 1982: 79–88). Finally, although the Callaghan government avoided any moves towards a statutory pay code, it must be remembered that by 1978 even a voluntary agreement to limit wage rises was now becoming unacceptable to the union rank and file (Donoghue 1987: 154–7).

Alongside these experiments with a prices and incomes policy came a radical new initiative to restructure the 'voluntary' tradition of British labour law. Although differing from each other in various ways, both the Wilson government's White Paper, *In Place of Strife*, and the Heath government's Industrial Relations Act contained a number of common proposals which challenged this traditional feature of British industrial relations. These included: the setting up of a Registrar of Trade Unions whereby only registered trade unions were to have legal rights and enjoy certain legal immunities; the drawing up of a new Industrial Relations Code of Practice, as well as a new National Industrial Relations Court (NIRC) to adjudicate in cases of dispute; the right of the Secretary of State to apply to the NIRC to defer a strike (the so-called cooling-off period) and to ask for a ballot before further action; and the stipulation that all collective agreements would be legally binding unless otherwise stated (Marsh 1992: 10–15).

From the above discussion, it is not difficult to trace the destructive effect of these policies on the autonomy and governing competence of the Court at this time. A good example of this process is the implementation of the Industrial Relations Act (1971). Spurred on by the TUC's plea for non-cooperation with the Registrar, the unions proceeded to make a mockery of the legislation. Faced with a strike by the National Union of Railwaymen in 1972, the government responded by first calling for a cooling off period, and then requesting a strike ballot before further action. The vote was 5–1 in favour of continuing the strike. The legislation had worked perfectly, yet had only succeeded in strengthening the position of the unions! Similar conclusions can be reached concerning the new NIRC, which found itself in conflict with the existing legal system over a number of decisions. One example was the judgement of Lord Denning at the Court of Appeal, who quashed a £55,000 fine imposed by the NIRC on the Transport and General Workers Union, arguing that the union was not responsible for the action of certain militant officials who were guilty of 'blacking' containers in a dispute on the docks. Instead, the judgement decreed that any official who continued the action would be personally liable and faced the threat of fines and imprisonment. Not surprisingly, the dockers were not shy about getting themselves arrested, and what was essentially a local dispute became a national controversy (Marsh 1992: 16–21; Campbell 1993: 459–60).

If the Industrial Relations Act generated counterproductive effects when implemented, it also seems reasonable to argue that the Court's experiment with a prices and incomes policy proved to be unsatisfactory. Grievances concerning this policy were at the heart of both the Miners' Strike (1974) and the Winter of Discontent (1978/9); strikes which were generally perceived to have brought down the Heath and Callaghan governments respectively. Whether the importance of these strikes has been exaggerated or not by recent historiography is beside the point. The more general point is clear. At a time when the bargaining strength within the trade unions movement was moving from the national to the shopfloor level (Marsh 1992: 29), intricate and time consuming negotiations over pay codes, which could then be applied across British industry, took up large amounts of the Court's time and energy. This loss of autonomy was particularly frustrating, especially as the Court subsequently watched nationally agreed deals founder against the resistance of increasingly powerful shop stewards.

EU Membership as a Response to Supply-side Failure

Faced with the increasing politicization of economic management, the efficient secret of this period was that the Court continued to hanker after external solutions to or escape routes from these problems. Put another way, while this period witnessed the gradual alteration of its governing code to stress the importance of discretionary policy instruments, the Court continued to promote the link between supply-side reform and external market solutions. Of course, the importance of the Commonwealth/OSA declined during this period. The new external support was supposed to be the EU, or 'Common Market' as it was referred to at the time. That said, it is important to be clear that politicians were not attracted to this policy solely or even primarily on the basis of its economic merits. What the Court found attractive about entry into the EU was the governing advantages that it conferred. Membership of this Common Market would help to re-establish the principles of automatism and neutrality at a time when the Court's autonomy and governing competence were increasingly being challenged. Faced with the domestic economic problems and constraints outlined above, the Court secretly welcomed the Europeanization of economic policy.

While it is not difficult to find evidence of British politicians making a public link between these domestic economic problems and EU membership, as noted in Chapter 1, the relationship between this policy idea, the motives of the Court and the implementation of policy needs to be problematized and unpacked. Two points are worth highlighting in this context. First, the academic community at this time was by no means united in its assessment of the effects of Community membership on the British economy. At best, the likely effects were uncertain. At worst, many of the 'facts' suggested that membership might impose a burden on the balance of payments. Second, although all British political leaders at this time were aware of the precariousness of the economic arguments, they were by no means neutral or unbiased in the evidence they chose to accept and reject. Memoirs of leading politicians of the time suggest that they were capable of selectively interpreting or even ignoring some of the advice they were given in order to put as optimistic a gloss as possible on the likely effects of membership on the British economy. These points will be elaborated below.

For supporters of EU membership, the economic case could be reduced to one simple proposition: growth by association. This statement contained two further claims. First, supporters of this argument pointed out that the Community Six had performed consistently better during the post-war period. Not surprisingly, they deduced that this superior performance stemmed from the fact that all these countries enjoyed preferential access to an enlarged home market of 170 million people. The removal of tariffs between the Six and the subsequent increase in intra-Community trade and competition had the effect of concentrating production in areas and firms where such goods could be produced the most cheaply and efficiently. Exposed to this larger market, European firms had been able to take advantage of economies of scale, leading to lower unit costs and prices and higher standards of living. In fact, by 1971, both the Heath and Wilson governments had gone further, by suggesting that, in addition to the removal of tariffs, the future challenge for the Community was to build a common industrial and technological community. This would further increase the performance of European firms by encouraging mergers and making available research and development into the latest technological advantages (HMG 1962; Cmnd 4715, 1971: 13–15; Lord 1993: 20).

The second proposition, not surprisingly, was that, if British industry gained access to this dynamic market, it too would enjoy the benefits of its European competitors. Politicians had to admit that the exact outcome of this policy would depend to a large extent on the way British industry reacted. A radical change in business planning, investment, production and sales effort would be needed. However, ministers were hopeful that the policy would increase the efficiency of British firms and with it their performance in international markets. They were certainly quick to point out that this judgement was supported by British business, both in policy statements and in its actions (HMG 1962: 38–40; Cmnd 4715, 1971: 12–13; A. Douglas-Home, *Hansard* (Commons) 21 October 1971: cols 912–24). In fact, EU membership represented something more to Conservative ministers. By joining this regional association, they hoped to engender a new sense of national purpose and pride (Aughey 1978: 12). As one Tory official put it, 'Europe was to be our *deus ex machina*; it was to create a new, contemporary argument with insular socialism, dish the Liberals by stealing their clothes, [and] give us something new after 12–13 years' (quoted in Lieber 1970: 164).

However, it was not difficult to find academic studies which questioned these benefits. Two criticisms are worth making in the light of the pro-Community case outlined above. First, a number of academic studies cast doubt on the argument that Community membership was responsible for the superior economic performance of the Six. Studies conducted by Scitovsky and Johnson estimated that the likely effect of the removal of EU tariffs on British welfare would not exceed 1 per cent of GDP. It was pointed out at the time that one reason for this disappointing figure was that, at the time of entry, the British tariff rate was comparatively low at 7.5 per cent (quoted in Cohen 1983).

Instead, a number of policy advisers pointed to other more indigenous factors to explain these favourable growth rates. It was reported at the time that the French government's conscious attempt to maintain a high level of demand in the economy, with little regard for the level of the exchange rate, was a more plausible reason for the impressive growth rates achieved. Other economists, such as Kaldor and Kindleberger, suggested that the relatively backward structure of many Continental economies was another important variable. After the war, with many of their industries destroyed, European governments were able to transfer a surplus of labour from low productivity agricultural sectors to new high productivity industries with little threat of wage inflation or other bottlenecks (quoted in Cohen 1983: 196–8). There is evidence from Macmillan's memoirs that such an analysis had filtered through to politicians at this time:

> Of course, if we had succeeded in losing two world wars, wrote off all our debts – instead of having nearly 30 000 million in debt – got rid of all our foreign obligations, and kept no force overseas, then we might be as rich as the Germans. It makes one think a bit. (Quoted in Horne 1989: 239)

Second, a number of studies also questioned the proposition that British industry was at a competitive disadvantage because British markets were too small. A study by Pratten (1971) concluded that the UK market was perfectly large enough to enjoy economies of scale. Indeed, as already noted, the striking feature of British post-war industrial development was that, despite little change in average plant size, the largest one hundred companies had enjoyed an increasing share of the total British manufacturing output (quoted in Cohen 1983: 191–2). The pertinent question, as Crosland pointed out at a Chequers strategy meeting on Europe in 1966, was, if the economic arguments were so contested, why were most industrialists in favour of joining? Jay replied at the time:

> But he knew as well as I did that if you asked most industrialists what effect they estimated higher food prices would have on their labour costs, most of them did not understand the question. The truth was that few industrialists had thought it out. (Jay 1980: 366)

Moreover, to admit that they might not be able to compete in this new dynamic European market would be tantamount to confessing that they were inefficient; a confession that few British industrialists were willing to make.

When it comes to evidence of ministers and civil servants selectively interpreting the advice they received on this matter, Jay's (1980: 354–6, 386) account of the decision of the Wilson government to apply for membership in

1967 provides a rich source of information. He complains of the lack of serious analysis in Whitehall concerning the overall effects of membership on the balance of payments before 1966. When he tried to present his own calculations in a paper to Cabinet, various techniques were used to try to suppress it. For example, Wilson argued, somewhat obscurely, that there were difficulties concerning the circulation of papers which were not inter-departmentally agreed. Although Jay seems to have ignored this put-off, when again trying to get his paper circulated, Wilson wheeled out a new doctrine which stated that ministers' papers should not be distributed until after the Cabinet had completed its analysis of studies by officials (Jay 1980: 361–2, 382–4). As a result, former Cabinet ministers now accuse Wilson of deliberate obfuscation in his handling of the economic case at this time. Instead of beginning with an overall discussion on the likely effect on the balance of payments (which was likely to show a negative effect, at least in the short-term), the Cabinet was asked to consider separately how Community policy at this time was likely to affect each sector of the British economy. Castle agrees, arguing that by compartmentalizing the discussions and swamping them with detailed papers Wilson prevented ministers from evaluating what she thought were the more important issues, such as the primacy of EU law over British law and the constraints this would impose on a future Labour government's freedom to implement socialist measures. Thus, during the detailed Cabinet studies on the economic case for membership, she can be heard to moan: 'He [Wilson] has succeeded in guiding us into a discussion of details which is more effective than anything else in making principles look less important' (Castle 1984: 236).

Finally, when detailed official estimates of the likely overall effect of membership were produced, they were ignored. Ironically, by estimating the negative effect to be between £400 and £920 million a year, official studies were slightly more pessimistic in their conclusions than Jay's own calculations. That said, Jay argues that the additional weight of these arguments had little effect on policy. Wilson admitted there was no positive economic case. Jenkins argued that he had committed himself for so long that he could hardly turn around and admit that he was now wrong. Crosland suggests that because the exact impact of membership could not be calculated, the effects may eventually turn out to be negligible, while Callaghan suggested that an extra load of £600 million on the balance of payments might be 'manageable'. As Jay concludes,

> the tragedy was that Brown, Wilson, Jenkins and others mainly in the Foreign Office, reached conclusions before they had made any serious effort to estimate the economic consequences at all. That was indeed the basic truth in the whole tangled story of Britain's plunge into EU membership. (Jay 1980: 386–8)

The question remains: how can we explain the attraction of the Court to the

EU during this period? One answer might be to assert that economic factors played no part: the whole thrust of policy was dominated by geo-political motives. Indeed, many accounts of British policy during this period prefer to stress such 'political' variables. In this context, the main worry for the Court was Britain's growing isolation in a world fast dividing into a number of regional blocs. Some authors suggest that one important motive behind Macmillan's original application was his concern at the growing economic and political weight of the Union. They point to his own sense of impotence at the Paris Summit in 1960 and his nervousness about de Gaulle's schemes to develop machinery for political cooperation within the EU at this time. Others suggest that a link was also explicitly made between membership and preserving the 'special' relationship with the USA. The Macmillan government feared that, as the EU grew in strength, Washington would increasingly turn to this regional bloc as its major partner in the free world, thus leaving Britain further isolated. This analysis remained influential right up to the early 1970s, although by the time of the Heath government it had been given a slightly new spin. Now the main worry in Whitehall was whether the USA would decouple itself from the defence of Western Europe. Although always played down in official publications, it was acknowledged that Europe had to do more to contribute to its own defence. In this context, membership was vital to ensure that Britain was at the forefront of any new discussions on the development of a Union defence capability (Camps 1963: 274–83; Cmnd 4715, 1971: 8; A. Douglas Home, *Hansard* (Commons) vol. 823, 21 October 1971: cols 912–24; E. Heath, *Hansard* (Commons) vol. 823, 28 October 1971: cols. 2202–4; Roll 1985: 103; Lord 1993: 11–13).

While not wanting to deny the importance of these geo-political motives in understanding Britain's decision to enter the EU, this chapter concludes by arguing that the economic arguments remained important. However, it was the governing advantages of these ideas which the Court found attractive. At a time when it was experiencing implementation problems with its attempts to develop discretionary policy instruments, EU membership offered an opportunity to return to the governing principles which ensured some element of domestic autonomy and governing competence before 1960. Take, for example, the principle of automatism. Faced with the uncertain economic climate of the early 1960s, EU membership seemed to provide an *automatic* solution to the Court's governing problem. Of course, leading politicians and officials were careful to state that the exact effects of membership on the British economy were hard to predict. As already suggested, much would depend on the efforts of British industry once it became exposed to this new external opportunity. However, their faith that the 'dynamic' benefits of membership would eventually materialize and that 'on balance' the aggregate effect on the balance of payments would be positive seemed to confirm the view that the Court hoped that the EU would automatically resolve its supply-side problem (HMG 1962: 39–40; *Hansard* (Commons) vol. 645, 2 August 1961: col. 1489; Cmnd 4715, 1971: 160).

Second, the EU seemed to provide a *neutral* external discipline which would shock British industry out of its outdated methods and practices. This viewpoint was known in some circles as the 'cold shower' thesis. Ministers made little attempt to hide the fact that some industries would benefit, while others would be penalized. As Maudling argued in the first debate on the EU after the initial announcement to join had been made:

> I think that the great effect of going into a wider European market will be that the efficient firms will prosper and the inefficient will go down. That, surely, is precisely what we must see in this country if our economy is really to expand and our growth is to be more rapid. (*Hansard* (Commons) vol. 645, 2 August 1961, col. 1605; see also *Hansard* (Commons) vol. 746, 8 May 1967, cols. 1062–3)

However, the great advantage for the Court was that responsibility for supply-side restructuring could be off-loaded on to British firms, who would either sink or swim in the new markets which Whitehall had provided for them. Membership represented the equivalent of a giant European 'invisible hand', which would reorder and revitalize the British economy according to the logic of the market. As a result, the Court could avoid the need to intervene in the economy directly: a policy which it found so troublesome.

Similar considerations can be detected in the Cabinet debates in the Wilson government during the 1960s. One prevalent theme was the effect of EU membership on 'discretionary' regional policy. Crossman describes Douglas Jay as presenting a very effective paper arguing that entry into the Common Market would remove both the carrot and stick with which the Labour government got industrialists to settle in certain regions. For Crossman, the defence developed by Wilson was 'captivating'. He did not deny the strength of Jay's arguments. Instead he pointed out that what regional policy really provided was a general expansion of capital investment. According to Wilson, this would be the exact effect of Common Market membership, producing a rise of 20–30 per cent in industrial investment. Such a policy would work better than 'any artificial scheme a British government could think up' (Crossman 1976: 303). This was nothing short of a conscious attempt partially to hive off responsibility for policy to the European level.

Indications that the Court longed to return to automatic, neutral market solutions to its economic problems provoked charges of 'escapism' from opponents in both parties. For example, this line of argument could be found on the right of the Conservative Party in the person of Enoch Powell. Writing in 1971, Powell was clear: 'When we consider the various arrangements we might make with other countries, we are not a drowning man clutching at a rope or screaming for someone to throw him a lifebelt. . . . So let's have none of this 'eleventh hour' stuff please. (Powell 1971: 12).

He went on to argue:

> Since the end of the last century it has been an article of faith with the
> British that they were wealthy and prosperous – or to pitch it lower, they
> survived – because Britain was at the centre of a world-wide Empire.
> This belief, which was buttressed by the adoption of Imperial Preference
> in 1932 ... was almost devoid of any foundation. ... So inbuilt,
> however, was this belief that, when the Empire dissolved ... the people
> of Britain suffered from a kind of vertigo: they could not believe they
> were standing upright, and reached out for something to clutch. It
> seemed axiomatic that economically, as well as politically, they must be
> part of something bigger. (59–60)

A similar line of criticism could be found in the writings of a well known
Labour pragmatist, Richard Crossman. Commenting on the original decision
to join the EU, Crossman thought it was possible to see the advantages of
putting the problems of the supply side of the economy up to the Community
level. In an article for *International Affairs*, he argued that, for Macmillan, EU
entry was: 'an extemporised device for propping up a failing government – an
escape into Europe from domestic problems that had become insoluble'
(Crossman 1963: 743; see also Lieber 1970: 164). Similarly, winding up for
Labour in the August 1961 debate on EU membership, Wilson cautioned the
government 'not to regard their decision about Europe as an exercise in
economic escapism. We shall survive – inside or outside Europe – only as a
result of our own efforts.' He went on to warn Macmillan: 'There is no more
dangerous illusion than that laissez-faire and the cold east wind will do the
trick. Positive, purposive, economic planning will be needed' (*Hansard*
(Commons) vol. 645, 3 August 1961: cols 1653–7).

Of course, this line of argument was to be expected from the opposition
front bench, in the 'adversarial' atmosphere of the House of Commons.
However, of more interest and significance was the reaction of Crossman to
Wilson's first bid to join the EU after the failure of the national planning
experiments in the mid-1960s. As Crossman pointed out, domestically, the
demise of the national plan left the party saddled with an unpopular short-
term policy of deflation, continual balance of payments problems and the
perennial threat of a sterling crisis. In January 1966, he could be seen
lamenting: 'an escape from the endless sterling crises seemed to be offered by
entry into Europe. Britain clearly depended on the economic and financial cooperation of the EU and would derive considerable advantage from
participation in its wider markets' (Crossman 1975: 442).

Similarly, writing against the background of the July 1966 crisis, he admits
that:

> very soon we shall be faced with the choice between devaluation and
> intensive deflation. I suppose to some of my colleagues the idea of
> escaping from this terrible choice into the Common Market is attractive

because once we are members, the blame for the deflation, the blame for the suffering, could be put, not on the British government, but on conditions inside the EU. That was really the reason why Macmillan suddenly became an enthusiastic marketeer . . . and I suspect much the same pressures were now working on Harold Wilson. (Crossman 1975: 557–8; see also M. Foot, *Hansard* (Commons) vol. 746, 8 May 1967: col. 1120)

More importantly, other members of Wilson's Cabinet made the connection between the Common Market and domestic policy failure. By April 1967, Barbara Castle can be seen complaining: 'We are going into Europe because we haven't applied economic policies which are a real alternative. It is *that* which matters' (Castle 1984: 245, original emphasis; see also pp. 236–7, 248). Five days later, Crossman argued that Wilson, Brown and Callaghan were attracted to membership because 'they've recently experienced the difficulties of trying to introduce socialist planning outside a great block and they're determined to escape from these difficulties by getting inside' (Crossman 1976: 335).

The connection between the intractable question of British supply-side economic reform and EU membership remains a common theme in the Labour government of 1974–9. Once again, most of the evidence comes from the left wing of the Labour leadership. As already noted, Wilson had lost faith in the policies of nationalization and planning agreements to achieve lasting restructuring in British industry. However, Benn went further, complaining that his attempts to implement these policies from the Department of Industry were being frustrated by the leadership's continual advocacy of EU membership. Two examples from Benn's memoirs are worth noting in this context. In March 1974, he complained that his attempt to intervene in the steel industry to control prices was overruled by Callaghan, the then Foreign Secretary, who pointed out that this might be in breach of the European Coal and Steel Treaty (Benn 1989: 128). Castle confirms that the Labour leadership was aware that the Paris Treaty conflicted with Section 15 of the Iron and Steel Act (1967), which gave power to the Secretary of State to control investment in the private sector. Heath had repealed Section 15 as a condition for joining in 1973. Castle notes that Wilson was mandated by Cabinet to go to Dublin in 1975 to work out how these powers could be recovered, but this was never done (Castle 1980: 323).

The second specific example from the Benn diaries concerns a financial support package for British Leyland (BL). Benn documents the case of a note in his red box from the European Office of the Department of Industry, advising him that when putting his case for financial support for BL he should tell the Commission that it was only an 'act of public ownership'. Benn admits this would be a case of clear deception, as the purpose of the aid was not acquisition. According to Benn, the aid had a threefold purpose: to subsidize BL, which would otherwise collapse, in order to preserve jobs and capacity which would be replaced by EU imports; to provide long-term loan capital at non-commercial rates, in order to re-equip and improve capacity; and to make BL more internationally competitive than would be the case if it was left to market forces. Benn is in little doubt at the time that these policy instruments were in breach of Articles 92–94 of the Treaty of Rome. This elicits a cry of frustration: 'it is madness to unarm ourselves at the moment when we were about to adopt a new policy' (Benn 1989: 142–3, 349–65).

At a superficial level, this looks like a classic case of policy bungling or irrationality, especially when it is also borne in mind that the TUC had come out against EU membership in the early 1970s (Bilski 1974). That said, it is possible to detect evidence highlighting that senior members of the Cabinet were more than willing to accept the Europeanization of Britain's supply-side problems, realizing that this had advantages in terms of governing autonomy and competence. Benn's diaries record how, in a Cabinet discussion, some Labour leaders stressed the political advantages of enmeshing this problem of industrial reform within the structures of European interdependence. For Harold Lever (27 February 1975), 'international disciplines must be enforced' (Benn 1989), while, according to Reg Prentice (18 March 1975), we need to strengthen the power of Parliament over the pressure groups at home and we must institutionalize our external interdependence' (Benn 1989). Indeed, two months before, in a New Year's message to his constituents, Benn himself accuses his pro-European colleagues of this sort of political manoeuvring. He begins by arguing that EU membership challenges the democratic rights of the British people because it blurs the lines of accountability between politicians and the electorate, thus boosting their autonomy from societal pressure. He goes on to assert:

> British membership of the Community, by permanently transferring sovereign legislative and financial powers to Community Authorities, who are not directly elected by the British people, also permanently *insulates* those Authorities from direct control by the British electors who cannot dismiss them and whose views, therefore need carry no weight with them and whose grievances they cannot be compelled to remedy. (Benn 1974: 40) (emphasis in the original)

Admittedly, the passage is ambiguous, but put in the context of the overall document, Benn seems to suggest that British politicians were aware of the autonomy advantages of the EU and that this was one reason why they remained wedded to membership.

Unfortunately, when it comes to studying the Heath government, there is little direct evidence to suggest that the leadership was attracted to membership of the Community as an external device for avoiding the problem of supply-side reform, although, at this point, analysis suffers somewhat from a paucity of literature. There are three reasons why such a connection might be unexpected. First, Heath dominated the government's policy towards the Community at this time. Second, his commitment to the Community was consistent and principled and largely unrelated to his views on other policy areas. Finally, by temperament, Heath was a technocratic problem-solver, largely uninterested in developing a wider strategy which knitted his various beliefs concerning foreign and domestic issues into some kind of relatively coherent whole (Holmes 1982: 4, 77; *Contemporary Record* (1990).

That said, those commentators who have analysed the Heath government accept that a crude link between measures to reform the supply side of the economy and Community membership existed. First, EU membership was seen as playing a supporting role to the government's plans for the implementation of its free market strategy under the so-called 'quiet revolution'. It was hoped that new competitive pressures emanating from EU membership would promote an efficient allocation of resources and improve productivity. Furthermore, once industry had been freed from the obstacles and shackles of the supply side of the economy, the Common Market would provide an external outlet to channel the extra production and output it was hoped would result. It was also hoped that membership would strengthen Britain's trading position in the sense that it would provide an additional source of funds in the event of balance of payments problems (Holmes 1982: 5; Campbell 1993; Lord 1993: 23). Most interesting, however, is an additional factor cited by Lord in his analysis of the Heath government's European policy. He suggests that it was realized within the Conservative leadership 'that the pains of competitive transformation would strain the administrative capacity and political authority of any British government; it was thus wise to rely to a degree on greater exposure to the autonomous operation of external economic disciplines' (Lord 1993: 23). Frustratingly, no source is cited for this judgement and Lord himself chooses not to elaborate on it.

While the economic arguments dominated discussion of EU membership, it should finally be noted that the constitutional aspect of this decision was played down by the Court at this time. For most MPs, the EU was just like any other international organization. Few understood, or were concerned enough to highlight the fact, that Section 2 of the European Communities Act 1972, which provided for the primacy of EU law, conflicted with the convention of parliamentary sovereignty. Membership now seemed to contradict the understanding that: Parliament had the right to make and unmake any law; no person or body was recognized by the law as having the right to override or set aside the legislation of Parliament; and no Parliament could bind its successors (Judge 1993: 182). White Papers produced by both Labour and Conservative governments at this time accepted that a future Parliament might have to refrain from passing inconsistent legislation, but instances such as these were expected to be few and far between (Cmnd 3301, 1967: 9; Cmnd 4289, 1970; Cmnd 4715, 1971: 8–9; Gregory 1983: 71). In short, there was little appreciation that the EU, with its own Court and developing body of law, had the potential to penetrate domestic politics in a way no other external commitment had done.

Conclusions

When it comes to understanding Conservative responses to the European-ization of economic policy after 1979, this historical survey contains three conclusions which are relevant to the analysis that follows. Historically, the Court has perceived itself to be structurally constrained in its ability to develop instruments or capacities for promoting reform in the supply side of the economy. As a result, it developed a governing code which stressed the importance of limited responsibility, neutrality and automatism in the conduct of economic policy. The role of external policy was to support those domestic governing principles. In particular, this code stressed the link between domestic supply-side problems and external market solutions. Through this connection, the Court was able to preserve its autonomy, authority and governing competence.

However, after 1960, against the backdrop of British economic decline, this governing code came under increasing strain. Many of the contributions which went to the heart of the debate concerning Britain's comparatively poor economic record reflected criticism of the Court's governing principles and style. As a result, some of those principles were dropped; others were added. More particularly, the Court accepted the necessity of developing discretionary policy instruments capable of intervening directly in the supply side of the economy. However, it attempted to develop this interventionist strategy while, at the same time, hoping to avoid the need to discriminate between actors in British markets. Not surprisingly, this inconsistency did not help in the promotion of policies which militated against the 'voluntarist' tradition in British industrial relations. By the mid-1970s, this experiment in Tripartism had collapsed, as did the Court's autonomy and reputation for governing competence.

At the same time, the Court continued to hanker after external solutions to its domestic problems. As the period wore on, it gradually came to understand that the economic ideas behind Common Market membership provided a solution to its governing problem. Put another way, membership offered an opportunity to revitalize the old pre-1961 governing code. Entry into this new 'dynamic' market would provide a new neutral, automatic, external discipline (a European 'invisible hand') which would shock British industry out of its outdated beliefs and practices. The Court could appropriate external (European) structures to hive off responsibility for the task of supply-side economic reform. The traditional link between supply-side problems and external market solutions could be restored, along with all the benefits of domestic autonomy.

CHAPTER THREE

Resurrecting the Old Autonomy Code: 'Monetarism in One Country' and the Challenge of International Economic Forces

Since the 1920s, external policy has always played a vital role in the Court's governing code. More particularly, it had provided the crucial function of supporting the Court's attempt to preserve its 'core' belief in the need for governing autonomy from domestic forces in the area of economic management. By stressing the important link between problems in the supply side of the economy and the fortunes of British industry in foreign (Empire) markets, external policy helped to support a number of instrumental beliefs linked to this autonomy code. Such beliefs included the importance of neutral economic frameworks or rules which apply to the whole economy, a distaste for discretionary, interventionist, industrial policies and a preference, wherever possible, for automatic or semi-automatic instruments of economic management. Even when this code came under challenge in the 1960s and had to be altered, the Court remained privately wedded to many of these principles. As a result, one of the efficient secrets of this period is how EU membership gradually appealed to an increasing number at the Court as a sort of external escape from the growing pressure of implementing discretionary Tripartite policies in the 1960s.

Having provided a historical perspective, this chapter makes three main claims. It begins by arguing that, at its core, Thatcherism should be partly understood as a Statecraft strategy aimed at repairing the pre-1961 autonomy code. Second, if the actions of the Conservative leadership reflected a desire to reconstruct a semblance of governing autonomy and competence, this experiment was domestically based. It paid little attention to the problems of implementing monetarism within a small and relatively 'open' economy such as Britain's. Moreover, while party publications were generally positive concerning membership of the EU, there was no evidence to suggest that Conservative leaders envisaged a supporting role for this organization, *vis-à-vis* their domestic concerns. Finally, if benign neglect of the external environment was considered acceptable in 1979, this chapter finishes by arguing that it was not an option by the mid-1980s. More specifically, 'monetarism in one country' was undermined, or was perceived to be undermined, by a combination of domestic and external forces. As a result, a number of prominent figures with the Court grew restless. In this context, they sought entrenchment of this autonomy strategy through the Europeanization of policy. This theme will be taken up in Chapter 4.

The New Conservatism and the Quest for Governing Competence, 1975–79

While the lessons of Europeanization took longer to realize, in opposition the new Thatcherite leadership began to address the problem of how a future Conservative government would protect its autonomy and governing competence in the face of the existing problems of enforcing supply-side economic reform. The result was what Lawson has termed the 'New Conservatism', which represented many things. What is important here is the renewed commitment to sound money, a balanced budget and free markets. These policies are popularly viewed as a New Right inspired economic theory which provided a plausible response to the main problem facing the British economy by the late 1970s, that of inflation. However, this chapter suggests an alternative interpretation. New Conservatism represented a new Statecraft project, aimed at repairing the pre-1961 governing code which had been compromised as a result of the Tripartite experiments of the 1960s and 1970s. More particularly, it represented an attempt to rediscover the principles of limited responsibility, neutrality and automatism and, with it, to recreate a semblance of autonomy and governing competence in the field of economic management. As Lawson put it in a policy tract in 1980: 'to describe the New Conservatism purely in terms of an approach to economic policy would be manifestly inadequate: it goes a great deal wider than that' (Lawson 1992: 1041; see also Thatcher 1977: 1).

That New Conservatism represented a reassertion of limited responsibility for policy by the Court can be demonstrated by the significant 'reversal of assignments' in economic management. Interestingly, this change meant resurrecting the formal, pre-1961, division of responsibilities between the state and peak groups in the economy. Once again, the Court defined its responsibilities in restricted terms. Its primary task was to provide a sound nominal framework for British industry through the pursuit of low and stable inflation. In rediscovering this old tenet of political management, Monetarism as a theory allowed the Court to reject the cost-push theory of inflation, which deemed that rising prices were directly linked to rising wages in the real economy. According to Monetarism, inflation was related to the level of the money supply circulating around the economy. Moreover, the fact that public expenditure (which was directly controlled by the Treasury) made up approximately 40 per cent of the total money supply made the policy doubly appealing. Some new institutional flesh was put on this theory through the creation of the Medium Term Financial Strategy (MTFS), which emphasized centrally defined and published targets for the money supply, interest rates and public expenditure. When it came to charting the level of inflation, sterling M3 (defined as all notes and coins in circulation, plus bank deposits) became the centrally important money supply target, because its growth was understood to be directly linked to the size of the Public Sector Borrowing Requirement (PSBR) (Pepper 1998). That said, while the policy instruments might be new, the Court clearly had historic parallels in mind when it drew up the policy. In the words of Ridley, monetarism 'was not revolutionary, it was a return to orthodoxy ... it was a return to good housekeeping' (Ridley 1992: 167; see also Lawson 1992: 1054).

At the same time, responsibility for 'real' economic variables, such as productivity, economic growth and employment, was hived off on to groups in the supply side of the economy. This is not to say that the government had no role at all. Conservative leaders maintained that they had an important responsibility to establish and maintain the right legal framework under which these groups, particularly business, could prosper in domestic and international markets. And, of course, the government fully expected that it would have to undertake specific supply-side measures to help to free the domestic market (Lawson 1992: 413–43; Thatcher 1993: 14). So in a move which distinguished it from politicians during the inter-war period, the Court presided over a cautious programme of industrial relations reform designed to weaken the position of the unions (Marsh 1992: 82–109).

Just as important to the Court were measures brought in to liberalize British financial markets. Most notable were: the abolition of exchange controls on overseas investment by financial institutions in October 1979; the ending of the Supplementary Special Deposits Scheme ('the Corset') in June 1980, under which banks were restricted from creating credit due to the fact that they had to lodge additional deposits with the Bank of England; the abrogation of hire purchase controls in July 1982; and the 'big bang' in the City of London in October 1986, which in effect brought about a liberalization of practices in a number of areas in the Stock Exchange rule book. As we shall see, these changes, combined with broader movements in the international economy, undermined, or were perceived to undermine, the implementation of monetarism in practice.

With this move to limit its responsibility for economic policy, the Court hoped to resurrect the benefits of a neutral policy framework. For Lawson, the MTFS, in particular, represented a clear attempt to replace discretionary economic management by adherence to known rules. These self-imposed and publicized rules were seen as the best guard against the 'arbitrary' demands of societal groups. As Lawson points out in his memoirs:

Governments that believe in unfettered discretion are likely to be led astray by short-term pressures and the politically expedient. A government that simply reacts to the pressure of events is likely to make more mistakes than one constrained by rules embodying experience accumulated over a long period. (Lawson 1992: 66–7; see also 1021, 1040)

Moreover, an explicit connection was made between the principle of neutral rules and the benefits of governing autonomy and competence. To quote Lawson again: 'A government of rules ... is less intrusive and – in the long run – more acceptable to the public at large than a government of men' (Lawson 1992: 1025).

Furthermore, the Court hoped to restore the benefits of semi-automatic economic management. By off-loading responsibility for aggregate demand, growth and unemployment on to the market, the Conservative leadership believed it could avoid the endless wrangling with societal groups, particularly the unions, over the objectives of national plans and incomes policies. Lawson was once again explicit concerning the autonomy advantages of abandoning discretionary policy instruments, which had 'conferred undue importance on trade union leaders ... [enabling them] to hold previous governments to ransom' (Lawson 1992: 437). This point is also illustrated by Thatcher in her memoirs: 'I was determined that the Government should not become enmeshed as previous Labour and Conservative administrations had been, in the obscure intricacies of "norms", "going rates" and "special cases" ' (Thatcher 1993: 93; see also 1995: 223–30).

It follows that this dramatic reversal of assignments in economic policy stemmed partly from a concern within the leadership about the problems the party was likely to face when implementing economic policy goals within the institutional confines of the British polity. In particular, it provided an answer to a question that had continually dogged the leadership throughout the 1960s and 1970s: 'How would the party deal with the unions?' Or more pertinently after the experience of the Heath government: 'How would the unions deal with the party?' For as long as the leadership accepted the analysis of Jim Prior, then shadow Employment Secretary, that inflation was caused by wage rises and that the only way to contain such rises was to institute some kind of incomes policy, the party consequently had to deal with the question of why it, rather than Labour, would be better at getting the unions to cooperate with a pay policy. The seeming inability of the so-called 'Wets' to come up with a credible answer to this conundrum just compounded the problem. Gilmour's (1977: 252–3) solution was for the party 'to reconcile competition and corporatism'. How was this to be achieved? Gilmour suggested a Public Industrial Forum, where industrial leaders would have to argue their case for wage rises against other industrial leaders. On the pertinent question of how this would avoid the problems experienced by the Heath government, Gilmour provided no real answer. Instead he fell back into pessimism verging on defeatism: 'at the end of the day, none of it may make very much difference. Governments have little power and influence, and well established attitudes may be immune to government persuasion or action'. By concerning itself solely with the task of controlling inflation, and denying a link between wages and prices, monetarism provided an altogether more satisfactory, if contested, answer to the problem.

Furthermore, by abandoning such Tripartite instruments of economic management, the Conservative leadership hoped to revitalize what was perceived to be the atrophy of British democratic institutions, particularly Parliament. With one eye obviously firmly rooted on the recent experience of governments in the 1960s and 1970s, Thatcher claimed that the use of Tripartite structures frequently meant that 'the proper channels' were discredited. Elaborating on this point at her first party conference as leader, Thatcher scrutinized Wilson's claim that Labour was now the natural party of government because it was the only one the trade unions would accept:

> Labour's failure . . . to look at national problems from the viewpoint of the whole nation, and not just one section of it, has led to a loss of confidence and a sense of helplessness, and with it goes a feeling that Parliament which ought to be in charge, is not in charge and decisions are taken elsewhere. (Thatcher 1977: 30; see also Thatcher 1995: 233; Conservative Central Office 1977: 5–7)

By restoring the role of Parliament, re-establishing what the party perceived to be the rule of law and focusing once again on the national interest, the leadership hoped to depoliticize the conduct of economic management.

In short, by resurrecting a governing code which put a premium on the importance of a neutral domestic framework of public rules for the conduct of monetary policy and which avoided discretionary economic management as a rule, the Conservative leadership hoped it would avoid the embarrassing and highly damaging U-turns, the strikes, the state of emergencies and the general atmosphere of overload which surrounded British politics in the 1970s. In other words, it hoped to recreate some semblance of governing competence, which in the longer term would lead to electoral benefits. To quote Thatcher again in her memoirs:

> We had to stress continually that, however difficult the road might be and however long it took us to reach our destination . . . I would have to struggle to ensure that this time the Conservative government kept its nerve. If we failed, we would never be given another chance. (Thatcher 1993: 15)

If this New Conservative statecraft project was conceived partly as a domestic response to the problem of maintaining autonomy and competence in the face of the likely domestic pressures that would result from attempts at restructuring, it was possible to point to a number of problems and contradictions even before the party entered office in 1979. Three in particular are worth noting in the context of the argument below. The first problem was that the New Conservatism presented a real challenge to the post-war social democratic consensus, yet seemed to offer little in the way of solutions to deal with the opprobrium that was likely to fall on Conservative leaders as a result of the implementation of specific policies. In a speech to the Institute of Directors in 1976, Thatcher admitted that the proposed reforms 'totally reject the concept of Britain living in the nostalgic glories of the previous industrial revolution based upon manufacturing techniques and products which may have very little relevance to our future pattern of wealth. Of course, such a challenge has social implications' (Thatcher 1977: 78). What worried the party faithful was the almost complete absence at the time of palliatives for such consequences (Behrens 1980). For example, in the same speech the leader suggested that the answer might lie in a far-sighted social policy. Exactly what this meant, and what the implications were for the government's stress on firm control of public expenditure, was not made clear. At other times, Thatcher fell back on even more platitudinous statements: 'It is the politician's job to warn the people of the consequences and to win their support for the prudent course of action, because ultimately its success will depend on the measure of consent it commands' (Thatcher 1977: 71).

In particular, what disturbed the former followers and supporters of Heath, variously called the Wets, Ditchers or One Nation Tories was the over-reliance that the leadership was placing on the market mechanism as a kind of magic, invisible, hand which would cure all the structural problems of the British economy. They warned that this market equilibrium would be unhinged by union monopoly power which operated in key sectors of the economy, particularly the public sector. Moreover, they worried that the abandonment of an incomes policy would pave the way for a return to free collective bargaining and the bad old days of leap-frogging pay claims in total disregard of profitability and output (Gilmour 1977: 236–45; Behrens 1980: 73–5). Finally, many within the party wanted to know how the Conservative leadership would deal with the real risk of higher unemployment and the opposition that this was likely to provoke. This question received no substantial treatment before 1979 (H. Young 1989: 316–17). Not surprisingly, when the political fall-out from the unemployment question arrived, some in the party urged a return to the Tripartite methods of the 1960s and 1970s.

Second, this over-reliance on market forces extended to the area of foreign economic policy. As already noted, the international orientation of British business and the fact that sterling was still traded widely as an international currency meant that the British economy was small but 'open' in comparison with its main competitors. By the end of the 1970s, the value of UK exports was 33 per cent of GDP compared with 21 per cent in the mid-1960s.

Alternatively, the value of UK imports was 30 per cent of GDP as compared with 23 per cent over the same period (Panic 1982: 37–8). Despite this fact, party publications were largely silent on the relationship between movements in the value of sterling and domestic monetary policy. *The Right Approach to the Economy* (1977) 'trotted out' the meaningless platitude that any attempt to foster a new climate of responsibility in Britain would have to take place in the context of 'financial constraints within which the solvent nation, like the solvent company, must operate' (Conservative Central Office 1977: 7). On the more specific role of the exchange rate, the party stuck close to the established orthodoxy, which rejected the argument that devaluation was the route to greater competition: instead, that policy option risked fuelling inflation and exacerbating Britain's relative economic decline (Conservative Central Office 1977: 8). While the MTFS contained targets for the money supply and public expenditure, there was no similar benchmark for the value of the pound. In this context, it is important to remember that North Sea oil had now come on stream, making sterling very sensitive to price movements in this commodity.

A third problem facing the party leadership was that the question about the exact role of government in the economy and society was one of the most contentious issues within the party itself. Hence, although the majority of the parliamentary party seemed to acquiesce in the shift towards a new emphasis on sound money and free markets, genuine enthusiasm for the new approach was limited to a hard core of the leadership. One obvious example of this was the lack of support Thatcher had when she appointed her first Cabinet in 1979 (H. Young 1989: 138–49). However, even so-called supporters of the new policy found the rationale behind it difficult to swallow. Lawson admits that a number of members of the Cabinet were against this self-imposed discipline or framework of rules. Biffen was one, 'believing that governments should never impale themselves on hooks in this way, since it reduced their room for manoeuvre as circumstances changed'. Of course, for Lawson this was exactly the point, and he put this point in more striking language in a policy tract published in 1980. British governments in the past had allowed inflation to get out of control because they had printed too much money. Lawson's explanation was that 'political forces have played a prominent part. . . . In so far as they have, it is legitimate to strive politically to weaken those forces' (quoted in Lawson 1992: 1042).

Similarly, when it came to checking the small print of the various position papers put out by the party between 1975 and 1979, there was a marked difference between the rhetoric and the reality. One example of the continuity with the Heath period was in the area of industrial policy. For example, having first been threatened with abolition, the National Enterprise Board was kept on, while at the same time having its powers restricted. The issue of industrial subsidies provides another example. While the leadership could often be heard condemning the practice of bailing out loss-making firms with taxpayers' money, in reality specific proposals allowed for a number of exceptional cases where subsidies might be needed (Behrens 1980: 103–13). Consequently, in the face of their relative isolation within the party, the Thatcherites had to move cautiously in opposition in developing this state-craft project.

The Conservative Party's Discourse on the European Union

If this New Conservative statecraft project represented an attempt by the leadership to protect its autonomy from the expected domestic challenges to its free market strategy, there was little direct evidence before 1979 that the leadership intended the EU to play a supporting role in this project. Party publications during this period do not give an impression of any radical new thinking on this issue. Instead, manifestos and campaign guides were domi-nated by party political point scoring. This literature pointed to the fact that Labour had changed its mind four times since 1961 (five times by 1984) as evidence of its *inconsistent* record on the EU. It quoted Benn's own enthusiastic promulgation of his own obstructive tactics in the Energy Councils in the mid-1970s as evidence of Labour's *half-hearted approach*. Finally, it cited Labour's policy of renegotiation, backed by the threat of a referendum on membership, as evidence of Labour's *unprincipled* approach to the EU. Renego-tiation, it lambasted, had nothing to do with securing better terms for Britain. It was a cynical ploy aimed at overcoming the deep divisions in the party over the European issue. Put another way, Labour was unprincipled because the leadership had committed the grave folly of allowing crucially important questions of foreign policy to be affected by the short-term needs of domestic party politics (Conservative Research Department 1979: 5–9; Conservative Research Department/European Democratic Group Secretariat 1984: 4–5). Ridley confirms this general impression of inactivity. No policy group was set up on Europe, simply because no one saw the need for one (Ridley 1992: 136).

This is not to say that party publications during the period in opposition adopted the negative tone that was often to infuse relations with the EU after 1979. On the contrary, the leadership constantly employed the theme that the Conservatives were the 'party of Europe' in Britain. They reminded voters that it was a Conservative administration under Macmillan, which was responsible for Britain's first application to join the EU back in 1961. Moreover, they emphasized the role of Heath in maintaining the party's consistently positive approach to the EU throughout the 1960s, before finally securing Britain's membership in 1972 (Conservative Research Department 1979). Indeed, after the election victory in 1979, Roy Jenkins, then President of the Commission, admitted that he expected the Conservatives to play a more positive and constructive role than his own party had in the last five years (*The Poisoned Chalice*, BBC2, 23 May 1996).

This expectation was shared by the Conservative leadership itself. Party publications stressed two changes in approach which would allow the new government to put membership back on a more positive footing, after what was seen as Labour's incessant wrangling over the questions of a common energy policy and the EU budget (George 1994: 99–104, 117–34). First, they would restore Britain's 'bargaining strength'. In order to do this, the leadership intended to show faith and commitment to the EU's purpose. Or, to put this another way, it would start exercising the sort of leadership role that many pro-Europeans had been calling for since Britain first entered the EU in 1973. This would involve producing its own suggestions for the future development of the EU and attempting to implement these by building coalitions of support for them at the EU level. In what subsequently looked like a frivolous gesture of goodwill in the heat of the election moment, the party promised to take sterling into the EMS if it won the 1979 election (Conservative Research Department 1979: vii, 283).

Second, while maintaining this general positive stance, Conservative leaders stressed that any new initiatives would avoid any gap between the rhetoric it would use to dress up its policy commitments and the reality of what it thought could be achieved at the EU level. Party publications continually stressed the virtues of focusing on the practical and suggested that the EU would be better built if it was constructed more gradually. Moreover, the party was not beyond chiding its EU partners for falling into the trap of promising more than they could deliver: 'Europe has seen and heard many of its politicians fix ambitious goals and make far reaching declarations. Expectations have been raised rather than satisfied; and consequently public opinion is becoming dangerously sceptical' (Conservative Research Department 1979: vii).

Moreover, it should be noted that the link between domestic policy problems and external European solutions was not totally forgotten, even if it was only articulated occasionally. In fact, when party publications addressed the subject, they were quite frank about the general limits to self-government in an increasingly interdependent world. Thus, Francis Pym, then shadow Foreign Secretary, can be seen writing in the introduction to the party's campaign guide for the 1979 elections to the European Parliament: 'We all know that on our own we can no longer command the influence in world affairs we once did. Britain needs a long-term national objective. . . . Membership of the EU is the way forward.' In language which suggested the influence of Foreign Office officials, Pym went on to argue that British membership would 'enhance our effective sovereignty' by giving the British nation more power over its own affairs. On the economic front, party publications continued to point to the economic benefits of European cooperation, pointing to the increasing reliance of British exporters on the EU market. On the foreign policy front, publications stressed the enduring contribution that the EU had made to peace and prosperity (Conservative Research Department 1979: v–vi, 282–3).

That said, Conservative leaders were quick to emphasize that this more positive approach to the EU in no way represented a move by the party towards the goals of a federal Europe. In an interview in *Europa* in 1977, Thatcher was adamant that the EU must remain open and outward-looking: 'I do not believe that nation states in Europe will wither away.' Likewise, the Conservative Research Department dug up a speech by Hurd, then a member of the opposition foreign policy team, delivered to the party conference in 1978 on the subject of the EU: 'some people see us moving inexorably towards a federal state. That is not my view. Nor do I believe that it is the view of the majority of the Conservative Party. If future generations want that, let them achieve it' (quoted in Conservative Research Department 1979: 3–4).

If it was possible to point to limitations and contradictions in the Conservative leadership's domestic statecraft project, these positive, yet largely uncritical, policy intentions in the sphere of EU policy also contained problems. Despite all talk of the need to restore Britain's bargaining strength, it remained unclear on a more philosophical/ideological level which other European governments the party would target in its quest to build alliances around this more positive, constructive approach to the EU. This point is graphically illustrated whenever party publications on elections to the European Parliament came to the section describing the British Conservative Party's relations with other European political parties. The conclusion of this section remained steadfastly the same throughout the first half of the 1980s: 'In sum, the European Conservative Group [containing the British Conservatives and the Danish Conservatives] has not found it easy to establish close alliances within the European Parliament.' Although alliance building theoretically should have been relatively easy with these fellow 'Conservatives', a number of barriers stood in the way. Publications of Christian Democratic parties in Europe consistently stressed their commitment to the ideal of a federal Europe, something with which, as noted above, British Conservatives would have no truck. Moreover, European Christian Democratic parties have their origins in the withdrawal of the Roman Catholic Church from politics. Finally, many of these European Christian Democratic parties were dependent on trade union support in their countries and explicitly needed to keep open the possibility of coalitions with parties of the left. As a result, they found the new Thatcher government's mix of secular, liberal, free market policies, tinged with moderate pro-Europeanism, largely unappealing (*Campaign Guide* 1979: 57–67).

Ridley (1992, 136–7) acknowledges this point in his memoirs. He argues that not only do political parties on the Continent have a different philosophical outlook from the Conservative Party in Britain, but this is reflected in their different policy objectives. In particular, Ridley highlights what he calls the half-hearted commitment of the majority of EU countries to free trade, singling out the Common Agricultural Policy (CAP). Not only did the CAP represent a gross distortion of free trade principles, but it was actually held up by governments as the classic example of a successful EU policy. This leads him to conclude that 'it is not surprising that Britain has been a half-hearted member of the EU, and that others describe us as intransigent and laggard'.

Monetarism in One Country and the Challenge of International Economic Forces

If the Conservative Statecraft project had been designed with little thought having been given to its relationship with the external environment, by 1985 many figures within the Court realized that such benign neglect was not an option. Put another way, the policy was exhibiting a number of implementation problems. Policy-makers found it continually difficult to establish a reliable relationship between the money supply and inflation. Furthermore, while party leaders had expected some increase in the level of unemployment after 1979, they seemed unprepared for its meteoric rise to three million by 1981 and the obvious domestic criticism this level evoked. By the middle of the second administration, an increasing number from within the Court began to develop an argument highlighting the destabilizing effect of international economic forces on monetarism. Moreover, while the exchange rate had replaced monetary targets as the chief instrument through which inflation would be controlled, dissatisfaction with the policy led many to conclude that the statecraft project needed bolstering or entrenching. As we shall see, the organization of the EU was to play such a role.

If monetarism represented a statecraft strategy designed to recreate domestic autonomy and governing competence, by 1985 it had been undermined by a combination of domestic and international economic forces. The evidence for such an assertion is not difficult to accumulate. In the realm of monetary policy, both Howe and Lawson experienced real difficulties in establishing a reliable relationship between the money supply in the British economy and the rate of inflation. Indeed, Lawson devotes a specific chapter in his memoirs to dismissing the 'myth' that the implementation of monetarism was all plain sailing in the 1980s. In essence, the main problem facing the Treasury was finding an accurate measure of the money supply. As noted, in the early 1980s the Treasury's chosen target was sterling M3. Yet as Lawson laments, despite bringing inflation down to 3 per cent by 1984, the government had only managed to hit its M3 target twice. This led Lawson to experiment with other monetary targets, such as M1, PSL2 and M0, none of which enjoyed much credibility with the financial markets (D. Smith 1987: 106–28; Lawson 1992: 413–22, 447–55; Pepper 1998: 37–44).

While neglect of the international dimension of economic policy came to play an important role in government analyses about the problem of monetarism, part of the difficulty stemmed from internal contradictions within the policy itself. Government measures to reduce controls in the banking sector had encouraged these institutions to expand into areas where their activities had previously been restricted, most notably the personal mortgage market. Unfortunately, for the Court, the growth in bank lending which ensued had a number of unforeseen effects on policy. On the one hand, such lending led to a month-on-month increase in sterling M3 when Bank of England officials expected a one-off increase.[1] On the other hand, this more competitive stance by the banks led to a collapse of the building societies cartel in the early 1980s, unleashing a fierce competition for mortgage business. However, as Lawson lamented, sterling M3 did not even include building society deposits (Lawson 1992: 448). In short, even before the 1983 election victory, supply-side reforms had made the relationship between the money supply and inflation increasingly difficult to chart.

The Court's gradual response to this problem was to increasingly take into account the importance of the exchange rate when setting policy. By the March 1981 budget, monetary policy was gradually relaxed in an attempt to bring down the high level of sterling in response to pressure from business. Indeed, the policy worked too well, the pound fell too far and interest rates had to be raised to guard against the possible resurgence of inflation. By 1983, the Court had accepted that the monetary targets (both old and new) were not sacrosanct, and that a broader mix of factors, including the exchange rate, would be taken into account when formulating policy (HC 21, 1983: 399, 401). By the time of Lawson's Mansion House speech in October 1985, the target for M3 had been abandoned and, with it, any pretence that a reliable relationship between monetary targeting and the level of inflation could be established. Instead:

> The acid test of monetary policy is its record of reducing inflation. Those who wish to join the debate about the intricacies of different measures of money and the implications they may have for the future are welcome to do so. But at the end of the day the position is clear and unambiguous. The inflation rate is judge and jury. (Lawson 1992: 480–1)

Unfortunately, if the government's own supply-side reforms had undermined 'monetarism in one country', international economic forces immediately subverted 'monetarism at one remove'. Indeed, with the gradual substitution of the exchange rate for monetary targets as a way of controlling inflation, a continual theme of the second term was the inability of the Court to effectively monitor the pound as it oscillated wildly in the winds of international currency markets. For example, in July 1984, the pound was dragged upwards in the wake of a rising dollar fuelled by figures showing a rapid rise in domestic economic growth. By January 1985, the pound had gone into free-fall, touching $1.10, after comments by Ingham suggesting that Mrs Thatcher was happy to let the pound sink to one pound to one dollar if that was what the markets decreed. As a result, Lawson began to argue with more frequency that such exchange rate volatility could, in the short term, contribute to inflationary pressures. 'Benign neglect' was not an option (Lawson 1992: 467–71, 476; see also evidence by Headley-Miller and Peretz, in HL 39, 1983: 8–10).

Part of the reason for this increased volatility can be traced to a process which some academics have fashionably called 'globalization' (for an introduction to this topic, see Hirst and Thompson 1996). This is not the place to go into an extended discussion concerning the literature on this subject. That said, two post-war developments in the international economy seem particularly pertinent to the argument below. First, as a number of authors have asserted, capital movements rather than trade have become increasingly important to the activities of both national governments and firms. To put this point in a slightly different way, by the 1980s, the financial world was operating independently of the real world in a way not experienced by policy-makers before. The most obvious example of this phenomenon was the growth of the Euro-dollar market in the late 1960s. Through this market, large amounts of financial capital moved across national boundaries in search of ever higher rates of return. Estimates of the value of this market in the mid-1980s put the figure at US$75 trillion a year (Drucker 1986). Not surprisingly, these movements became important determinants of international currency values, particularly the dollar (Gilpin 1987: 114).

This development clearly had important implications for the second feature of the post-war international economy which contributed to exchange rate volatility in the 1980s: the collapse of Bretton Woods in 1973 and the spread of floating exchange rate management. In this era, it was initially hoped that because national economies were no longer linked to one another, domestic economic management could largely be isolated from broader structural changes or shocks. Unfortunately, the meteoric rise of the pound in response to a second hike in oil prices in the late 1970s put paid to any illusions on this front. One could add that these problems were not helped by the de-stabilizing effect of Reaganomics, whose mix of tight monetary and lax fiscal policy led to high interest rates and a high dollar (Gilpin 1987: 143–5). The close link between movements in the dollar and the behaviour of sterling meant that these developments across the Atlantic exacerbated the already intense pressures on a rising pound.

Not surprisingly, key figures within the Court were soon quick to make the connection between these volatile and constraining international economic structures and forces and the domestic policy problems they were encountering at home. For Heseltine, the evolution of global 24-hour financial markets had unleashed a number of economic forces which begged the question: 'But can governments be sovereign in today's financial world?' (Heseltine 1991: 72; see also D. Smith 1992: 52). What worried Lawson was that, with confidence in domestic monetary targeting having been lost, the exchange rate during this period could also fluctuate in ways which were becoming very difficult to predict, and could not be justified by the underlying state of the economy.

Take, for example, his analysis of the 1984–85 Sterling Crisis. Lawson signals a combination of temporary factors to explain the rise of sterling in the second half of 1984. These included a short-term rise in the dollar, the psychological impact of the Miners' Strike on the financial markets and erratic money supply figures. As a result, interest rates had to be raised to 12 per cent, the highest 'real' level since the war and hardly justified by domestic condition alone. Moreover, as already noted, Ingham's indiscreet comments suggesting that Thatcher was indifferent to the level of the pound led to a free-fall of sterling to almost one dollar to the pound in January 1985 (Lawson 1992: 461–71). The important point here is that, where monetarism was supposed to provide a predictable, rule-based governing code which allowed the economy to be run as automatically as possible, this level of uncertainty was most unwelcome. Put another way, the statecraft strategy had lost its discipline or anchor in this increasingly unsettling financial climate. A common theme of commentators at this time was how Lawson was 'flying by the seat of his pants' (D. Smith 1992: 63, 85–91). In short, not only did the policy need adjustment, but this rule-based strategy needed bolstering or entrenching.

At the same time, international economic forces were partly responsible, or perceived to be partly responsible, for challenging the credibility of the Court's market-based supply-side strategy. Once again, the facts of the story are well known and the details need not concern us here. In the context of the argument being pursued, the decision by OPEC to raise oil prices by 15 per cent in 1979, at a time when North Sea oil was rapidly coming 'on stream', served to boost sterling to uncompetitive levels. At a time when the government was also increasing interest rates to cope with inflation, sterling's rise served to choke off British exports, leading to three million unemployed by 1981. Interestingly, the Court initially saw the opportunities in linking this unemployment problem to the development of international market forces. This led it to produce the argument that the plight of the British jobless was the unfortunate but necessary product of a worldwide shake out of restrictive manufacturing practices. Of course, by blaming Britain's unemployment problem on the changing nature of international capitalism, the Court had hoped to avoid responsibility for this issue (Howe 1982: 6–8; Butler and Kavanagh 1984: 3). However, with renewed levels of economic growth failing to make any impression on these jobless figures by 1984, clearly Conservative ministers had to find an alternative response to deal with this supply-side economic problem.

Figures within the Court accepted that its statecraft project needed bolstering in this area. What is interesting about Lawson's memoirs is that the subject of policy entrenchment gets a general airing. In a section on what makes a good politician, Lawson (1992: 250–3) discusses a number of qualities in turn. As well as man-management qualities, media skills and the ability to perform in Parliament, he argues that a good politician should also possess the ability to think strategically. Because Lawson's comments are of central importance, it is worth quoting them in full:

> Those who write about politics tend to be concerned with the visible side: that is, what a politician says in public and what is said about him. But to my mind the most important yet most overlooked dimensions of being a politician are the least visible. These range from being a loyal and reliable colleague to being a fertile source of workable political ideas and able to make correct political judgements. ... Effective political judgement, moreover, involves thinking more or less simultaneously on two levels: assessing both the likely short-term electoral consequences and the longer-term political consequences. ... *These range from how to entrench – that is to say render unlikely to be reversed – a particular policy, how to affect the longer-term political climate. This sort of strategic and tactical thinking was probably my strongest suit, even if I was sometimes less successful in persuading others of my judgement.* (Lawson 1992: 253; emphasis added)

If Lawson understood the importance of policy entrenchment in general terms, more specifically the leadership needed a more positive initiative which responded to the problem of unemployment. A policy of benign neglect in this area was not considered an option during the second term of office. This point was acknowledged by Howe in a policy paper as far back as 1982:

> In part, we are to blame. Language and tone are often as important as content and policy. ... We must make it a prime aim ... [to correct the image that Monetarism supports] wealthy heartless individuals, selfishly pursuing their own interests. ... The perception that our policies coincide with people's interests is not sufficiently widespread. We must make it so. (Howe 1982: 5–6)

Moreover, in his Mais lecture in June 1984, Lawson accepted that monetarism had not been well understood, and that Conservatives needed to respond to the question: 'Where will all the jobs come from?' (Lawson 1992: 413–16, 423–34). On the domestic front, this task led him to push forward with a number of initiatives to further deregulate the supply side of the economy.

In this analysis, these leaders could point to incidents indicating less than forthright support for government policy. In no particular order of importance, one could point to: threats from the President of the CBI of a bare-knuckle fight with the government; a protest letter to *The Times* from 364 economists calling for a policy of sustained reflation and specific measures to deal with unemployment; and the bitter and sometimes violent miners' strike during the winter of 1984/85 (see *The Economist* 9 June 1984; see also *The Economist* 23 June 1984, 29 September 1984, 27 October, 1984, 24 November 1984, 12 January 1985). By June 1984, unemployment topped every poll as the political issue which most concerned the British electorate. Survey results suggested that half of voters suspected the government was deliberately maintaining high levels of unemployment, in order to curb union wage demands (H. Young 1989: 299). The Conservative leadership itself admitted that many within the party itself were 'anxious' and 'downright critical' of the consequences of monetarism (Ridley 1992: 172–5; see also H. Young 1989: 16–17, 302–3). Of course, the so-called Wets were neutralized and the party went on to win the election with an increased majority. However, for certain members of the Court, this electoral support represented little more than public acquiescence (see Alt 1987; Gilmour 1992: 36). The Court's statecraft strategy remained vulnerable to reversal by a future left-of-centre government.

This was particularly the case when it proved difficult to come up with alternative supply-side measures which provided a credible response to this criticism. It was true that a number of schemes were introduced aimed at upgrading the skills of young people and creating a new enterprise culture. These included a whole range of youth and adult training schemes, job creation projects and start-up grants for small businesses. Yet commentators doubted the real and lasting changes that these schemes would introduce. As *The Economist* noted, these more interventionist measures ran against the grain of the general economic programme that the Court was trying to introduce. Trying to instil market discipline into the nooks and crannies of the British economy, the Conservative leadership was unwilling to make such intervention its principle priority and shied away from turning this effort into political credit (*The Economist* 6 October 1984; Hall 1986). Instead, Labour's policy of advocating a good old Keynesian reflation package was regarded as the best way of dealing with the problem (*The Economist* 23 June 1984, 29 September 1984, 27 October 1984).

Political Argument Hegemony

In short, international economic developments were perceived to be undermining the Court's governing code. However, as noted in Chapter 1, Statecraft also involves political support functions such as Political Argument Hegemony and party management, and these require consideration here. When it came to the battle for political ideas, developments at the EU level were making a mockery of the party's stated commitment to play a more positive role in this area. More particularly, claims to restore Britain's bargaining strength and to work within the framework of the EU to achieve Britain's interests looked misconceived. Like the Labour governments before them, the Conservatives had become embroiled in an intransigent battle over the level of British contributions to the EU budget. In a notable episode, Thatcher attempted to invoke the Luxembourg Compromise to veto an agreement on agricultural prices in 1982/3, a move which was dismissed by the other Heads of Government. Although an automatic settlement of the budget problem was achieved at Fontainebleau in June 1984, if George is right, Thatcher's awkwardness prevented the Court from securing the same deal a year earlier (George 1994: 155–8).

If the budget dispute called into question prior Conservative claims to be 'the party of Europe', Labour attempted to exploit this inconsistency in the battle for Political Argument Hegemony. Although defensive and badly split on the issue, opposition figures attempted to link the issue of EU membership to the problem of unemployment. Two arguments in particular are noteworthy. Reviving the sceptical arguments from the 1960s and 1970s, Labour leaders suggested that Britain's economic problems were at least partially related to the effects of EU membership. They pointed to the ever-increasing cost of the CAP and the problems which the Conservatives were having in controlling the EU budget. They linked these issues to the fact that Britain's visible trade balance with the EU had declined from a small surplus at the time of membership to a large deficit by the early 1980s. Once these connections were made, and faced with daily evidence of bankruptcies and redundancies in British manufacturing, it was not too difficult to extrapolate the evidence and suggest that membership might actually be making a contribution to British unemployment (Castle 1983). Second, Labour leaders pointed to the acrimonious and intractable negotiations over Britain's budgetary contribution, as evidence that 'negotiation from within had proved as abortive as negotiation from without'. In this context, great play was made of the failed attempt to invoke the Luxembourg Compromise noted above. As a result, the party finally came to the conclusion that the logical policy was to negotiate withdrawal from the EU, if and when it achieved victory at the polls in 1983 (Shore 1983).

However, it is important not to overstate the difficulties faced by Conservatives in this rhetorical battle. Labour's divisions over the European issue allowed the Conservative leadership to parry these arguments with relative ease. Three main counter-arguments were employed. First, on the supposedly deleterious effects of membership on Britain's visible trade balance, Conservatives revived a popular ploy of the Euro-enthusiasts in the 1960s and 1970s. Put simply, they argued that drawing up a balance sheet estimating the economic effects of membership was a difficult job. Other variables, such as the effect of domestic economic policies and the changed international economic environment, also needed to be taken into account. Second, the leadership chose to sidle around the facts concerning Britain's deteriorating manufacturing trade performance with the EU. Instead, ministers countered by claiming that over 40 per cent of British exports now went to the EU and this export market was increasing more quickly than any other at this time. To pull out of this expanding 'home market' would have a disastrous effect on the British economy.

Third, Conservative leaders argued that 'going it alone' would also have a disastrous effect on levels of investment and employment. They were fond of pointing out that one of the reasons why Britain had been so successful in attracting inward investment from the United States and Japan was that these companies saw British membership of the EU as a 'gateway' to this larger European market. At the same time, ministers were quick to claim that this inward investment was now playing a vital role in regenerating a number of regions in the UK which had suffered as part of the deindustrialization of the British economy in the 1970s. Moreover, Conservative Party publications during the 1983 general election took advantage of recently released estimates by the CBI that two and a half million jobs could be put at risk if Britain withdrew from the EU.

The salience of these arguments is confirmed by Butler and Kavanagh (1984: 91–2, 199) in their study of the 1983 general election. They highlight a story in the *Daily Mail* on 16 May 1983, which had the headline, '35,000 Jobs Lost If Foot Wins'. The paper alleged that Nissan would pull out of a planned £5 billion investment if Labour attempted to withdraw from the EU after an election victory. Interestingly enough, soon after the story ran, Nissan qualified its comments, arguing that the company's plans would not be significantly altered if Labour won the election. This was largely due to the fact that the actual legal process of extracting Britain from its treaty commitments would almost certainly have been a long drawn-out affair.

Party Management

To the extent that the party cared about this issue, evidence suggests substantial backbench support for Thatcher's 'resolute' approach on the question of Britain's budgetary contributions. To be sure, a number of traditionally pro-European figures on the Conservative back benches voiced criticism over Thatcher's belligerent stance. Heath wrote an article in *The Times* as early as 5 January 1983, which called for an end to British quibbling over the budget issue and urged the need for a more concerted effort to provide leadership to the EU. These claims were supported by Pym when he returned to the back benches in 1983, and by David Howell, who criticized the government for fighting too much on nationalist issues in the European elections campaign of 1984 (*The Times* 5 January 1983, 1 June 1984, *Agence Europe* 1 July 1983). This theme also found resonance among the ex-ranks of the diplomatic service. In an article in *The Times* (26 June 1983), Nicholas Henderson warned the Thatcher government that, although Britain's EU partners might by then have realized the justice of the budgetary case, they expected London to be more positive about Europe in the future.

That said, in the general debates at Westminster over the government's EU policy, support for this resolute approach generally held up well. Reporting back to the House of Commons on the failure to get an agreement at the Athens Summit in December 1983, Thatcher took a robust stance that was the subject of a wide range of cross-party applause, even among a number of prominent Europhiles, such as Geoffrey Rippon and Roy Jenkins. Similarly, when she reported the details of the Fontainebleau deal to the House a year later, the majority of Conservative members contributing to the debate accepted the deal and the need for the toughness shown by Thatcher in holding out for it (*Hansard* (Commons) vol. 100, 27 June 1984; vol. 63, 10 July 1984, cols 890–972). In short, there is a lack of evidence to suggest that the Continent's portrayal of Britain as an awkward partner caused much consternation around Westminster.

However, in private a number of figures within the Court became increasingly concerned that Thatcher's belligerent style towards Europe was being fuelled by pressure from Euro-sceptical backbenchers. It is certainly possible to witness the existence of Euro-sceptical sentiment during the early 1980s. For example, writing in *The Times* during this period, Teddy Taylor described how the philosophical basis of the EU militated against the current neo-liberal economic policies of the Conservative government. In particular, he pointed to an article in the *New Socialist* by two of Tony Benn's advisers, which expressed sympathy for the Common Agricultural Policy, the European Monetary System and calls for a common European industrial strategy. For Taylor, the Treaty of Rome could provide a foundation for socialist policies Europe-wide. His conclusion was to urge the Conservative leadership to work for substantial institutional reform of the EU, or go for associate status, although he admitted that this approach might have the effect of excluding Britain from other EU policies (Taylor 1982; see also Wood 1981; Palmer 1982; Story and Taylor 1982; *The Times* 25 March 1982, 11 November 1982, 20 March 1984).

Sir Michael Butler confirms that these backbenchers threatened to strengthen Thatcher's Euro-scepticism because

> they had very much been her friends when she managed to get voted leader instead of Ted Heath after the 1974 election. If she had to, she would often not do what they advocated, but she didn't go out of her way to pick things which irritated them. But understand, they had been her supporters for the leadership. (Non-attributable interview with the author, 21 February 1995)

Another official at the Cabinet Office at the time agreed that this Euro-sceptical group brought a lot of pressure to bear through private meetings and correspondence. When it was suggested to him that this only seemed like a small group, he replied that a group of 20 'can still be a powerful force' (non-attributable interview with the author). For the pro-European elements within the Court, this problem of party management was something that needed to be addressed, as we shall see in Chapter 4.

Conclusions

It is often argued in the literature that Thatcherism represented a decisive break with post-war consensus politics (see, for example, Kavanagh 1990; Kavanagh and Morris 1994). The picture presented here is a more complex blend of continuity and change. Indeed, one of the paradoxes of Thatcherism was the old-fashioned nature of this 'new' ideological project; for example, its promotion of Victorian principles of self-help and limited government, and its return to 'good housekeeping'. This chapter also argues that Thatcherism reflected a continuity with the governing practice of earlier governments. More particularly, it attempted to resurrect the old pre-1961 governing code, which stressed the link between governing autonomy and a limited, neutral and automatic policy framework. However, by the mid-1980s, the policy faced a number of implementation problems, not least because of the earlier lack of attention to the possible impact of external forces on this strategy. As a result, a number of figures within the Court, most notably Howe and Lawson, came to argue that this statecraft project needed entrenching. Clearly any revision of policy would have to take the link between external and domestic politics more seriously. It is to this topic that the book now turns.

Note

1. For example, after the removal of 'the corset' in the summer of 1980, Threadneedle Street expected sterling M3 to be affected by a one-off boost of 3 per cent. In fact, this monetary target expanded by 8 per cent during July and August, leading it to miss its 7–11 per cent growth band by 7 per cent (D. Smith 1992: 40).

CHAPTER FOUR

The Europeanization of Conservative Statecraft

If domestic monetarism had been undermined by international economic forces and Thatcherite Statecraft needed bolstering, the main argument of this chapter is that an increasing number of figures at the Court realized that such entrenchment could be secured through the Europeanization of British economic policy. More specifically, it makes three claims. It begins by documenting the Europeanization of the Court's discourse towards economic policy. On the one hand, it details the development of the Court's argument for the Europeanization of its supply-side market strategy, promoted through its enthusiasm for the Single Market and implemented through the negotiation of the SEA. On the other, it documents the increasing attraction of ERM membership to figures within the Court, a policy which nevertheless remained the subject of private and intense debate. Second, it argues that the Europeanization of economic policy during this period cannot be explained solely in terms of the leadership's belief in the economic merits of these ideas. Both policies were contested within the academic community, debates which the Court were perfectly cognizant of.

Finally, the chapter argues that this policy change partially reflected Statecraft concerns. For an increasing number within the Court, ERM membership offered an alternative rule-based, disciplinarian framework through which domestic autonomy could be maintained. At the same time, by getting its free market philosophy accepted as the centrepiece of the SEA, Conservative leaders hoped to legitimize these policies, while providing a more attractive solution to the problem of unemployment. More fundamentally, the SEA offered other advantages. It helped to ease tensions within the Court which had developed over the future direction of policy towards Europe. Moreover, this initiative had beneficial spin-offs for the leadership's political support functions (Political Argument Hegemony and party management).

The Europeanization of a Statecraft Strategy

The earliest indication of this change of strategy was indicated by the Court's increasing enthusiasm to promote the Europeanization of British supply-side policy. Of course, politicians did not refer to this shift in quite these terms. Nevertheless, by 1984 the Conservative leadership began to articulate an explicit link between the completion of the Single Market in Europe and the supply-side problems which continued to manifest themselves. Indeed, this initiative became one of a number of suggestions for pulling the EU out of one of its periodic bouts of Euro-pessimism. If monetarism in Britain had failed to convince critics that the problem of British economic decline had been reversed, the EU was also wracked by a collective sense of sclerosis at this time. Of particular concern was the perception in many capitals that the Union's performance on the issues of growth and job creation remained relatively poor compared with the USA and Asia. Part of the problem was seen to be the persistence of national economic strategies in response to international challenges that all member states shared. A number of commentators demonstrated this argument by pointing to the continual fragmentation of the Common Market (as it was still perceived). The persistent use of the veto by member states to protect their own industries had resulted in the maintenance and proliferation of a number of non-tariff barriers to trade in goods and services. While it was in no way inevitable, the initiative to complete the Single Market in Europe by 1992 became the centrepiece of a programme to relaunch the EU, as we shall see (Hoffman 1989; Sandholtz and Zysman 1989; Grahl and Teague 1990: Introduction and Chapter 1).

The first official pronouncement of the Thatcher government's new policy could be found in the White Paper 'Europe: The Future'. First introduced by the British delegation at the Fontainebleau Summit in June 1984, it represented the origins of a more *communautaire* incursion into the European domain. At first glance, however, one could be forgiven for overlooking the importance of this new initiative. The paper contained nothing more than a general statement of aims, some of which did not look entirely compatible. In particular, the layout of the paper, where a section on 'Strengthening the Community' (points 6–12) was followed by a section stressing the need for a more 'flexible Europe', looked inconsistent (HMG 1984: 73–81). Moreover, the fact that the two central policy proposals in the paper, the completion of the Single Market and measures to strengthen European Political Cooperation, had been called for continually during the previous decade or more did not suggest that there was any deep or radical thinking behind the new document.

However, more detailed consideration of this paper reveals the re-emergence of the old connection between problems in the supply side of the British economy, such as unemployment, and the importance of exporters having access to international markets. Certainly, the precise details remained to be worked out, but there was no doubting the more positive tone of the proposals. When referring to the future development of a policy for European industry, the paper talked of the need to examine 'urgently whether more can be achieved, or can be achieved more economically, by action on a Community basis rather than nationally' (HMG 1984: 75). In her memoirs, Thatcher also refers to this change of tone: 'When we prepared our own paper ("Europe – the Future") on the Community's future for the forthcoming [Fontainebleau] Summit, I accepted that it should be liberally sprinkled with communautaire phrases' (Thatcher 1993: 540). More importantly, candidates for this 'reverse subsidiarity' were exactly those supply-side responsibilities that continued to plague the Conservative leadership, despite its more general election success. In an analysis similar to that noted in the 1930s, point 6 argued:

> If the problems of growth, outdated industrial structures and unemployment which affect us all are to be tackled effectively, we must create the genuine common market in goods and services which is envisaged in the Treaty of Rome. (HMG 1984: 74)

This meant addressing rather dull issues, such as the harmonization of standards, more rapid and better coordinated customs procedures, the mutual recognition of professional qualifications and the liberalization of trade in services. However, there was no mistaking the significance of the initiative. These awkward supply-side problems were now being partially hived off to the European level for solution.

Soon after the launch of 'Europe: The Future', Conservative leaders began to publicly make the link between the completion of the Single Market and the problem of British unemployment. A couple of examples are enough to make the point. Reporting to the Commons just after the Fontainebleau European Council, at which 'Europe – the Future' was first presented, Howe maintained:

> If we seize the opportunities available for a really expanding Europe-wide market in services and goods, we will create jobs throughout Europe. . . . It is a matter of selling such insight not only to the people of this country, but to those in the Community as a whole on the basis that it is not founded on the interests of any one state. (*Hansard* (Commons) vol. 63, 10 July 1984: col. 898)

In a speech at the opening of the third biennial conference of the Franco-British Council, Thatcher made the same link. Urging her EU partners to 'work for the substance . . . [not] talk in the shadow', she called on Europe to strengthen its cooperative effort in tackling unemployment. For Thatcher, the completion of the Single Market was a vital ingredient to this effort (*The Times* 1 November 1984). Finally, reporting to the House of Commons on the conclusion of Britain's budgetary deal at Fontainebleau, Howe outlined Britain's plans for future EU development:

With the Fontainebleau agreement behind us, Britain has been able to make completion of the Common Market by 1992 the top priority of the Commission and member states alike. The effective establishment of a single large market will not only give us an opportunity to exploit our strength and skills; it is crucial to the creation of wealth and jobs and to the generation of profits that can stimulate research and the successful exploitation of our inventive skills. (*Hansard* (Commons) vol. 81, 25 June 1985: col. 803; see also Thatcher, *Hansard* (Commons) vol. 82, 2 July 1985: col. 188)

By the late 1980s, the Commission had published official reports to add empirical weight to these sometimes rather vague and woolly claims. The analysis of these reports began by pointing out that, after 30 years of membership, the European Single Market remained incomplete. It continued to be hindered by a number of non-tariff barriers, such as border controls, divergent standards and regulations, conflicting business laws, protectionist public procurement practices and capital controls. A study by Emerson *et al.* (1988: 3) suggested that the total cost of all non-tariff barriers was 2 per cent of company costs. If only these were removed, all the EU countries, including the UK, would experience a number of benefits. The Commission predicted that by removing these barriers, costs and prices would come down, thus triggering a one-off competitive supply-side shock to the EU economy. The Cecchini Report estimated that the average drop in prices would be 6.1 per cent. Business, under pressure from increased competition, would have to undergo a process of restructuring, leading to improved efficiency. The Emerson Report estimated that efficiency gains would lie within a range of 70–190 billion ECU. At the same time, greater competition would lead to technological innovation, producing a number of more 'dynamic' gains in growth and unemployment. Cecchini estimated that the policy would increase EU GDP by 4.5 per cent, while predicting that the medium-term impact on employment would be 1.8 million jobs (on the Cecchini Report, see Tsoukalis 1993: 78–97; see also Emerson *et al.* 1988: 1–10).

In the context of the argument being pursued, it is important to note that a number of policy-makers interviewed for this book emphasized that the Court's attachment to the Single Market policy was largely a matter of 'blind faith'. When it was pointed out to one official that many of the Commission's own claims had been contested, he replied:

Well you have to realise that we were in a period where the Conservative government was dominated by a number of simple ideas. I'm sorry to come back to it, but this was the case. Of course there were lots of people in lots of departments who said this was going to be very difficult for the aluminium industry and so on. In the whole range of public services in Britain, people did examine their own responsibility for certain areas of industry and came back and said that there were certain things that they didn't like. So there was a certain amount of blind faith in the whole thing. (Non-attributable interview with the author)

Adam Fergusson, special adviser to Howe during this period, confirms this view:

Well I made a speech many times that the way to get and keep unemployment down, to get inflation down and to get industry moving, was to open up the Common Market. And I believed in it then and I believe it now. I think it was genuine enough. Margaret Thatcher's belief that free markets, as a way of getting the economy moving and getting unemployment down was totally genuine. I cannot think why anybody would have cynically embraced an economic policy of such depth unless they thought that it was going to deliver economic results. I think in politics, one believes everything about eighty per cent, but experience tells you that there is always a possibility that the policy may not work. (Interview with the author, 27 September 1995)

More specifically, on the link between the supply-side problem of unemployment and the completion of the Single Market, one official admitted:

In government, I think there was certainly a considerable confidence that employment would pick up much better than perhaps a more considered analysis would have shown. The shedding of labour was pretty substantial in industries like British Steel, and British Shipbuilding. So, even if the economy was growing fast, and new industries were developing, one would have foreseen that there would still be serious problems with unemployment, which were probably underestimated. It was thought that, after finally opening up the internal market completely, and the bonanza of opportunities for British industry to expand, things would pick up, not only in terms of growth, but also in terms of jobs. My experience is that contemporary Tory governments have been extremely attached to the view that, if you got growth, you got employment. Quite contrary to the view of other governments of the world, the US for example, who consider that growth is an essential condition for employment, but that the employment content of growth is also extremely important and can be varied. (Non-attributable interview with the author)

At the same time, although official policy on ERM membership remained that sterling would join when 'the time was ripe', this platitude served to conceal an increasingly heated private debate at the Court concerning the Europeanization of monetary policy. Two features of the Court are worth noting before the details of this argument are focused on. First, although the arguments were real and sometimes acrimonious, it is important not to overstate the disunity within the Court at this time. Even in 1985, Thatcher was largely isolated in resisting arguments for ERM membership during this period and could only rely on the consistent support of Ridley and Biffen in Cabinet. While Tebbit was to emerge as an arch Euro-sceptic in the 1990s, Cabinet discussions at this time indicate that he came out in favour of ERM entry largely for party political reasons (see below). Similarly, while Parkinson, Lilley and Redwood were later to gravitate to the Euro-sceptical wing of the party, they supported a decision by the party's manifesto group on economic policy in 1987 to endorse entry as a future policy goal (Lawson 1992: 489, 633–64; Thatcher 1993: 698; Thompson 1996: 58–9).[1] Second, this increased enthusiasm for the Europeanization of monetary policy seems to have emerged quite quickly. As we shall see, Lawson's support had its origins back in 1981. However, according to Smith, the decision to pursue this policy was only taken in the first three months of 1985 (D. Smith 1992: 52). This point may be of little significance. However, it is clear that these calculations reflected more than long-held ideological beliefs.

As noted in Chapter 3, prominent figures within the Court had become increasingly disillusioned with the operation of the Medium Term Financial Strategy and turned to the exchange rate as an instrument for controlling inflation. For this growing band of Euro-enthusiasts, the first attraction of targeting sterling within an actual system of semi-fixed exchange rates was that this move merely represented a formal and logical extension of policy. The adoption of a public target would certainly lend the policy more credibility, thus avoiding continual speculation as the markets attempted to discover the floor and the ceiling of an implicit rate. Of course, this shift had to be justified in academic terms. However, that did not pose too much of a problem as Treasury officials soon wheeled out the doctrine of international monetarism to fill the vacuum. Its main propositions were as follows: in the long term, the currency value of a country reflects its relative inflation rate; this assertion stems from the theory of purchasing power parity, which stipulates that an exchange rate will adjust so that a basket of goods costs roughly the same wherever purchased; it follows that if one country allows its money supply to grow at a faster rate than that of its competitors, it will suffer a fall in its exchange rate, leading to an increase in inflation; indeed, in an open economy like that of the UK, fluctuations in the value of the pound represented an important transmission mechanism for inflation. In short, in the absence of a reliable relationship between domestic money supply targets and rising prices, committing the value of a currency to a fixed level might provide an alternative way of discovering the virtuous cycle of non-inflationary growth, as long as the right level was established (D. Smith 1987: 54). Not surprisingly, many commentators dismissed the new policy as a U-turn. Lawson himself was forced to admit that it was 'monetarism at one remove'.

This Europeanization of monetary policy could be further justified by the Court's 'apparent' experience with exchange rate management at this time. Once again, the major theme of the Euro-enthusiasts' argument was the

73

unpredictability of policy in a global world where outcomes increasingly failed to reflect underlying economic conditions. Take, for example, the sterling crisis of 1986, where the Court failed to foresee the substantial devaluation of the pound. A decline in the price of oil, as well as downward pressure on the dollar, meant that the authorities were initially able to account for the concomitant fall in sterling and raise interest rates accordingly. However, the pound seemed to stabilize after the March budget, leading Lawson to reverse these earlier cuts. Unfortunately, the value of sterling plunged unexpectedly in the second half of the 1980s, despite the fact that movements in oil prices were less dramatic. For Lawson, the implication was clear; this uncertain climate led to mistaken policy choices which had adverse knock-on effects for inflation in the late 1980s (Lawson 1992: 647–57). However, others suggest that the importance of these unpredictable global conditions has been deliberately overstated. For Thompson, the Sterling Crisis of 1986 was discursively constructed and this helped to disguise the fact that the Thatcher government was presiding over the covert devaluation of the pound as part of a pre-election growth strategy (Thompson 1996: 74–5). In the context of the argument being pursued here, discourse was more important than reality.

While the academic consistency in this transformation was arguably dubious, a number of commentators and policy-makers were much more impressed with the actual operation of the European system of semi-fixed exchange rates – the ERM. Despite the initial scepticism of policy-makers in the late 1970s, the ERM had not suffered the same fate as 'the Snake' earlier in that decade. More than this, it could be said with some confidence that this system had generally been successful in fulfilling its objectives of promoting monetary stability and policy convergence among its members. Lawson and others could point to a record of greater stability in nominal exchange rates compared with the period before the system was introduced. One did not need a degree in economics to extrapolate from these figures and assert that a general reduction in exchange rate volatility between countries would boost trade volumes, leading to higher investment, output and employment. At the same time, low and stable inflation would be assured on account of Germany's dominance within the system. The German economy's post-war record on inflation was second to none in Europe, and the independence of the Bundesbank would guarantee that this remained the case. By tying oneself to the ERM, the British economy could enjoy the benefits of German policy 'by association' (Scott 1986: 194–8; see also the CBI Memorandum to HC 57II, 1985: 97; Heseltine 1991: 69–73; Lawson 1992: 494–5).

However, to argue that the Thatcher government gradually promoted the Europeanization of economic policy at this time because it was attracted to the merits of these policy ideas is too simplistic an explanation. Put simply, the economic merits of these ideas were contested, something which the Court was more than aware of. To understand why ministers supported the Single Market project (including signing the SEA) and why an increasing number became attracted to ERM membership, we need to explore factors apart from the influence of the academic community. To the extent that the Court listened to this advice, it was selective in the messages it chose to receive. How can we explain this apparent example of partial 'lesson-drawing'?

Take, for example, the case for completing the Single Market by 1992. A number of economists criticized the Commission's reports on both theoretical and empirical grounds. Theoretically, these criticisms drew attention to the fact that no previous study of trade liberalization had ever come up with such large estimates about possible economic benefits. Indeed, a number of commentators made the point that trade theory, as an academic discipline, was not well placed to analyse the so-called 'dynamic' benefits of completing the Single Market. Such theory rested on a number of imperfect assumptions about the nature of trade, such as homogeneous products, perfect competition and constant returns of scale. Moreover, as Jacquemin and Sapir (1989) have argued, attempts to generate new models which can take into account deviations from this theory are fraught with difficulty and controversy (see also Cutler et al. 1992).

Economists also contested the empirical estimates of the Commission. First, a number of writers questioned whether the short-term gains from reducing the Union's non-tariff barriers would be as large as the Commission was projecting. More to the point, such gains would only be a one-off event. The real test of the Commission's case lay in its estimates of the dynamic gains. Here, economists encountered a number of qualifications. In terms similar to the debates during the period before Britain's entry into the EU, the Commission argued that these dynamic gains would depend on two unproven assumptions: the willingness of business to take advantage of what it believed to be a credible project; and the willingness of governments to support these strategies with well coordinated, growth-oriented, policies. Finally, if attempts to project the dynamic gains of completing the Single Market relied on a number of unquantifiable assumptions, officials in Brussels admitted that their studies had next to nothing to say about the likely distribution of the costs and benefits between different EU countries and regions. Based on past history, where the UK trade balance with the EU had experienced a huge deficit since membership, a case could be made for suggesting that the policy may be just as likely to harm as to benefit the British economy overall (Emerson et al. 1988; Davis et al. 1989: 8–9).

At the same time, the Court was also aware that the positive economic gains from completing the Single Market were largely hypothetical and unquantifiable, but largely ignored these sceptical arguments. One official in the Cabinet Office at the time agreed that the Thatcher government did not see the Single Market project as a panacea for its economic problems at this time: 'it wasn't that naive' (interview with the author). Asked by John Evans how much unemployment would fall as a result of the completion of the Single Market, Thatcher wisely refrained from producing a precise figure. Instead, she replied, 'the hon. Gentleman is aware that it might be right for him to ask the question, but it is most unwise for anyone at this Dispatch Box ever to answer it' (*Hansard* (Commons) vol. 76, 2 April 1985: col. 1067).

Similarly, the economic advantages of sterling's entry into the ERM were a matter of lively debate in the first half of the 1980s. The difference is that while sceptical arguments about the benefits of the Single Market were largely ignored, differences in opinion on the latter became a matter of dispute within the Court. To begin with, Thatcher, backed up by arguments from Alan Walters, disputed the intellectual case for international monetarism. First, Thatcher constantly reminded her colleagues of the need to be crystal clear about the implications of using the exchange rate to control inflation. Interest rates could not be used for the purpose of controlling domestic money supply *and* the exchange rate. To give primacy to the latter would lead to a severing of any direct relationship between interest rates and the former. Of course, this separatism did not matter as long as sterling joined the ERM at a rate which was reasonably consistent with stable, non-inflationary growth. However, the second argument employed by the Euro-sceptics was to cast doubt on the proposition that there was a fundamental or natural real exchange rate for sterling. As Walters pointed out, while all economists had their own idea concerning what such a rate might be, they found it very difficult to operationalize such a target for the purposes of policy-making. As a result, the possibilities of an exchange rate misalignment were very real, as were the concomitant adverse consequences for the trade performance of British industry (Walters 1990: 35–7; Thatcher 1993: 688–9).

This argument was partly confirmed by the conclusions of the Treasury and Civil Service Select Committee's investigation into the subject of Britain's membership of the ERM. The committee did not rule out sterling's entry in the long-term. However, the difficulty of securing an appropriate rate was one of the main reasons for the Committee's recommendation that the pound remain outside the system in the short term. Of particular relevance to this conclusion were sterling's over-valuation at this time and the real constraints concerning the realignment of a currency within the ERM. Such a revaluation was a matter for negotiation: no member state had secured the full percentage of change which had originally been asked for. Britain should not expect any kind of special treatment. Moreover, if one combined this fact with the reality that Britain experienced a nine billion pound trade deficit (six billion with West Germany) at this time, there seemed few incentives for existing members to allow any significant devaluation at all (HC 57II, 1985: xxxiii, xix–xx).

Finally, even if the authorities were clever (or lucky) enough to fix sterling's exchange rate at the right level within the ERM, even for a short period, Euro-sceptics within the Court argued that nominal exchange rates were a dubious indicator of domestic monetary conditions. They did not contest the fact that the exchange rate was one of the channels through which inflation was exported between countries. However, as Walters argued, in practice, the exchange rate was affected by a number of intangible pressures which were impossible to predict and monitor. These included such things as future political prospects and something as vague and unquantifiable as 'confidence' in the markets (Walters 1990: 33–4). Such factors led Thatcher to conclude that the exchange rate was a more 'wayward' indicator of domestic inflation than monetary targets (Thatcher 1993: 689). Furthermore, the level of exchange rate reserves needed to defend sterling and the possible inflationary consequences of this action continually bothered her (Thatcher 1993: 696–7; Lawson 1992: 784).

The Euro-sceptics were also less impressed with the supposed benefits of the ERM in practice. As Walters (1990: 73–4) noted, in ERM countries the average rate of inflation decreased more slowly in the 1980s than that in the rest of the OECD countries. At the same time, convergence on inflation took longer within the ERM than in the OECD as a whole. It should be added that the UK managed to achieve convergence on the issue of price levels, despite being outside the system and not tracking European currencies in a stable way. As for the beneficial effect of semi-fixed exchange rates on trade growth and investment, Walters asserted that, for the former, the unweighted average over the period 1979–84 was 0.6 per cent, whereas in non-ERM countries it was 4.1 per cent. At the same time, growth in investment was slower in the ERM over the same period (see also Scott 1986: 191).

The question remains: how can we explain the gradual yet increasing interest in these European solutions to domestic policy problems? It is argued below that the Court became attracted to the Europeanization of economic policy, not because of the perceived merits of these policy ideas alone, but because of the governing advantages they conferred. More particularly, the ERM was perceived as an external, rule-based, disciplinarian framework which would allow the Court to protect its autonomy from domestic groups. Similarly, the promotion of the Single Market (and the signing of the SEA) would help to entrench the Court's free market strategy by getting it accepted at the European level. At the same time, Britain's cooperative approach had other advantages. On the one hand, it helped to ease tensions within the Court over the government's diplomatic style towards this regional organization. Moreover, negotiating the SEA largely had a beneficial impact on the battle for Political Argument Hegemony and party management.

With the operation of the MTFS having become increasingly distorted by global financial forces, forcing a more discretionary monetary regime on Whitehall, an increasing number within the Court perceived ERM membership as a way of bolstering domestic autonomy in this uncertain external environment. It will be recalled from Chapter 3 that, from a Statecraft point of view, the MTFS served as a domestic, rule-based framework designed to discipline the behaviour of domestic groups. In policy terms the ERM looked like a radical abandonment of monetarism, but in Statecraft terms it reflected an alternative policy support to achieve this same governing end. Proponents of this shift certainly expected this system of semi-fixed exchange rates to impose the desired disciplinary effect on British industry. Lawson's paper to the November 1985 Cabinet meeting on the subject made this very point:

> We all know that the most intractable problem apart from unemploy-
> ment itself, and with which it is indeed closely linked, is the persistent
> tendency of British industry to allow its labour costs per unit of output
> to rise faster that its competitors. (Lawson 1992: 1058; see also Scott
> 1986: 198)

Lawson went on to argue that industry was more likely to control its costs if it knew that the possibilities of insulating its position through an exchange rate devaluation 'had been rendered unlikely by virtue of our joining the exchange rate mechanism ... a step incidentally which ... they themselves have called for (Lawson 1992: 1058).

Interestingly, the same theme lay behind Lawson's attraction to the ERM as far back as 1981, although this time, this policy instrument was to serve as an external discipline on the outspoken backbenchers who were less than enamoured with the initial results of monetarism in practice. In a long memorandum to Howe, Lawson distinguished between two types of financial discipline needed to control inflation. The Conservative leadership could operate a self-imposed explicit monetary target, as it was doing at the time, or an externally imposed exchange rate discipline. Although Lawson at this time preferred the former, he ruminated out loud whether an externally imposed exchange rate discipline might not be more effective in helping the leadership to impose financial discipline on the Wets: 'Those of our colleagues who are most likely to be pressing for the relaxation of monetary discipline, are those that are keenest on the UK joining the EMS [European Monetary System]. In other words, we turn their swords against them' (Lawson 1992: 111–12). Howe concurred by arguing that membership of the ERM represented a 'buttress' for monetary and fiscal policy, 'a reassertion of the disciplined philosophy which had inspired the Medium Term Financial Strategy' (Howe 1994: 639).

One could add that behind this shift lay an increasing lack of self-confidence within the Court concerning the possibilities for governance in an increasingly interdependent world. In language more often associated with European politics, leading politicians seemed increasingly resigned to their loss of sovereignty at this time and sought to strengthen their position by embracing European institutions. Indeed, some saw the opportunities for diffusing blame that such a policy provided. One theme of Lawson's memoirs is to use Thatcher's veto over ERM membership to diffuse blame for subsequent policy mistakes. While he denies that this decision totally absolved him for responsibility,

> it undoubtably made the conduct of economic policy more difficult, and thus errors more likely. In particular, it was very difficult outside the ERM, to handle the effects of the 1986 oil price collapse and prevent sterling from falling too far. Moreover, the advantages of rules over discretion in the conduct of economic policy is not merely that this can save policy-makers from their own mistakes. It also – and this is equally important, although usually overlooked in the discussion of the subject – affects decision-makers in the private sector, persuading them to conduct their affairs in a more prudent way. (Lawson 1992: 504)

Although writing after his resignation in 1986, the normally ebullient Heseltine was even more pessimistic concerning the possibilities for self-government in the changed global world of the 1980s:

> What was clear in 1971 is even more so today. The conditions which made it possible for Britain to be semi-detached from Europe for so long have vanished for ever. There is no Empire to sustain us; we are no longer an industrial superpower; we can no longer pretend that Britain is in anyway an equal partner of the United States. There is nowhere for us to go except as part of a European consortium. In 1989 few British citizens would, I think, deny this truth. (Heseltine 1991: 13–14, 27)

Indeed, a perusal of Howe's memoirs uncovers evidence of such an attitude as far back as his 1951 Parliamentary speech attacking the Attlee government's decision not to take part in discussions over the Schuman Plan:

> Why ... should 'foreign' be a word of disapproval unless designed to rouse the most insular of prejudices? Why should the 'surrender of British sovereignty' be 'unjustified' simply because is was 'unprecedented'? To say that 'we can perfectly well stand on our own feet as we have done in the past' struck me, I said, as 'unduly optimistic, and quite out of touch with the realities of our day and age'. (Howe 1994: 21)

At the same time, the Court understood that the Single Market programme and the signing of the SEA offered governing advantages. Of course, as we shall see in Chapter 5, ministers initially resisted the decision at the Milan European Council to set up an Intergovernmental Conference to discuss this treaty amendment. However, by getting the Single Market proposals accepted as the centrepiece of the Act, not only would this policy provide a plausible solution which could be pedalled in the domestic arena, it would also help to legitimize the Court's free market strategy by giving it European sanction. Howe certainly showed an awareness of how external support for a policy could fortify its acceptance at the domestic level. In a policy paper in 1982, his concern with the public image of government policies led him to defend its free market strategy by pointing out how, even in 1982, the international community was increasingly coming to share Britain's emphasis on sound money and free markets. For him, the international coordination of these policies over the medium term was an important part of the solution to the unemployment problem in Britain. He went on to conclude:

> It would be a tragedy if the real advantages of trade and jobs which flow from EU membership continued to be obscured by unfair budgetary arrangements. That underlines the importance of securing a fair and lasting settlement of the European budget problem. It means promoting and defending a liberal trading system throughout the world. (Howe 1982: 8)

Reflecting in his memoirs six years later, Howe (1994: 445) recalled how he continually tried to stress the link between economic and foreign policy and the extent to which the Conservative emphasis on free markets was now being accepted in Europe and was gradually gaining a position near the international centre of gravity. In a pamphlet written shortly after the ratification of the SEA, Howe proclaimed 'around the world, our message that markets really work has become the established orthodoxy of the day' (Howe 1988: 5).

If the Conservative leadership was aware that it could boost the authority of its statecraft project by entrenching it at the EU level, a number of Labour politicians were also aware of the dangers of this policy for their own economic strategy. Both Eric Deakins and Michael Foot observed in the Second Reading of the European Communities (Amendment) Bill (which was drawn up to insert the SEA into British law) that future British governments would be unable to institute import controls, place restrictions on capital movements and use state aids to support declining, but politically sensitive, industries (*Hansard* (Commons) vol. 100, 26 June 1986: col. 593; 27 June 1986: col. 604). Furthermore, when pressed, one official confirmed that the Conservative leadership understood that by signing the SEA, it would make any return to interventionist supply-side policies much more difficult (non-attributable interview with the author).

If the Single Market project helped to entrench the Court's free market supply-side policy and the autonomy concerns which it supported, it also conferred a second more basic governing advantage on the Conservative leadership. It helped to preserve the cohesion of the Court at a time when differences were evident over the government's future policy towards the EU. We have already noted real tensions within the Court over ERM membership. Interestingly, these differences seem to have extended on to the subject of the most appropriate style of British diplomacy towards Britain's European partners. As already noted, Thatcher's resolute approach towards the budgetary question enjoyed broad support within party ranks. This view was not shared by officials in the Foreign Office, who drew different conclusions from the episode. According to Adam Fergusson, 'the conflict over the budget made us terribly unpopular' (interview with the author, 27 September 1995). Another official at the Foreign Office during this time agrees that Britain had lost a lot of goodwill:

It was partly because of the budget dispute and partly because of what was seen as our negativeness across a whole range of policy issues. Underlying the whole argument was the suspicion that all the British were really interested in was having a free trade area. (Non-attributable interview with the author; see also comments by Tom King in *The Times* 30 May 1984)

Similarly, in taking up his appointment as Howe's special adviser on Europe, Fergusson became immediately aware of the contrast of style between Number 10 and the Foreign Office:

I came from the European Parliament, where I had been from 1979–84, as a pro-European, whatever that phrase means. And I was anxious to push the British government into a more pro-European stance. Not so much for its own sake, but because, by being pro-European, we stood a much better chance of getting our way than by being confrontational. When I got to the Foreign Office, I very quickly found out that the Foreign Office was not the problem.

Instead, Fergusson found himself

working with the grain of the Foreign Office which was trying to get No. 10 to take a more civilised and sensible view of how to get on with these people. But the effect of No. 10's policy was to polarise European opinion, with us at one end of the spectrum, and everybody else at the other. The trouble with that approach, which got progressively more confrontational as the 1980s went on, was that it made it impossible for doubts to emerge within the other member states. (Interview with the author, 27 September 1995)

Fergusson's view is supported by an official at the Cabinet Office who was closely involved with policy at this time. Asked about the different departmental interests between the Foreign Office and Number 10 on Europe, he replied:

It isn't really the case that different Ministries have different views which they advance. You are all trying together to advance the cause of the government. The Government's policy is set down by Mrs Thatcher, and you're all working out how best to promote that. However, what the Foreign Office does tend to see is that Britain's interests lie in the EU, and you actually advance your cause better by playing a full part in that. (Non-attributable interview with the author)

Faced with these growing tensions and divisions, the SEA became important because it helped to maintain the cohesion of the Court. On the origins of 'Europe: The Future', Adam Fergusson argued that this White Paper was a carefully worded document drawn up by the Foreign Office

> which was aimed as much at Number Ten as our Community partners. Almost everything that came out of the Foreign Office to do with Europe in those years, was crafted so that No. 10 would find it acceptable. This is not to say that the Foreign Office ever deceived No. 10, but policy papers were always written with No. 10's highly critical and often anti-European eye in mind. (Interview with the author, 27 September 1995)

The same point was made by an official at the Foreign Office when interviewed about the origins of the Howe Plan on Political Cooperation, which flanked the Single Market policy at this time (see Chapter 5):

> What was this approach all about? It was basically a ploy to try and overcome a problem which we faced in our relationship with the Europeans. Under Margaret Thatcher's direction, we were essentially negative to any developments in Europe. What we were looking for on Political Cooperation was to come up with a proposal which, in its essence, was a very forthcoming, go-ahead idea. So, we proposed having a new treaty on Political Cooperation, but which, by its nature, represented not only no step forward, but actually was something that one could present to Margaret Thatcher as being an opportunity to prevent any developments that we didn't like. In other words, you encapsulate all the progress that has been made in the preceding years, put it all in a treaty and at the end of the process all you've got is no more than you've got today, but the ability to control further developments as well. So you've got a policy that looks positive, but doesn't constitute any new step. And Margaret Thatcher thought that was brilliant. (Non-attributable interview with the author)

In short then, the Europeanization of economic policy at this time reflected more than just the perceived merits of these economic ideas. This policy change also represented an elite strategy to bolster its governing autonomy from domestic forces, while at the same time, cementing over a number of cracks which had appeared within this narrow ruling bloc. As we shall see, by 1990, this strategy had crumbled, leaving the Court deeply divided over the appropriate response to the EU. The reasons for this collapse will be taken up in Chapter 6.

Political Argument Hegemony

To the extent that the Conservatives had any problems in this area, the policy towards Europe drove home their 'victory' in the battle for Political Argument Hegemony. By 1987 EU membership was no longer questioned as the right goal for British foreign policy and the Conservatives could argue that they were the only party which could be trusted to continue to carry out this European role. For Howe, the government's recent initiative to complete the Single Market showed that the Conservatives

> are clearly committed to the success of the Community [and] are more likely to make progress than those who base their negotiation on a never ending threat to leave the Community. Britain is an integral part of Europe and is there to stay ... withdrawal [is no] longer an option in Community affairs. (*Hansard* (Commons) vol. 63, 10 July 1984: col. 890)

This theme is also taken up by Malcolm Rifkind, the Foreign Office Minister with chief responsibility for EU affairs at the time. Rifkind began by stressing the Conservatives' positive and constructive approach to the EU during this period and defended its Single Market initiative as an attempt to secure a major improvement in the working of the EU. He went on to argue that, at last, Britain under the Conservatives has been able to start playing the leadership role expected of it in so many quarters since it joined in 1973: 'A significant factor in the past twelve months has been the extent to which, for the first time in many years, the Community has ceased to be obsessed with the single dominant issue of the United Kingdom's relations with the other states' (*Hansard* (Commons) vol. 81, 20 June 1985: col. 466).

It should be added that government promises to push for the completion of the Single Market struck a chord with British business, which had been pushing for the same action itself for a number of years. For example, in April 1983 the Institute of Directors (IoD) could be seen savaging the European policy of the Thatcher government as 'vague and next to useless'. This criticism was combined with a plea for ministers to seize the initiative and push for the completion of the internal market (*The Times* 29 April 1983; *Sunday Times* 4 March 1984; *The Economist* 26 May 1984; *Agence Europe* 3 March 1983, 1 July 1983, 12 October 1983, 4 February 1984). By responding to this plea, Conservative leaders could present the impression that they were listening to the needs of business, a claim which was subject to much derision in business circles during the first four years of government.

In particular, ministers stressed that the City would be ideally placed to gain from this policy development. Britain's financial services were among the most competitive in Europe, if not the world, and the City was bound to experience an increase in business as barriers in Europe were broken down. In the Cecchini Report, issued by the Commission, on the implications of the completion of the internal market, the liberalization of financial services occupied a crucial position in its analysis of the overall macro effects of the study. One-third of the predicted additional GDP growth was expected to come from the expansion of services once the reforms were complete (quoted in Tsoukalis 1993: 92). Here was an issue over which the British could provide real leadership (see speech by Thatcher, *Hansard* (Commons) vol. 100, 27 June 1984: col. 1005–6; G. Howe *Hansard* (Commons) vol. 63, 10 July 1984: col. 898; Tugendhat in *Agence Europe* 21 September 1983).

At the same time, it is not difficult to chart a gradual change in the policy of the Labour Party from one of advocating withdrawal to one of grudging acquiescence. Although this is more noticeable in tone rather than substance, an article by the new Labour leader, Neil Kinnock, led the way in pointing to a gradual retreat, and it is noticeable that, although the right to withdrawal was maintained, it was played down. At the October 1983 Conference, Labour did not debate the EU question at all; a partial reflection of the fact that the leadership was divided over the subject. By 1984, a National Executive Committee (NEC) document, *Campaigning for a Fairer Britain*, contained a section on the EU which also seemed to reflect a less hostile approach. The document called on the party to campaign vigorously in the elections for the European Parliament in 1984. At the same time, it sought to remind its audience that, by the likely date of the next election, Britain would have experienced fifteen years of membership and this fact would be reflected in Britain's economic and political relations overseas (quoted in *The Times* 15 May 1984). By 1987, the policy of withdrawal was quietly being discarded.

Part of the reason for this was that there was some evidence to suggest that *the parties themselves perceived* that the more positive stance of the Conservatives had conferred electoral benefits on the party. The Conservative Party's Campaign Guide of 1984 argued that Labour's policy of withdrawal was 'an important reason' for its defeat at the 1983 election. To give substance to this argument, it utilized what looked like an attempt by Hattersley to set in motion a post-election reappraisal of policy:

> We fought the election primarily as the Party that would put Britain back to work and the overwhelming judgement of the people, and the overwhelming judgement I think of the economists, was that leaving the EEC would reduce our employment prospects rather than improve them. The people knew that our objection to the EEC was the objection of a half thought-out slogan. (Quoted in Conservative Research Department/European Democratic Group Secretariat 1984: 6)

Party Management

To the extent that the Euro-sceptics were contributing to tensions within the Court, the SEA provided a policy which the vast majority of the party could unite around, thus relieving inter-party stress. By June 1984, Teddy Taylor could enthuse about the need to 'co-operate in getting trade barriers broken down . . . [thus creating] more jobs, more investment and certainly more unity in the Continent of Europe' (T. Taylor, *Hansard* (Commons) vol. 63, 10 July 1984: cols 934–40; see also the speeches of Michael Knowles and Sir Anthony

Kershaw). Not surprisingly, the Wets concurred. As far back as January 1983, Pym had written that the completion of the Single Market 'must be an important part of the answer to the appalling problems of unemployment which afflict all Community countries' (*The Times* 10 January 1983). Despite disagreeing with many aspects of government policy, even Pym could support an initiative he himself had championed while in office.

It helped that, at the time of ratification, the SEA was not perceived as a controversial measure in Britain. The Conservative leadership played up the completion of the Single Market and played down the institutional change that might be involved. While no one could disagree that the harmonization of professional qualifications or the liberalization of insurance services was not important, it was dull, esoteric stuff. Put another way, the legislation to bring down the non-tariff barriers was a long way away from the theoretical and political debate between intergovernmentalists and federalists about the future of the EU which was always likely to animate the divisions between the Europhile and Europhobe elements within the party. As one official closely involved with policy observed in a interview, 'we did have quite a good run [between 1984 and 1986] mainly because we never took a general theoretical view that Europe mustn't develop this way or that way' (non-attributable interview with the author).

That said, it is possible to detect the faint rumblings of discontent among a few backbenchers during the ratification of the SEA. Of particular interest in the context of the argument developed below were nascent worries concerning the effect of this autonomy strategy on the authority and legitimacy of the Court. More specifically, Euro-sceptics began to highlight the perceived deleterious effects of EU institutional change on the role and function of Parliament within the general structure of the British polity. Most notable was the increased role of the European Parliament on matters pertaining to the completion of the Single Market. As discussed in Chapter 5, the SEA strengthened the cooperation procedure, which effectively gave the MEPs a second reading over legislation in this area. During the first reading, acting on a proposal from the Commission, the Council of Ministers could adopt a common position, but only after taking into account a preliminary opinion from the European Parliament. The Council of Ministers could then send its proposals to the Parliament. If an absolute majority of MEPs voted for amendments to the Council's decision, both the Commission and the Council would be obliged to take these amendments into account. If, during this stage, the Commission agreed to change its original proposals to accommodate the Parliament's amendments, the Council of Ministers could accept the Commission's amended proposals if supported by a qualified majority. If the Commission rejected the Parliament's amendments, only a qualified majority vote would be needed to adopt the Commission's proposals.

What particularly worried the Euro-sceptics was that at the second reading stage the Commission and the Parliament could work together to push through common proposals, if they so desired. Sceptics were quick to note that, although ministers retained the final power to veto proposals which ran counter to British objectives, in practice achieving unanimity in the Council of Ministers could be very difficult. At bottom, the control of UK ministers over policy had weakened and, as the only channel of influence that parliament had over EU policy was through elected politicians in the Council of Ministers, the Bill posed a threat to parliamentary democracy (see speech by E. Du Cann, *Hansard* (Commons) vol. 100, 26 June 1986: col. 490; Cash 1986; Johnson 1986).

It followed that this loss of influence would have detrimental consequences for Parliament's legitimating function. What particularly worried the Euro-sceptics was what they saw as the growing gap between the public perception and political reality of Britain's relations with the EU and the effects this relationship was having on the domestic political process. Put simply, they suspected that the majority of the British people were not aware that power was being transferred from their own elected representatives to what they saw as less accountable politicians and officials in Europe. If, and when, the British public woke up to this fact, the Euro-sceptics warned that the consequences might be malign for British politicians. The comments of Labour member Ron Leighton on this subject accurately reflected the thoughts of this small number of Euro-sceptical backbenchers at this time:

> I agree that in future, if constituents come to us to complain about this and that, we will have to say: 'its no good coming to us, you must go and see Herr somebody or Senor somebody on the Continent because the powers are there'. People come here to lobby us. I sometimes feel a little bit cynical about that. What do they think they are achieving by lobbying us? But it is right and proper that they do. Think of the situation if they felt that it was not worth coming to the British Parliament. Where would they go? (R. Leighton, *Hansard* (Commons) vol. 100, 26 June 1986: col. 526)

In other words, the search for autonomy can be taken too far. In such circumstances, its relationship to authority and governing competence becomes inversely proportional. We return to these arguments in Chapter 7.

Conclusions

In Chapter 3 it was argued that by 1984 international economic forces were perceived to be undermining the Conservative leadership's strategy aimed at re-establishing domestic autonomy and governing competence. This chapter has asserted that the Court gradually became attracted to the Europeanization of economic policy as a way of responding to these implementation problems.

ERM membership became increasingly attractive to policy-makers because it provided an alternative, external discipline which could replace the MTFS as a route to governing autonomy. At the same time, the Court promoted the completion of the Single Market as a way of entrenching its free-market supply-side strategy, which supported these autonomy concerns. Finally, this policy conferred more basic party political advantages on the Conservative leadership. It helped to preserve the unity of the Court at a time where friction existed over the government's future policy towards Europe. Moreover, Europeanization had beneficial spin-offs for the Court's political support functions: Political Argument Hegemony and party management.

Note

1. It should be noted that Redwood did indicate public dissent, but went along with the unanimous recommendations anyway.

CHAPTER FIVE

The Negotiation of the Single European Act: Institutional Legacies and the Problem of Foreign Policy Implementation

Chapters 2, 3 and 4 have been concerned with delineating the domestic sources of Europeanization in the area of economic policy. Perhaps the main conclusion is that this process should partly be understood as an external product of a domestic strategy aimed at entrenching the perceived governing benefits of neo-liberal economics. The rest of the book turns to the consequences of this action. The main focus of this chapter is the Thatcher government's experience in negotiating the Single European Act (SEA). Paradoxically, this period represented the zenith of Conservative influence in Europe in the 1980s and also the origins of its decline. In June 1984, the Thatcher government was isolated and unpopular when putting forward proposals to complete the Single Market. Although other member states supported this goal, majority opinion argued that institutional reform was the best way to drag the Community out of the period of Euro-sclerosis it had been experiencing. However, by December 1985, the programme to complete the Single Market had become the centrepiece of the Act, while proposals for institutional reform had gradually been watered down over the negotiating period. While it was true that the Thatcher government had accepted more majority voting, this was supposedly strictly confined to matters necessary to complete the Single Market. Having started from this weak position, and bearing in mind the supposed awkward style of Thatcher towards the EU, how can we explain the British government's apparent success in implementing its objectives? Moreover, how can we account for the rapid decline of this influence in the second half of the 1980s? What were the more general implications for the ability of the Conservative government to manage this external environment so that its domestic political objectives were promoted? These questions are the subject of the next three chapters.

With these issues in mind, this chapter makes the following arguments. First, despite Britain's relative isolation and unpopularity, the Court showed itself capable of adopting a varied and flexible negotiating strategy to try to build support for its objectives during this period. British negotiators attempted to support a core policy position on the Single Market by building an alliance with the French and German governments and developing a more pro-European discourse towards the Union. Moreover, when this tactic failed at Milan, it will be shown how the Thatcher government reverted to a more reactive, yet largely successful, approach during the Luxembourg negotiations. Second, faced with the failure of alliance-building, the British delegation adopted a more reactive approach and successfully exploited a gap between rhetoric and actual policy positions of many member states at Luxembourg. In other words, to the extent that the Court could talk of successfully implementing its objectives during this period, it did so despite, not because of, attempts to employ the intergovernmental bargaining techniques highlighted in Chapter 1. Finally, where the Thatcher government failed to influence the negotiations over the SEA, this chapter draws attention to the importance of the EU institutional context. Again, the most dramatic example of such a defeat was at the Milan European Council, where the British delegation was outmanoeuvred on the issue of convening an Intergovernmental Conference (IGC) to discuss amendments to the Treaty of Rome. The discussion suggests that this failure had less to do with the specific bargaining techniques employed. Of more importance was the impact of EU institutions on the negotiations, as outlined in Chapter 1. Moreover, bearing in mind that the SEA itself involved further institutional reform, we should expect such institutional factors to play a more prominent role in Chapters 6 and 7.

An Isolated Partner

As noted in the introduction, British negotiators were starting from an isolated and unpopular position as they began to plan a more cooperative and constructive offensive at the Community level after June 1984. The problem facing the Thatcher government at this time was broadly threefold. First, the British were generally unpopular in Brussels after five years of acrimonious wrangling over the question of Britain's contributions to the EU budget. Despite the Conservative Party's constant criticism in Opposition that the Labour Party had frittered away Britain's bargaining strength through its policy of continual renegotiation in the 1970s, things had not improved after five years of Tory rule. By June 1984, the Thatcher government's belligerent style towards the British budgetary dispute had used up a lot of goodwill among Britain's partners. Writing in melodramatic style after the collapse of the Brussels European Council in March 1984, the European correspondent on *The Times*, Ian Murray, lamented that, if British negotiators persisted with their combative approach, they risked splitting the EU. John Ardagh quoted the feelings of the French five days later: 'that woman is an old fashioned nationalist with no feeling for the European ideal' (Murray 1984; Ardagh 1984; *The Economist* 23 June 1984: 15; George 1994: 160).

The speeches and behaviour of some politicians across the Channel seemed to confirm this general picture of unpopularity. In May 1984, Dumas, the French Foreign Minister, ruminated aloud about the possibility of a two-speed Europe in which member states could opt out of certain policies, leaving the rest to cooperate. In his speech to the European Parliament, Mitterrand's call for a conference of interested governments to discuss amendments to the Treaty of Rome, backed by Chancellor Kohl, was interpreted by the British government as a coded threat that Bonn were prepared to create such a multi-tiered Community, without Britain if necessary (*Agence Europe* 3 May 1984, 25 May 1984; *The Times* 25 May 1984).

Second, if the Thatcher government was unpopular, it was also largely isolated in the battle of political ideas surrounding the future of the EU. The debate at this time was dominated by proposals for institutional reform which would alter the decision-making structure of the EU in a way that challenged the supremacy of the Council of Ministers. The starting assumption behind this alternative position was the view that the Community 'is now in a state of crisis and suffers from serious deficiencies'. It followed that 'the establishment of a new institutional balance' was needed both as a way to more efficient decision-making and to pull the Community out of this malaise (*The Draft Treaty Establishing European Union*, in HL 226, 1985, Appendix 3, xxxix–lxv). Finally, this increasing pressure for institutional reform took place against a backdrop of federalist rhetoric which made ministers in London uncomfortable. The most obvious manifestation of this was the call for a new 'European Union' in the Draft Treaty of the European Parliament (also known as the Spinelli Treaty). However, references to 'European Union', 'European unification' and 'European integration' could also be cited in the Genscher–Colombo plan and the Stuttgart Declaration.

Perhaps the most contentious proposals from London's point of view were those which aimed to increase the legislative role of the European Parliament.[1] Reflecting a long-term trend stretching back to 1960, both the Genscher–Colombo plan (1981) and the Stuttgart Declaration (1983) reaffirmed the central importance of the European Parliament and its direct involvement in the decision-making process of the EU. However, concrete suggestions went little further than extending the Parliament's rights of consultation on the appointment of the President of the Commission and decisions relating to the accession or association of new member states to the Community (*Bulletin of the European Communities* 14(11), 1981: 89). Although Whitehall could just about claim that these proposals did not add up to an increase in the powers of the European Parliament, ministers would not have been happy with the Stuttgart Declaration's objective to 'improve' and 'extend' the scope of the 'conciliation procedure' (*Bulletin of the European Communities* 16(6), 1983: 26;

Hansard (Commons) vol. 25, 17 June 1982: col. 1106; Jacobs 1990: 162–9). More worrying were the Parliament's own proposals in its Draft Treaty. Calling for a 'new institutional balance', Article 38 set out a new cooperation procedure giving the Parliament an increased input into the legislative process of the Community. What was significant about these proposals was their provision for a second reading of the Council's decisions. After the first reading, the Council's decision would then be returned to Parliament, where it could do one of three things within a six-month deadline. It could approve the text, reject it or propose amendments. Parliament's decision would then go back to the Council, where after taking note of an opinion given by the Commission, it could approve the Parliamentary text by majority vote or reject it by unanimity. If it proved impossible to secure the majorities outlined above after the draft was put to the vote, a 'conciliation procedure' would be triggered. This involved setting up a committee composed of representatives from the Council and the Parliament, who would then undertake an elaborate process to try and reach a 'joint position' (HL 226, 1985).

A second area of concern was the increase in calls for the greater use of majority voting in the Council of Ministers. The Thatcher government was particularly sensitive on this issue after its Community partners had pushed through a decision increasing agricultural prices during the Falklands War. Although ministers could live with the aspirations of the Genscher–Colombo plan and the Stuttgart Declaration to take advantage of every opportunity to increase majority voting, the specific proposals of the European Parliament's Draft Treaty were unacceptable. These called for the incorporation of the Luxembourg Compromise into the Treaty of Rome, where it would have a ten-year lifespan before being abolished. During this period, the veto could only be invoked in the case of 'vital' national interests, to be judged 'objectively' by the Commission (HL 226, 1985: Appendix 3).

If the debate at the European level was dominated by federalist rhetoric and proposals for institutional reform at this time, what made the problem worse was that the Thatcher government was largely isolated in its enthusiasm to complete the Single Market. This can be seen by briefly reviewing the various policy papers and proposals circulating around Brussels at this time. In 1981, the Genscher–Colombo plan for a new European Union drafted by the German and Italian Foreign Ministers was largely aimed at developing European Political Co-operation (EPC) and put forward a number of suggestions with this in mind. It did call for the completion of the Single Market as part of the more general process of achieving greater economic integration of the economies in Europe. However, this was nothing more than a general statement and was well down the list of policy priorities (*Bulletin of the European Communities* 14(11), 1981: 88–91).

Furthermore, there was little hope of the Thatcher government building an alliance with Paris at this time. In its *Memorandum on the Revitalisation of the EC*

(1981), completion of the Single Market is relegated to the third section under the heading 'Industrial Policy'. Until March 1983, French foreign policy was concerned with other priorities, most notably the export of its socialist programme to other parts of the globe (Levy 1987: 175; Haywood 1993: 278; Cole 1994: 119). Even after the abandonment of this socialist programme and the adoption of a more positive approach to the EU, French initiatives were often in areas which Whitehall found largely unappealing. Calls for a European defence policy in November 1982 were unattractive to a Conservative leadership which still placed great emphasis on the importance of NATO to Europe's security interests. Finally, up to 1984, the French government continued to block progress in the newly created Internal Market Council, by linking it to the 'parallel' creation of a new trade policy instrument (*Bulletin of the European Communities* 14(11) 1981: 92–100; *Agence Europe* 11 April 1983, 22 June 1983, 22 September 1983, 3/4 January 1984, 8 March 1984). This argument is confirmed by Lord Cockfield's analysis of the *Solemn Declaration on European Union* at the Stuttgart European Council in June 1983. He maintains that the completion of the Single Market was not a priority at Stuttgart, only appearing on page 14 of the English translation. Moreover, despite the tabling of 'Europe – the Future' by the British delegation, there was no discussion of the Single Market at Fontainebleau (interview with the author, 22 February 1995).

Similar conclusions can be drawn once the ten member states began discussing proposals for the future development of the Community in the Dooge Committee (also called the Institutional Committee or Spaak II Committee). First, discussions were dominated by terms of reference which were biased against the position of the British negotiating team. In his introductory report to the Committee, the representative of the French government, Faure, taking the lead from Mitterrand's recent support for the principles of the Spinelli Treaty, stated that the problem faced by member states was how to generate a political will allowing the present Community to develop into a new dynamic political entity. His preliminary conclusions stated that only reform of the Community's decision-making processes would be enough to achieve progress towards a meaningful European Union (*Agence Europe* 1 October 1984, 13 October 1984). Not surprisingly, the discussions that followed were dominated by suggestions for increasing the legislative role of the Parliament, whether there could be an objective measurement of a country's national interest and the need for an IGC to implement such reforms (*Agence Europe* 19 January 1985, 23 January 1985, 30 January 1985). Predictably, the British government found itself in the 'minority group' when the Committee's report was finally published.

Third and finally, the British government's desire to complete the Single Market, a project which had been stalled in the Council of Ministers for a decade, only seemed to confirm this logic for institutional reform. As Howe (1994: 407) states in his memoirs, the vital question facing ministers at this time was whether there was 'a need to amend the Rome Treaty itself, if we were to make headway even on our own basic British objective of the Single Market'. Implementing this policy was proving very difficult because of the unanimity rule. The problem for the British, however, was that to abolish the unanimity rule by amending the Treaty of Rome would mean having to convene an IGC leading to 'any and every possible constitutional amendment ... being discussed'. Howe's special adviser, Adam Fergusson, agrees:

> Every time you change a treaty, the whole treaty can become unstitched because more and more people try and get something changed. The process goes on and on, and it's very difficult to stop it. So do not change the Treaty of Rome. By all means include a protocol if you feel this is necessary, but don't change the Treaty. (Interview with the author, 27 September 1995)

These recollections suggest that the Foreign Office (although not necessarily Number 10) was not against limited institutional reform itself. What worried the British was that an IGC which would open up a Pandora's Box of reforms and alter the structural framework of the Community regime in ways inimical to the future interests of the Thatcher government.

A second reason for the opposition to an IGC and Treaty amendments at this time was that the Thatcher leadership saw it as against their domestic political interests. According to one Whitehall official:

> It was going to cause her a lot of aggravation back home, mainly in Parliament. In such negotiations, she would inevitably be pushed in directions that she didn't want to go ... and she was constantly being held back by her own backbenchers. The opposition to the government at this time came from her own party, not the Opposition. (Non-attributable interview with the author)

As already noted, this view is confirmed by other interview material in this book.

To conclude, the Thatcher government was largely beginning from an unpopular and isolated position in its attempts to promote the completion of the Single Market. After five years of acrimonious wrangling over the question of Britain's contributions to the EU budget, the British were generally unpopular in Brussels. Furthermore, in the battle of political ideas surrounding the future direction of the EU, the Conservative leadership was largely isolated in its enthusiasm to promote the completion of the Single Market as the way forward. Instead, the debate was dominated by proposals for institutional reform of the type which made ministers nervous. Finally, the Thatcher government lacked a credible policy response to these proposals for institutional reform. Indeed, its own desire for the completion of the Single Market, a project which had been stalled in the Council of Ministers for a decade, only seemed to confirm the logic for at least some increase in qualified majority voting, despite its own reservations and the possibility of unrest back home. Although the British negotiating team appeared to be genuine in its assertion that completion of the Single Market was the most 'European' contribution that member states could make to the future development of the Community, other European governments suspected that London was reverting to its old strategy of trying to turn the Community into a glorified free trade area.

From Isolated to Cooperative Partner:
The Response of the Thatcher Government

Instead of exhibiting awkward behaviour towards its Community partners at this time, the Thatcher government responded to this dilemma by pursuing a positive, if not especially imaginative, negotiating strategy. This was centred on a core of building up momentum behind the Single Market project, while trying to frustrate momentum for institutional reform, largely coming from the European Parliament at this time. This core was supported or flanked by additional initiatives aimed at constructing a more general alliance with the French and the Germans. Ministers produced limited reforms to strengthen the process of European Political Cooperation and a conscious effort was also made to develop a pro-Union discourse to accompany these proposals.

The Core: The British Government and the
Implementation of the Single Market

We have already discussed, at length, the domestic motivations of the government's attractions to this policy goal at the time. Logically, one would expect the British negotiators to be taking centre stage in pushing for this goal at the Community level. While there can be little doubt that British negotiators were constantly promoting the Single Market goal, the role of the Court was also more subtle and ambiguous. However, before we assess this role, it is important to address Lord Cockfield's argument that the Thatcher government made little contribution to the implementation of the Single Market proposals. For Cockfield, the implementation of the Single Market project was largely the product of his own efforts. He acknowledges the commitment of the government to the Single Market at the rhetorical level, but he argues that this did not match the reality of actual policy preparation at this time. Not only was he 'horrified' at the paucity of the briefing material he received as he left to take up his post as the Internal Market Commissioner, he also alleges that this material was excessively concerned with budgetary matters. As an example of this lack of preparation, he points out that the main briefing document produced for the visit to London by Delors in 1984 was only nine pages long and the section on the Single Market ran to a mere seven lines (Cockfield 1994: 37–8).

While it may be accurate to point to a lack of preparation behind the government's commitment to the Single Market, the role of the Thatcher government deserves more attention. To begin with, it is worth remembering that Britain's relations with the EU until Fontainebleau were dominated by the question of getting a fair solution to the issue of Britain's budgetary contributions. At this time, it is not surprising that little detailed thinking had been done on additional policies. Moreover, despite the lack of detail, Conservative leaders were constantly emphasizing throughout the first half of the 1980s that this stress on the budgetary question was the first part of a broader twofold approach to the Community. The tough diplomacy of the Thatcher government over the question of the budget may have left the British negotiating team open to charges of excessive negativism, but future British policy priorities, such as the completion of the Single Market, could not be embarked on until the EU had reformed its finances. As the Conservatives' manifesto for the 1989 European elections put it, 'First things first: you cannot build on unsound foundations. Before moving forward to the creation of the Single Market, we knew it was crucial to reform Europe's chaotic budget.' The parallels with domestic policy indicated at least some coherence at this time (Conservative Central Office 1989; but see also British paper to the special council on the Stuttgart Mandate, *Agence Europe* 22 September 1983; G. Howe in *Hansard* (Commons) vol. 63, 10 July 1984: cols 890–9).

Once the Thatcher government did turn its attention to implementing the Single Market project, it recognized the importance of securing the right personnel at the Commission. As Howe remarks in his memoirs, if the British government was to make any progress, this 'turned above all' on the appointment of Lord Cockfield. He was chosen partly because of his background, but also because his qualities of commitment and determination were felt to be ideal in pushing the policy through at the European level (Howe 1994: 405). Cockfield's own account of events suggests that his nomination represented a conscious choice on behalf of Number 10 and the Foreign Office. One alternative expounded by Lawson at the time was for Cockfield to take over the budget portfolio. However, according to the latter, this would be a recipe for 'the familiar situation in which the United Kingdom was isolated in a minority of one'. What was needed was a more positive strategy. This involved filling the budget portfolio with a tough neutral (the Danish representative, Henning Christophersen), leaving Cockfield free to concentrate on implementing the Single Market and presenting the contribution of the British government in a much more positive light. Thatcher sanctioned this strategy by accepting Cockfield's arguments over those of Lawson (Cockfield 1994: 25–6).

Moreover, once Lord Cockfield set to work on the details of the Single Market project, the Thatcher government gave broad support to his reform efforts. Interviews with former officials suggest that some Whitehall departments did have problems with various measures to bring down non-tariff barriers by 1992. The Treasury is known to have displayed concern at suggestions to harmonize VAT rates, a concern which was shared by Number 10. MAFF, it could be added, was said to be anxious about proposals on animal and plant health. However, broad political support from Number 10, the Foreign Office and the Cabinet Office was helpful in overcoming these pockets of resistance. As one official remarked on the initial response of the British government to Cockfield's White Paper,

> the conclusion was that we should welcome it, and it was strongly welcomed. ... We understood there were difficulties for different departments, but it was not in our interests to try to be negative about this. The broad thrust was obviously right. It was promoted by a British Commissioner and we ought to support it. (Non-attributable interview with the author, 19 July 1995; see also Cockfield 1994: 55, confirmed in an interview with the author, 22 February 1995)

Finally, it is important to remember that, although differences over specific elements of the White Paper were to develop later, the strategic approach of Cockfield largely complemented that of the Conservative leadership until the Milan European Council. In his account, Cockfield provides a detailed description of the strategy and tactics employed to pioneer the Single Market. However, one point is particularly important. When presenting his proposals to the Heads of Government in Milan, Cockfield stressed that he inserted at the beginning of the White Paper the declarations of previous summits, which called for the completion of the Single Market: 'this was put in, not because they were driving it, but to illustrate to them that we were doing what they thought they were asking for' (interview with the author, 22 February 1995). In other words, the British government felt that it could give broad support for Cockfield's proposals, because they were aiming at nothing more than the implementation of outstanding policy objectives and commitments.

Frustrating Calls For Institutional Reform:
The Luxembourg Compromise Number 2

It was noted that the second part of the core negotiating position was a deliberate attempt to frustrate momentum for institutional reform, something which also reflected domestic motivations. In particular, what ministers wanted to avoid was a formal revision of the Treaty of Rome via an Intergovernmental Conference. As a result, the government responded with a number of more limited ideas to improve the decision-making machinery of the Community. On the issue of increasing the use of majority voting in the Council of Ministers, as long as there has been a thorough discussion of the issue, Conservative leaders argued, there was nothing in the Rome Treaty, or as a consequence of the Luxembourg Compromise, which prevented the Chairman calling for a vote (where the Treaty allowed for it). However, if the chairman sensed that there was no unanimity among ministers, present practice meant that, after a debate, instead of asking for a vote to be taken, discussion was allowed to continue until a consensus point was reached. In evidence to the House of Lords Select Committee, Rifkind argued that these proposals would speed up decision-making on account of the fact that the veto was hardly ever invoked. No member state enjoyed the opprobrium that came with being held responsible for blocking progress in Europe (HL 226, 1985: 47). Another proposal suggested that individual governments abstain in the face of unpalatable policy decisions, rather than invoke the veto. When putting forward this suggestion, ministers particularly had in mind those directives pertaining to the completion of the Single Market under Article 100. In fact, Thatcher had suggested this reform as far back as the Dublin European Council in November 1979, arguing that this procedure could be adopted under Article 148. Under this article, 'abstentions by members present in person or represented shall not prevent the adoption by the Council of acts which require unanimity'. However, this proved unacceptable to other member states at the time (HL 226, 1985: 47–8).

The Thatcher government also adopted and championed a suggestion that any member state vetoing a specific policy in the Council of Ministers on the grounds of national interest should give publicly stated reasons for this decision. However, ministers resisted proposals, discussed at the time, which sought to derive some kind of 'objective' measurement of the national interest of each country. There was no sympathy in Whitehall for a proposal discussed in the Dooge Committee which suggested that, in the event of a member state blocking a proposal on the basis of its national interest, the Commission should be invited by the Council of Ministers to examine the problem with member states for a three-month period. The Commission would then present the Council with a new proposal which the Council would consider for up to three months before reaching a decision (*Agence Europe* 30 January 1985). In the face of these proposals, the Conservative leadership stuck steadfastly by its line that the definition of a country's national interest was a matter solely for the particular government in question (HL 226, 1985: 51).

During the period between Fontainebleau and Milan, there is evidence to suggest further movement by the British negotiating team, although it is difficult to judge whether this should be interpreted as a weakening of the British position. Howe provides details of British proposals for a constitutional 'convention'. According to this written but not legally binding gentleman's agreement, the Council of Ministers should proceed as though the unanimity rule had been set to one side on issues pertaining to the completion of the Single Market (Howe 1994: 407). This suggestion found its way into a paper tabled in the Dooge Committee by Rifkind. It proposed 'procedural changes' short of treaty amendments which would 'permit detailed implementation of selected policies [pertaining to the completion of the Single Market] by majority voting once agreement had been reached unanimously on the principles' (HL 226, 1985: 34).

Before we move on, this description of the British position deserves some comment. First, there seems to be a real contradiction between the twin policy objectives of the British government. Progress on completion of the Single Market, and many of the Commission's initiatives for removing the offending non-tariff barriers, had become stalled in the Council of Ministers for a decade or so. If the government wanted to give itself the means to implement this policy, it seemed inexplicable why ministers thought these proposals for a gentleman's agreement not to invoke the Luxembourg Compromise would succeed in unblocking ten years of inertia (*Agence Europe* 31 May 1985). This contradiction is particularly pertinent bearing in mind the consideration that senior Conservative leaders gave to the problem of implementing domestic policy, outlined in Chapters 3 and 4. How can we explain this contradiction?

Although ministers preferred to see the more general problem of Eurosclerosis in terms of a lack of political will rather than the need for institutional reform, there was a powerful case for accepting that institutional reform could prove a valuable aid to generating this political will. More specifically, formal treaty amendments stipulating the increased use of majority voting, particularly on matters pertaining to the completion of the Single Market, could be used by the British government as a way of locking recalcitrant member states into this policy goal. The gradual acceptance of this argument by the British negotiators largely explains why Thatcher accepted formal amendments to the Treaty of Rome on Single Market matters, despite consistent opposition to this policy before Milan.

Finally, it is possible to be bolder and suggest that even before Milan the Thatcher government was employing a twin-track strategy on this issue. As early as the start of 1983, Francis Pym, the then British Foreign Secretary, was reported as saying that the Thatcher government was not dogmatically opposed to the extension of majority voting, although this must be gradual and with the consent of all member states (*Agence Europe* 24 January 1983). In his evidence to the House of Lords Select Committee on the EU, Rifkind was careful not to rule out totally the possibility that the government might accept some institutional reform. He stressed that, once specific issues on which a common policy is desirable have been identified, a judgement will then be made to 'determine if it is necessary to have an institutional change to achieve these results' (HL 226, 1985: 42). An official at the Cabinet Office at the time has since confirmed that all governments have a 'hierarchy of objectives' when they approach international negotiations: 'given the importance of the Single Market for the British government, it was clear that it would be sensible to accept an extension of majority voting in this area' (non-attributable interview with author; see also David Owen, HL 226, 1985: 155).

What was more objectionable to the British government during this period was the issue of giving more legislative powers to the European Parliament. In a Memorandum submitted to the House of Lords Select Committee, the Foreign Office objected to Article 38 of the Spinelli Treaty because, according to its interpretation, Parliament would be able to adopt legislation without the consent of the Council of Ministers. This was unacceptable because it represented a substantial alteration of the external implementation framework facing British political leaders and could seriously hinder the ability of British administrations to achieve their future policy goals. In the words of the Memorandum,

> the balance of power between the Community institutions, as laid down in the Treaty of Rome, would be significantly altered. Strengthening the powers of the European Parliament would increase the probability that member states would find themselves under pressure to accept proposals which they judged to be against their national interests.
> (HL 226, 1985: 3)

In separate evidence to the Committee, it was this issue above all others that Rifkind judged would be hardest for London to accept (HL 226, 1985: 55–6).

The Flanking Proposals: The Howe Plan for European Political Cooperation

In order to support this core negotiating strategy, the Thatcher government attempted to draw up additional proposals designed to appeal to member states, thus, it was hoped, creating a broader alliance behind its position. In this context, two elements of the policy are worth mentioning: proposals for strengthening European Political Co-operation (EPC); and the attempt to develop a pro-Community discourse to promote the whole package. As Howe noted in his memoirs, support for the Single Market and the Luxembourg Compromise 2 proposals 'needed to be backed and flanked by a comprehensively positive attitude on most, if not all, the other European questions' (Howe, 1994: 408).

The British approach to EPC had traditionally been evolutionary and pragmatic, concerned with informally building up a body of procedure and precedent for cooperation where possible and desirable. This approach was evident in the response of the British government to the invasion of Afghanistan by the Soviet Union, which had produced a diverse reaction from the member states of the Community. Calling for a number of limited proposals for underpinning EPC, the Foreign Office suggested establishing a small Secretariat or troika to assist the Presidency in its work. This body would be staffed by officials from the present, preceding and succeeding Presidencies. There were also suggestions for a new crisis management mechanism, increased association between EPC and the work of the Commission, and inclusion of security issues in future discussions (Hurd 1981). Although the Howe Plan, drawn up and published in the first half of 1985, called for a new Treaty on Political Cooperation, it merely represented a codification of this existing procedure and practice and fitted in entirely with this traditional evolutionary and practical approach. That said, this plan now accepted that the status of any future Secretariat would have to be permanent. According to Nuttall, these proposals represented a real concession on the part of the Thatcher government (Nuttall 1992: 245–6; George 1994: 179).

Although it was hardly likely to fire the imaginations of its European partners, the government hoped that the Howe Plan would help to reintegrate Britain into the European policy process by building an alliance with the French and the Germans. However, the relationship and approach of the British government to the Franco-German alliance at this time remains unclear. Howe's memoirs suggest that the British government concentrated a large proportion of its time lobbying Germany rather than France. Kohl was invited 'unprecedentedly' to a Saturday Chequers meeting with Mrs Thatcher, at which she attempted, and failed, to get him to co-sponsor the Howe proposals. Although all officials interviewed spoke of the folly of trying to split the French and the Germans over this issue, no mention was made of any approaches to Mitterrand. It is also worth remembering that the French President's support for the idea of an autonomous and permanent political Secretariat ran counter to British thinking, which, as already noted, favoured a small advisory body (Howe 1994: 408).

Moreover, it was not lost on British negotiators that the evolutionary, practical approach of Whitehall in this area had historically commanded broad respect from the smaller states in the Community. French support in the 1960s for some sort of higher independent political authority or Secretariat has always elicited reservations from smaller member states. In particular, these worries centered on the implications for the Community method and a possible dilution of the Atlantic Alliance. Mitterrand's call for a similar organization twenty years on was likely to rekindle these traditional suspicions (Nuttall 1992: 241–4) and it would be surprising if the Foreign Office had not seen the tactical advantages of promoting a rival, but more limited, initiative.

Pro-Community Discourse

If the British government recognized that it needed to flank its Single Market policies with more positive proposals on EPC, a conscious effort was also made to develop a pro-Community discourse to accompany these proposals. It is possible to trace the origins of this discourse back to the start of 1983, if not before. As Sir Michael Butler has confirmed, by the Stuttgart Summit, the British perceived that a conclusion to the budgetary problem was in sight. The time was right for a restatement of the British approach to the future development of the EU. This was especially so when it was felt that British policy was not being fully communicated to Britain's partners (interview with the author, 21 February 1995). In an article in January 1983 entitled 'The EEC Must Be Our Future', Francis Pym set out many of the themes that were to recur as this *communautaire* discourse developed (*The Times* 10 January 1983; *Agence Europe* 24 January 1983).

This discourse almost always contained a preface arguing that Britain's commitment to the EU was 'profound and irreversible' (see Howe's speech to the German Foreign Policy Society and Anglo-German Society, *The Times* 18 October 1984) and that Britain's future economic success and political influence was dependent on Community membership. Once Britain's budgetary problems had been settled, the Thatcher government would be 'second to none' in its attempts to develop 'an extremely positive approach' to the Community (see Rifkind in *The Times* 12 July 1983; Howe's speech to the Berliner Pressekonferenz in West Berlin, *The Times* 12 December 1984). At the same time, threats by Britain's partners of a two-speed Europe were dismissed. If there was to be such a development, Britain would be in the fast lane and ministers continually pointed to the fact that it was making the running in working for the development of policies in a number of areas (see Howe in *The Times* 26 May 1984). Howe remembers it in his memoirs: 'I was seeking to demonstrate, explicitly, the range of Britain's European commitment and, by implication, to suggest that the Franco-German relationship should not be seen as the only cornerstone of the European Community' (Howe 1994: 403–4).

If the Thatcher government continually stressed the commitment of Britain to the EU, it also consistently argued that the successful development of the Community hinged on the implementation of a number of limited goals which were meaningful to the lives of European citizens. This incremental and gradual approach would stand a much better chance of reigniting enthusiasm for the Community than promising grand ideological blueprints which had little prospect of being achieved. As well as the completion of the Single Market in goods, ministers constantly pushed for lower European airfares and easier travel formalities. By the Milan European Council in June 1985, the European Movement had set up a campaign (with government backing) to support this policy position (see the *Sunday Times* 12 May 1985; Ridley in *The*

Times 14 May 1984; see also Rifkind's speech at Maison de l'Europe, *Agence Europe* 1 February 1985).

It should finally be noted that, up to this point, the development of such a discourse by the Conservative leadership represented a novel feature of British policy towards the EU. This fact is often overlooked in existing accounts of this policy area. Christopher Tugendhat drew attention to this argument in his evidence to the House of Lords Select Committee on the EU. He agreed with Committee members that part of the reason why the British government was constantly regarded as being out of step with her Community partners was because it is not in the British tradition to accompany Whitehall's often constructive initiatives with rhetorical flourishes of Euro-enthusiasm. Tugendhat concluded that Howe's speeches in Germany, 'show[ing] that he is trying to develop a rather a distinctive form of oratory', were a welcome response to this traditional shortcoming of British policy towards the EU (HL 226, 1985: 191).

If the Thatcher government attempted to play a more cooperative and constructive role at the Community level during this period, this approach was rejected by a majority of Britain's partners at the Milan European Council. The failure of this strategy can be easily demonstrated. A joint initiative by the French and German governments for a 'Draft Treaty on European Union' clearly represented a blow to earlier attempts to secure German support for the Howe Plan. The Draft Treaty was introduced without consulting London and, even more galling, represented little more than a rehash of Howe's proposals for Political Cooperation (George 1994: 181–2). Thatcher was said to be furious at the time. In a recent television programme on the subject, Ingham confirmed that Milan was the worst European Council he attended during his time as Thatcher's press secretary (*The Poisoned Chalice*, BBC2, 23 May 1996). Moreover, Howe's reflections ten years after the event also indicated the mood of frustration and bitterness that existed at the time: 'Milan had, in truth, been a miserable experience. . . . One was tempted almost to turn one's back on the whole thing. But it was too important for that' (Howe 1994: 409–10; *Agence Europe* 30 June 1985).

Moreover, the decision to convene an Intergovernmental Conference to put forward amendments to the Treaty of Rome represented another setback. It will be recalled that the Thatcher government opposed such a conference because it feared it might lead to a Pandora's box of institutional reforms. What particularly upset British negotiators was the behaviour of the Italian chairman who, failing to get unanimous support for the IGC on an earlier vote, forced the issue by calling for an unprecedented vote under Article 236. This procedure permitted the Council of Ministers to call for an IGC if a majority of member states approved. As a result, Thatcher found herself outmanoeuvred in a 7–3 vote in favour of the conference.

To sum up, despite beginning this period from an isolated and unpopular position, and despite seeming to lack the objective resources necessary for success in international negotiations, the Thatcher government adopted a positive, if not very imaginative, negotiating strategy from June 1984 to June 1985. This was centred on the core of the Single Market project, while attempting to frustrate momentum for institutional reform largely coming from the European Parliament at this time. This core was supported or flanked by additional initiatives aimed at constructing a more general alliance with the French and the Germans. Ministers produced limited reforms to strengthen the process of EPC, while making a conscious effort to develop a pro-Community discourse to accompany these proposals.

From Cooperative to Reactive Partner: Negotiating the Single European Act, July–December 1985

Despite the failure at Milan, a superficial comparison of the competing policy positions which dominated that European Council and the final text agreed at the Luxembourg European Council in December 1985 suggests that British negotiators achieved most of their aims. The completion of the Single Market was placed firmly at the centre of the Act, whereas the codification approach of the British towards European Political Cooperation is evident in Title III. At the same time, proposals for institutional reform were largely confined to the Single Market. As such, the paradox identified in Chapter 1 remains: after the 'miserable experience' of Milan, and the new challenge of the IGC, how can the apparent success of the British be explained? What do these conclusions tell us about the ability of the Conservative government to implement its foreign policy objectives at the EU level? This chapter finishes by making two arguments.

First, this success was partly dependent on the willingness and the ability of the Court to alter its negotiating strategy from a 'cooperative' to a more 'reactive' approach. Although not representing a complete break with earlier diplomatic methods, this change in style was distinguished by the following features. First, British negotiators produced no new initiatives themselves. Instead, they chose to subject the proposals of other delegations to the kind of 'rationalistic' probing with which Whitehall was more comfortable. Referring to one of his last acts before handing over to Sir David Hannay, Michael Butler confirms this point:

> After the Milan summit ... I got myself instructions to propose that everybody should lay down on the table the sort of amendments to the treaty which they wanted to see. Now I knew that they hadn't got anything in their lockers and, sure enough, they didn't have anything much. (Interview with the author, 21 February 1995)

Second, British negotiators generally avoided attempts to create new coalitions across issues, although cooperation was sought on a temporary basis wherever possible. That said, the success of this tactical switch depended on the absence of a united Franco-German axis around alternative policy suggestions. In adopting this 'reactive' approach, the Court hoped to expose the gap between rhetoric and reality which it had reason to expect existed in some capitals at this time, particularly over the question of institutional reform. In other words, to the extent that this approach was successful, it was despite, not because of, the ability of British negotiators to employ the intergovernmental bargaining techniques outlined in Chapter 1.

The Powers of the European Parliament

Perhaps the most appropriate place to begin in trying to demonstrate the importance of this change of approach concerns the negotiations over extra powers for the European Parliament. It is generally accepted that the final text of the SEA resembled a pale imitation of the initial proposals contained in the Spinelli Treaty. To recap, the treaty proposed a new form of joint decision-making under Article 38. After the first reading, the Council's decision would return to Parliament, where it could approve the text, reject it or propose amendments. Parliament's decision would then go back to the Council, which, after taking note of an opinion given by the Commission, could approve the parliamentary text by majority vote, or reject it by unanimity. If it proved impossible to secure the majorities outlined above after the draft was put to the vote, a 'Conciliation or Cooperation Procedure' would be triggered. This involved setting up a committee composed of representatives from the Council and the Parliament who would then undertake an elaborate process to try and reach a joint position. In addition, the Luxembourg Compromise was to be brought into the Treaty of Rome and given proper legal status, only to be phased out after a period of ten years. Finally, a variety of matters were to be brought within the concurrent competence of the Community, including competition policy, monetary policy and social and health policy.

By mid-October, Bonn had produced a revised text, which departed significantly from Spinelli. Instead of one legislative procedure, it proposed introducing three different procedures, which would vary according to specific areas. First, Parliament's consultation rights were to be extended to all normative clauses in the Treaty of Rome, except in well defined cases. Second, Parliament's suggestion for a 'Cooperation Procedure' was maintained, although it would only be applicable to a clearly defined list of articles (7, 43(2), 54(2) and (3), 56(2), 57(1) and (2), 63, 75(1), 87, 126, 235). Under this procedure, MEPs would be able to deliberate upon Commission proposals within a six-month deadline. Amendments could be proposed or the text could be rejected entirely, but such decisions would have to receive the backing of an absolute majority. The Council would then consider such proposals and, if it dissented, an independent conciliation committee with

Commission participation would be initiated to broker a decision. Third, a stronger joint legislative action procedure was suggested, whereby Parliament's consent would be needed for decisions. However, this was only to apply to a limited number of areas, such as association agreements with new countries (*Agence Europe* 14/15 October 1985; Lodge 1986: 214).

After protracted negotiations, the final text contained a further watering down of proposals. The provision for a second reading or 'Cooperation Procedure' was maintained, but further refined, with the effect of slightly strengthening the legislative powers of the Parliament on nine articles relating to the completion of the Single Market. This procedure corresponded roughly to a five-stage process. First, provision would be made during the drafting of legislative proposals for Parliament to make its views known to the Commission and Council. Second, the Commission's proposals would then be sent to the Council, where, after discussion, a common position would be adopted. Third, this decision would then be forwarded to the Parliament where MEPs would have the opportunity to discuss it and table amendments, providing they were backed by an absolute majority. The Council and the Commission would be under obligation to take into account any amendments which were passed. Fourth, if the Commission accepted the Parliament's amendments, the Council still had the right to reject these amendments, but the vote had to be unanimous. Alternatively, if the Commission rejected the Parliament's amendments, only a qualified majority would be needed in the Council to reject them entirely. Finally, if Parliament voted by an absolute majority for the wholesale rejection of the Council's proposal, the Council could still reject this verdict, although the Council decision had to be unanimous.

Two other concessions to the minimalist camp could be detected in the final text. The proposal for an independent conciliation committee in the event of stalemate was dropped, leaving effectively the last word on all legislation with the Council of Ministers. Moreover, as Howe pointed out in the second reading of the European Communities (Amendment) Bill, the domestic legislation incorporating the SEA into British law, apart from the extension of the cooperation with the European Parliament over matters pertaining to the completion of the Single Market, the Luxembourg Compromise remains in place 'untouched and unaffected' (*Hansard* (Commons) vol. 96, 23 April 1986: cols 321–2; Corbett 1987: 255–7). How can we account for what was perceived at this time to be a success for the minimalist version of institutional reform?

Although it was possible to point to a powerful alliance against the British position on paper, the Court had reason to suspect a certain amount of ambiguity in the support of the French and Germans for greater powers for the European Parliament. Academic observers at the time were dismissive of Mitterrand's support for Spinelli (see Levy 1987; Schmuck 1987; Burgess

1989). For Levy, this policy was supported by little detailed preparation and represented nothing more than the French President's more general predilection to engage in 'grand diplomatic initiatives' when faced with a crisis (Levy 1987: 185). That said, it is worth noting that Haywood (1993) and Cole (1994) provide persuasive evidence to suggest that Mitterrand's pro-Europeanism was a consistent feature of his political philosophy. Nevertheless, both authors accept that Mitterrand was capable of tailoring his beliefs to suit the political circumstances of the time. Moreover, the need for support from the French Communist Party in the early years of the Socialist government dictated that Mitterrand played down his enthusiasm for the European Union.

Even if Mitterrand's enthusiasm for Spinelli was genuine, it should not be assumed that this interest was shared by the French foreign policy community in general. This point was understood within the Court. As Rifkind notes from his experience of negotiating in the Dooge Committee:

> Without wishing to sound too controversial, it is worth remembering that, whereas some of the members of the Dooge Committee were either ministers or officials of their respective governments, others were not and therefore able to express personal views to a much greater extent. (HL 226, 1985: 45–6, 53)

At this time, Faure, France's representative on the Dooge Committee, was not a member of the French government, leading Rifkind to complain of the difficulties in interpreting the French position on Spinelli, because of the ambiguous signals coming out of Paris. This more general ambivalence continued into the detailed negotiations at Luxembourg. Even if it was sincere, Mitterrand's earlier support for Spinelli did not filter through to the French negotiating team.

At the same time, the Court could point to contradictions in German support for greater powers to the European Parliament. In a speech to the Bundesrat in February 1985 billed as an outline of his views on the future of Europe, Kohl acknowledged that it was necessary to give the European Parliament more power to monitor the policies of the Community. However, in what seemed like a contradiction of his earlier support for the Spinelli Treaty, Kohl wondered whether it was the right moment to give priority to the proposals contained in the Parliament's Draft Treaty (*Agence Europe* 11 February 1985; see also 14 February 1985, 17 June 1985). Writing in 1989, Kirchner also asserts that Kohl's views on European integration lacked clarity and drive at this time. In doing so, he quotes the EU correspondent of *Der Spiegel* complaining that the old enthusiasm for Europe no longer prevailed among the German leadership (Kirchner 1989: 428–34). In this context, we should not be too surprised at the limited nature of the final text in this area. One of Britain's chief negotiators at this time agreed that where Bonn would certainly have liked a stronger text, the German delegation was not particularly assertive during the negotiations. Put another way, the British government did not have to trade off concessions made by the Germans in this area for compromises elsewhere (interview with David Hannay, 16 November 1995).

Instead, this gap between rhetoric and reality was exploited by the British negotiating team, which had to fend off proposals from the Italian delegation. The main technique employed by the British was to wear down its opponents through 'rationalist' argument. As an official in Whitehall who was close to the negotiations at the time put it: 'the British were encouraging other governments to voice their doubts and concerns. We were trying to advance our cause by stealth' (non-attributable interview with the author). Two arguments in particular were deployed.

First, at a time when all national delegations were on record as wanting to make the Community's decision-making process simpler and more effective, the British team continually questioned how joint decision-making would contribute to this goal. Attention was focused on an Italian paper tabled in the Dondelinger Committee in mid-October. This proposed that the Council could adopt a decision after debate by qualified majority voting on a proposal from the Commission and after taking a preliminary opinion of the Parliament. The Parliament could then amend this decision if so desired by an absolute majority of MEPs. This ruling would then return to the Council, which, after debating by qualified majority voting and hearing the opinion of the Commission, could adopt, amend or reject the Parliament's text. If the Council decided to amend the Parliament's text, the decision would go back to the Parliament, which could then approve this new text, by an absolute majority, or reject it. If it chose the latter course, the proposal would then be dropped (*Agence Europe* 17 October 1985). Not surprisingly, British queries concerning how this would make decision-making simpler and quicker commanded substantial tacit support from many quarters in the maximalist camp (*Agence Europe* 10 October 1985).

Second, British negotiators emphasized that the proposals for extending the powers of the European Parliament threatened to alter the balance of power at the Community level to the extent that all national governments would be forced in the future to accept decisions that they deemed to be against their national interest. The argument stressed that the present institutional structure of the Community rightly gave the Council of Ministers the final say on legislative matters. Ministers were responsible to national parliaments and any interference with this institutional balance would be perceived in national capitals as a challenge to the influence of democratically elected national parliaments. More importantly, bearing in mind the importance the 'maximalists' attached to having a treaty of any kind, any challenge to the prerogatives of national parliaments was likely to place the ratification process in at least some jeopardy. Despite the public rhetoric, British officials remember receiving substantial tacit support for their arguments and some open support from the Danish delegation (*Agence Europe* 22 October 1985; *The Times* 23 October 1985).

Howe confirms this interpretation in his memoirs. Many governments at this time found it popular to champion the cause of the European Parliament: 'yet in truth all the Heads of Government had a common interest in maintaining their own joint and several authority, as represented by the powers of the European Council' (Howe 1994: 455; see also Lodge 1986: 213–15). However, it should be noted that, when interviewed, Hannay was clear that this support in no way represented an explicit alliance between the British delegation and other Community countries: 'it was a very complicated argument in which there were many nuances of position' (interview with the author, 16 November 1995).

European Political Cooperation

The reactive approach was also employed with success in the Political Committee set up to deal with the proposals for foreign policy cooperation. The success of the codification approach of the British delegation is demonstrated by four features of Title III. First, Article 30(3) maintained that all foreign policy decisions would continue to be made through consensus, although each member state 'shall, as far as possible, refrain from impeding' this process. Under no circumstances would national governments find themselves subject to foreign policy decisions that had been imposed on them. Second, and following on from this point, the jurisdiction of the European Court of Justice did not extend to Title III. Member states would not be held to account if they failed to observe their commitment to endeavour to reach common foreign policy positions. Third, the Secretariat would be a small advisory body which 'shall assist the Presidency in preparing and implementing the activities of European Political Co-operation and in administrative matters. It shall carry out its duties under the authority of the Presidency.' Nuttall goes on to expand further. The Secretariat was not to prepare papers on its own initiative, nor to act as a spokesman for the twelve. It was to be composed of seconded national diplomats on the 'enlarged support team' principle contained in the *London Report* (1981). The proposal by the Franco-German Draft Treaty for a Secretariat-General under the direction of a new Secretary General of the European Union, failed to make any headway after Milan (Nuttall 1992: 253–5).

Finally, the Committee shunned the idea of a separate Act of European Union, as tabled by Mitterrand and Kohl at Milan, and reintroduced by the French half-way through the negotiations. This was despite the fact that, when preparations for the Committee were first made, it was assumed that an agreement would eventually lead to a separate treaty. Looking at the official texts coming out of the Milan European Council, the section titled 'Institutional Affairs' supports such an interpretation. The third paragraph is particularly noteworthy, where the text discusses the convening of a conference and the exact format that the amendments to the Treaty of Rome might take. There is a proposal for a treaty on a common foreign and security policy as well as the amendments to the Treaty of Rome. In other words, it was intended that the two subjects be discussed separately (*Agence Europe* 30 June 1985; Nuttall 1992: 248).

An official at the Foreign Office who was closely involved in discussions in the Political Committee suggested that Number 10 was against a separate treaty along these lines. Although he suggested that this was not an especially controversial issue within Whitehall, he went on to say:

> I have a feeling talking about this that maybe Number 10 had some hang-ups about it being a separate treaty. I have a feeling that Mrs Thatcher or Charles Powell may have said that this must be tucked into the Single European Act because they didn't want another Treaty of Rome. (Non-attributable interview with the author)

Bearing in mind the general phobia towards treaty amendments exhibited by the Thatcher government, this reading of events seems plausible.

In explaining the success of the Thatcher government in getting most of its proposals accepted, evidence again points to ambiguities in the position of the Franco-German alliance. Despite hijacking the Milan European Council in a rather melodramatic fashion with their plan for a grand Act of European Union, Paris and Bonn seemed to lose interest in the proposals. Officials in the Foreign Office do not remember their French and German opposite numbers pushing an alternative agenda in negotiations. When asked how difficult it was to break down the support for the Franco-German Draft Treaty one replied that it wasn't that difficult:

> It [the Franco-German Draft Treaty] died after Milan and the French and Germans didn't come back to it. I don't think that either of their two Foreign Ministries were particularly attached to it and I think that was largely the reason that they didn't come back to it. There was never a sense that the rest of us were up against a Franco-German compact. (Non-attributable interview with the author)

Put another way, there was a gap between the rhetoric in Italy and the reality in Luxembourg.

In response, the British delegation did not attempt to reprise the tactic of building an alliance with Paris and Bonn in this area. As with negotiations over greater powers to the European Parliament, negotiators again favoured the alternative method of rationalistic argument, demonstrating the unsatisfactory features of various other proposals on the table. The question of the Secretariat was one of the few issues which caused fraught discussions in the Committee. One Foreign Office official close to the negotiations remembered 'one of the tactics for dealing with [the French proposal for a Secretariat General] was to propose the name of Genscher to be the first Secretary-General, which made the entire French delegation go pale' (non-attributable interview with the author).

In addition, the British delegation enjoyed substantial tacit support on the question of the Secretariat. Interestingly, this included support from the Commission, which was opposed to the Franco-German proposals, but for different reasons. Brussels favoured the British proposals for a small advisory body because it feared some sort of Political Commission growing up alongside it. However, this is not to say that the Commission would have minded a foreign policy directorate inside the Commission. Less surprisingly, the British desire for a small advisory Secretariat, as well as its more general emphasis on the codification of existing practice, received substantial tacit support from the smaller states of the Community. As Nuttall (1992: 241) has argued, the prospect of a Secretariat deriving its authority from the Heads of Government and unconnected with Community institutions, was bound to cause concern to partisans of the Community method.

However, officials are adamant that there was little prospect of, or attempt at, building alliances with other delegations by making linkages or side-payments either in the Political Committee or between it and the Dondelinger Committee. Although the British delegation conceded the principle of a permanent Political Secretariat in the Howe Plan, officials interviewed agreed that, by and large, such linkage did not take place. Two factors in particular militated against explicit trade-offs over policy between the two Committees. The first was the issue of Community competence. Officials pointed out that, when the British paper on EPC was drafted and discussed in negotiations, the British team was careful to keep political cooperation outside of Community competence. Yet clearly negotiations in the Dondelinger Committee were on various areas of reform which were inside Community competence. This barrier largely prevented concessions between the two areas, although it was suggested in interviews that 'there might have been some sense of give and take across policy areas in an informal way. But it was certainly not the kind of negotiating linkage that you would get, for instance, in the Uruguay Round.' Another official commented that, although he wasn't directly involved in negotiations in the Political Committee, he would have been surprised if the British delegation made much in the way of trade-offs between committees at this time. The British position on political cooperation was clear and consistent, so they would have had very little room for manoeuvre (non-attributable interview with the author).

Fiscal Harmonization

A similar reactive approach can be detected on the part of the British team in the negotiations over fiscal harmonization in Luxembourg. In its White Paper, the Commission had argued that, along with physical and technical barriers, variation in VAT and excise duties across Community borders represented another type of non-tariff barrier to the completion of the Single Market. A completely free internal market could only take place if there were measures to ensure a substantial amount of harmonization of these rates. Although no detailed proposals were put forward at this time, the Commission tabled a proposal at the start of October calling for an extension of majority voting to Article 99 (indirect taxation matters) 'as far as this was necessary with a view to establishing the internal market' (*Agence Europe* 7 October 1985). By the end of November, the Luxembourg Presidency had tabled a compromise proposal, which formed the basis of the final agreement and incorporated much of the British position. Decisions under Article 99 were to remain under the unanimity rule (*Agence Europe* 27 November 1985). However, it is important to note that the final text of the SEA recommitted the Community to work towards the goal of fiscal harmonization: 'to the extent that such harmonization is necessary to ensure the establishment and the functioning of the internal market within the time-limit laid down in Article 8a'. It was this commitment which led to the animated debate over the Commission's detailed proposals in this area in the late 1980s.

Although it is not suggested here that the British delegation single-handedly took on the Commission and 'won', the reactive approach it deployed made a significant contribution to securing a final outcome that was satisfactory to the Thatcher government. Again, the British delegation chose to wear down the Commission through rationalistic argument. Two main arguments were deployed to magnify the doubts that others had about the Commission's proposals. Although the Commission emphasized that approximation would be phased in gradually over the period to 1992, the British maintained that Cockfield's policy represented an unacceptable infringement upon the ability of all European governments to control one of the main levers of economic policy. As far as they were concerned, it didn't matter, as Cockfield pointed out in a heated exchange with Mrs Thatcher, that harmonization of fiscal policy was in the Treaty of Rome and therefore represented a treaty obligation (Cockfield 1994: 55–7). The Commission's proposals were an unacceptable challenge to the powers of the British Parliament to raise revenue. Just for good measure, Thatcher locked the government into this policy before the 1987 election campaign by pledging that under no circumstances would existing VAT policy change.

At the same time, the British negotiating team was quick to use figures provided by the Commission's White Paper, which pointed to a wide variation of VAT rates and excise duties, to argue that some member states would have to make substantial changes to their tax regimes and risk a substantial loss of tax revenue. Taking the example of excise duties, Rifkind reminded the French delegation that, if it were to harmonize its wine duty, it would have to increase rates by 229 per cent. In Germany, the approximation of excise duty on beer would require an increase of 223 per cent. In Italy, the approximation of tax on diesel would require an increase of 886 per cent. No wonder Rifkind was quick to conclude that 'this is clearly a matter of controversy in the Community' (*Hansard* (Commons) vol. 82, 20 June 1985: cols 467–8; Owen and Dynes 1990: 157). It should finally be noted, however, that this defensive position was combined with an attempt to inject a more constructive contribution into the debate. Highlighting the example of the United States, where different levels of sales tax exist in different states, Rifkind pointed out that this did not seem to have impeded the free flow of goods and services. As an extension to this analysis, Lawson suggested in the late 1980s that approximation was best achieved by the market, through the healthy competition of national tax regimes (Lawson 1992: 895–8).

To conclude, the Thatcher government did not have to produce initiatives, seek alternative coalitions or alliances and cement these with linkages or side-payments to achieve its objectives on this issue. Although officials involved in negotiations all agree that this was a contentious area, the British team was able to take advantage of a lack of strong feeling among those member states that supported a formal extension of majority voting. Instead, accounts suggest that most national delegations wanted to retain the unanimity rule for Article 99 and they lined up together against the Commission. The British delegation was certainly not in 'a minority of one' and, by continually deploying its position, it was able to win round support in a number of capitals (note the hesitation of Ruhfus, the German representative, as documented in *Agence Europe* 22 October 1985).

If the Court's apparent success depended on a relatively favourable institutional context, this was not to say that EU institutions were unimportant to the overall conduct of negotiations at this time. Of course, the Court did not achieve all its foreign policy objectives during this period. Indeed, it will not be lost on the reader that this chapter has so far played down the extent and importance of these defeats. The second and final argument of this section asserts that these failures cannot be solely explained by looking at the limitations of the Thatcher government's intergovernmental bargaining strategy. Instead, building on the theoretical insights of Chapter 1, we need to recognize the importance of institutional legacies to an understanding of the constraints on foreign policy implementation at this time. It should be noted that this argument is only detailed in the briefest of terms in this chapter: a fuller exposition is beyond the scope of this book. That said, these preliminary observations are developed further in Chapters 6 and 7.

The main and perhaps most interesting defeat for the Court during this period was at the Milan European Council. As already noted, the British negotiating team was outvoted on a decision to call an IGC and, by participating in the subsequent negotiations, conceded the possibility of treaty change. The question remains: why did a British-Franco-German triumvirate fail to emerge around a more limited set of reforms? We have already noted the ambiguity of Bonn and Paris over the issue of institutional reform, despite their public support for a new treaty. Moreover, as other accounts of this period note, the Draft Treaty represented little more than a rehash of the Howe Plan. The opposition of Italy and the Benelux countries confirmed this point. They resented the application of the term 'European Union' to a treaty proposal which was largely confined to Political Cooperation measures and brought no advances on the Community side. In fact, when it came to the minor differences in substance between the competing proposals, the British approach received a more favourable response. Belgium, as well as Greece and Denmark, distrusted the reference to a high-level Secretariat General for the European Council, preferring a smaller, advisory body along the lines of the British proposal (Nuttall 1992: 247; *Agence Europe* 29 June 1985; see also Howe 1994: 409).

This question becomes even more perplexing if we then suggest that the Draft Treaty did not reflect the results of a carefully prepared and crafted alliance around a number of delicately balanced compromises. Instead, it partly resembled a Pavlovian reflex, an instinctual attempt to reassert the Franco-German axis as an end in itself. One British official confirmed that the Franco-German plan represented a hurried joint personal initiative between Kohl and Mitterrand:

My French and German colleagues were as baffled as I was by the way this had come out and they hadn't really been consulted. This was largely the work of two men, the French President and the German Chancellor, and their own officials had been left out of it. (Non-attributable interview with the author)

When asked to explain the motivations of the French and German governments, Adam Fergusson agreed that the Milan episode was perplexing:

I don't know. It's fascinating. Maybe they didn't trust us. It was certainly never explained. I remember that we were amazed in the Foreign Office that this could have happened. It was just so blatant, the way they had stolen our ideas, repackaged them and, presented them as their own initiative. We couldn't understand why they hadn't said to us: 'look, the British are doing something good. Let's get together on these ideas and cooperate'. (Interview with the author, 27 September 1995)

How then, can we explain the sudden, almost visceral, emergence of a Franco-German axis at this time? One way forward might be to consider factors which are *outside*, but impinge on, the process of intergovernmental bargaining. On the one hand, we need to question the assumption that the EU provides a passive, stable and neutral framework when it comes to understanding the dynamics of Europe. On the other, we need to explore the importance of institutional legacies, particularly how they constrain the possibilities for foreign policy implementation over time. While only providing a thumbnail sketch, this discussion suggests the importance of two particular institutional legacies, while of course, accepting that this description of constraints in no way intends to be exhaustive.

As noted in Chapter 1, those authors who highlight the importance of indirect institutional power stress the ability of national actors to shape the contours of EU institutions themselves. Of central importance to the formation of the EU in the 1950s was an agreement between the French and German governments to cooperate within this new regional association. Originally, this agreement was largely instrumental. It formed part of the more general response to the so-called 'German problem' at the time: how was the resurgent power of West Germany to be contained as it went through a period of reconstruction after the war? In specific policy terms, successive French governments allowed Germany access to their markets in return for the development of the Common Agricultural Policy, which subsidized French farming interests. Put in different terms, the EU became a regional organization which simultaneously allowed Paris to control Germany's future economic development, while providing an internationally recognized base from which Bonn could set about rebuilding German power. However, as the EU developed, this relationship became an end in itself. Formally, it became institutionalized with the signing of the Elysee Treaty in 1963. Behind these formal arrangements developed a willingness on both sides to treat this bilateral relationship as a positive sum game – an arrangement which offered benefits to both governments (H. Wallace 1986: 136–44; McCarthy 1993).

Alternatively, those authors citing the importance of structural power argue that EU institutions can develop independent, impersonal sources of power which confer systemic advantages on particular member states. When applied to the historical development of the EU, originally the Franco-German axis described above had an important effect on the structural properties or norms of the EU. More particularly, Paris and Bonn, supported by the Benelux countries, Italy and the USA, recommended that the relationship between Germany and its counterparts within the EU should be infused with the principle of supranationality. If the revival of German power could not be stopped, it would have to be 'caged' within a new supranational organization which committed itself to the development of common policies. These would be formalized in a legally binding treaty, closely monitored by a new Commission and policed by a new European Court. However, as the EU developed over time, this principle of supranationality attained a normative importance in itself. It was believed to have contributed to the continued peace between France and Germany after 1945. On these grounds alone, this normative principle was not to be challenged or reversed.

Broadening our account of British diplomacy during the negotiation of the SEA by taking into account these institutional legacies helps to clarify some issues arising from the earlier discussion in this chapter. As already suggested, the absence of a 'dynamic' Franco-German 'motor' at this time helps to explain the relative success of the Court's more positive approach. Of course, the question remains: what would be the possibilities for sustaining this influence in the face of a more united axis? Second, this institutional analysis confirms the importance of the principle of supranationality and institutional integration *as an end in itself*, irrespective of the policies incorporated into this reform process. It followed that any bid to turn the Franco-German alliance into a triumvirate behind a policy package which did not accept the importance of supranationalism (as the British did in Milan) was always going to be unrealistic. While it is true that the commitment of member states to institutional reform could be questioned at this time, it was also clear that the dilution of the Community into a Thatcherite European Free Trade Area also militated against the structural properties of the EU; at least as the majority of other member states understood them.

It followed that policy defeats within the context of this institutional reform might hold adverse future consequences for the Court. Two defeats in particular are worth noting in the context of the discussion in Chapters 6 and 7. The first was over the question of Economic and Monetary Union (EMU). At Luxembourg, British negotiators resisted the inclusion of any new clauses on EMU, maintaining that enough articles and declarations on this matter existed already. As was the case with many of the other areas discussed above, on paper the British delegation faced a powerful coalition in favour of including an article on EMU in the SEA. As well as the Commission, France, Italy and the Benelux countries promoted this goal. Discussion in the Council of Ministers was based on a Dutch draft which suggested that reference to EMU be included in Article 2 of the Act. This policy was supported by two arguments. On the one hand, supporters protested that there was no point in this general reform effort if it did not embrace further moves towards monetary integration. This was imperative to achieve a critical total which would ensure that the whole exercise was a real success. On the other hand, Andreotti, the Italian Foreign Minister argued that the free movement of capital would be difficult to achieve without a common monetary policy (*Agence Europe* 27 November 1985).

Paradoxically, the commitment of Delors to EMU at this time was probably a lot greater than to many of those issues which formed the centre of negotiations in Luxembourg. A number of academics and biographers have documented that EMU was Delors 'great dream' and that completion of the Single Market was largely perceived as a means to that end (Grant 1994: 67; interview with Lord Cockfield 22 February 1995). This is perhaps best evinced by his comments on the immediate aftermath of the Luxembourg European Council. Although disappointed that the text did not go as far as the

Commission had hoped, he took solace in the analysis: 'You do not need to have a PhD in economics to understand the need for some kind of monetary union to establish the great Single Market' (*The Times* 5 December 1985). In what was to be an exception to the rule during this period, the Commission received powerful support from the French delegation. For once, there was no gap between rhetoric and reality in Paris.

Faced with this alliance, the British team had in the German government one possible ally and, after a bilateral meeting between Thatcher and Kohl in November, thought they had forged an alliance around a policy of maintaining the status quo. However, this initiative met the same fate as the Chequers rendezvous described earlier. After a 'threesome' with Mitterrand and Delors, Kohl accepted the inclusion of a commitment to continue to work towards the goal of EMU in the Preamble of the SEA, in return for the acceptance by Paris of the principle of free capital movement (Grant 1994: 73). As well as this, a new chapter was to be inserted into the Treaty of Rome which reiterated the present direction of monetary policy. Clearly disappointed, the British delegation stressed the clause in this chapter which stated that further institutional change in this area could only come about through unanimity, under Article 236. Yet it soon became clear that the wording of the chapter was ambiguous enough for all sides to claim a victory. In fact, as we shall see, these concessions, particularly over monetary policy, proved to be the foundation for a new structural framework at the Community level, which threatened to destroy the Thatcher government's domestic statecraft project.

A similar defeat could be recorded on the insertion of Article 118a into the SEA. This extended qualified majority voting to the issue of health and safety at work, while at the same time seeking to strengthen social and regional cohesion within the Union, as well as a 'Social Dialogue' between trade unions and business organizations. The Court opposed such a measure for a number of reasons. Having spent the first half of the 1980s deregulating the British market, ministers feared that any legislation introduced under this article would increase the costs to British business. Second, the government lived in perpetual fear that having introduced a number of reforms limiting trade union activity, any strengthening of the social dimension would provide a 'European backdoor' through which this peak organization could return to the domestic political stage (Bale and Buller 1996: 71). It should be noted that the Thatcher government did not put up blanket resistance to greater employee involvement at the firm level. However, it decreed that this goal should be implemented through a voluntary approach, leaving such decisions to negotiations at the company level. A legislative approach, whether of national or European origin, which forced British companies into a rigid constitution was firmly rejected (Conservative Research Department 1979: 165–6, 172–3).

As with other areas, the British negotiating team was largely in a minority over Article 118a. Hannay remembers finding it difficult to forge alliances during negotiations, a conclusion which would seem to be confirmed by the fact that Thatcher was alone in refusing to sign the Commission's Social Charter of fundamental rights for workers in 1989. Indeed, the discussions on Article 118a were among the last to be settled, spilling over into the period after Luxembourg. That an agreement was finally reached shortly before the signing of the SEA suggests how contentious the negotiations were. As we shall see in Chapter 7, Article 118a was to remain a controversial topic for debate within the Conservative Party in the 1990s (interview with the author, 16 November 1995).

Conclusions

When it comes to explaining the apparent rise and fall of British influence in Europe in the 1980s, this chapter has yielded two main conclusions. While the Court was capable of adopting a more cooperative strategy during negotiations, this approach had little obvious impact on the outcome at Luxembourg. The British team was more successful when it adopted a reactive approach, although this depended on the absence of a united Franco-German axis committed to an alternative policy prospectus. Second, analysts ignore broader institutional factors at their peril when studying British diplomacy towards this regional organization. This discussion has suggested that institutional reform represented an end in itself for many actors at the Union level during this period. When the Court ignored this feature of the external environment, it failed to secure its interests. Of course, institutional innovation can have consequences, both intended and unintended, which impact back on domestic politics. It is to this subject that the book now turns.

Note

1. The following proposals are not an exhaustive list of suggestions put forward during the period 1979–84. Instead, they represent the main areas of debate as the negotiations developed.

CHAPTER SIX

European Integration and the Challenge to Conservative Statecraft

This chapter attempts to explain the rapid and rather spectacular disintegration of the Court during the second half of the 1980s. Superficially, the reasons for this collapse are not at all obvious. On the domestic front, the Conservatives had secured a hat-trick of victories at the General Election in June 1987. In Europe, as already noted, ministers and officials were generally perceived to have played a constructive role in negotiations leading up to the signing of the Single European Act. Having secured the Single Market at the centre of this legislation, suddenly diplomatic discussions began to highlight a possible future leadership role for Britain in the European Union: 'Euro-Thatcherism' was in the ascendancy. Yet by 1990 the European issue had clearly become a deeply divisive one for the party leadership. It played a part in the fall of Lawson, Ridley, Howe and finally Thatcher herself. The question is obvious: how can we explain this rapid turnaround? What were the implications for the Court's statecraft project?

In response to these questions, this chapter makes two main arguments. It begins by detailing a number of shifts in the international environment which combine to set off significant pressure for further European integration during this period, particularly in the area of monetary policy. More importantly, it highlights the *related* nature of these structural changes, both to each other and to the existing institutional properties of the EU, as being responsible for the enduring nature of this structural pressure. Second, the chapter asserts that the relationship between these external structural developments and the Court's behaviour is not linear. It is not just the *realities* of this pressure which cause the divisions within the Conservative leadership at this time; the differing and developing *perceptions* of these movements within the Court are also crucially important. More specifically, the Court collapsed over the European question because the issue impacted on intensifying differences over the means to governing autonomy in an increasingly interdependent world.

Chapter 4 noted the nascent tensions concerning the Europeanization of this Statecraft strategy by the mid-1980s. At the end of that decade, the pressure of European integration had helped to destroy any semblance of unity that existed within the Court on this subject.

Related Structures, Emergent Properties and the Development of Unintended Institutional Power at the EU Level, 1986–90

To understand this argument, it is important to begin by delineating this changing external context as it would have appeared to the Court during the second half of the 1980s. The central point to emerge from this discussion is that a number of structural movements combined to 'set off' significant pressure for further European integration during this period. While, in some quarters, this pressure dissipated in the face of public resistance in the early 1990s, as we shall see in Chapter 7, momentum towards Economic and Monetary Union was relatively enduring. The main source of this endurance lay in the *related* nature of these structural changes – both to each other and to the existing properties of EU institutions as highlighted in Chapter 5. More specifically, three developments will be discussed: the problem of asymmetry within the EMS in the face of global financial pressure; geo-political shifts in the system of international relations; and the re-establishment of a Franco-German axis around a new project for economic and political union.

To understand how a renewed drive for economic and monetary integration emerged from these institutions, it is worth beginning by outlining some of the main features of the ERM as it came to operate in practice. As Tsoukalis (1993: 198–202) has argued, the ERM was perceived to be asymmetrical in two senses. One complaint referred to the unequal burden of exchange rate intervention and adjustment within the system. As has been documented exhaustively elsewhere, the ERM gradually became a German dominated zone of cross exchange rates which placed constraints on currency fluctuation. When the limit of fluctuation between two currencies was reached (normally 2.5 per cent either way of the central rate), the central banks of both countries were obliged to engage in what was termed marginal intervention (so-called because it took place right on the margins of the ERM bands). Not surprisingly, by the mid-1980s many countries found the last gasp nature of such marginal intervention increasingly unsatisfactory, and shifted to intra-marginal intervention (so-called because it took place before currencies reached their limits). One consequence of this shift was to circumvent the joint-intervention obligation which pertained only to marginal intervention, thus placing the burden of adjustment on weaker currencies. However, in practice, this made very little difference as the Bundesbank was very reluctant to engage in currency support, fearing the inflationary consequences of such a policy.

A second complaint concerning the asymmetrical nature of ERM institutions focused more generally on the disproportionate German influence over policy in this area. For member states with less than impressive inflation records, maintaining a roughly stable nominal exchange rate against the Deutschmark meant accepting an appreciation of the currency in real terms. It followed that most countries were experiencing trade deficits with Germany; a factor which they partly attributed to the persistent high levels of unemployment they were experiencing. Of all member states, France and Italy were the most critical of this German hegemony (Thompson 1996: 109; for an alternative view, see Grahl 1997: 59–76).

By 1987, international financial forces exposed the asymmetrical nature of this system, leading to calls for institutional reform. More particularly, having been a source of instability because of its persistent strength in the first half of the 1980s, the managed devaluation of the dollar as a result of the Plaza Agreement in January 1986 exposed the ERM to further tensions. The dollar's descent put sustained upward pressure on the Deutschmark. Facing similar difficulties, the French government eventually let the franc fall through the floor of its ERM band, thus displaying its displeasure with the policy, while at the same time compelling the Bundesbank to spend DM5 billion in a support operation (Thompson 1996: 73–4; Grahl 1997: 71–2). A post-mortem on the crisis carried out in Paris concluded that only the construction of supranational institutions would effectively insulate French policy-makers from destabilizing global pressures, while similarly diluting the power of the Bundesbank over European economic policy. By January 1988, this episode had produced a vitriolic response from French finance minister Balladur, who called generally for the 'monetary construction of Europe' and, more particularly, for the establishment of a European Central Bank (Gross and Thygesen 1998: 396). As noted in Chapter 4, similar global pressures were a major cause of Conservative leaders' increased attraction to ERM membership as a way of bolstering their economic strategy. One of the ironies of this period was that, just as they were reaching this conclusion, the debate at the Union level had begun to move on.

If international financial pressures set off momentum towards greater economic and monetary integration, this development was compounded by geo-political shifts in the international system in the late 1980s. In particular, two changes are worthy of note. First, the fall of the Berlin Wall and the collapse of communism in Eastern Europe raised important questions concerning the balance of power in Europe. While the Cold War may have been a source of much international tension, its structures did have the advantage of providing an environment which helped to diffuse concerns about renewed German power. The collapse of these structures in 1989 heralded the possibility of Germany loosening its ties with the EU and turning its attention eastwards. Second, the reunification of Germany did nothing to alleviate these fears. What most worried Bonn's European partners was the style in which this policy decision was made. It was announced in the form of a ten-point plan without any consultation. The response of most EU member states was one of uncertainty and anxiety. The German Question had re-emerged, thus strengthening the process towards greater European integration (Baun 1995/6: 610–12).

Finally, these related structural shifts led to the (re) creation of a balance of power configuration at the EU level which, on paper, did not augur well for British influence. More particularly, this took the form of a Franco-German consensus (powerfully supported by the Commission) which argued for the strengthening of European integration as a response to this uncertain external environment. In France, support for the notion of greater economic and monetary integration was not difficult to find. As already noted in Chapter 5, French negotiators were responsible for pushing for the insertion of a reference to EMU in the preamble of the SEA. In fact, French support for greater integration in this area had deeper roots after international financial pressures had forced Paris to abandon 'socialism in one country' in favour of the policy of competitive disinflation. According to this approach, the maintenance of low and stable inflation would become the primary economic goal, with commitment to a stable exchange rate *vis-à-vis* the Deutschmark inside the ERM serving as a vital external discipline for the realization of this objective. Behind this policy lay the hope that, in a world of relatively fixed exchange rates, a more successful inflation policy in France would help it to gain a competitive advantage over its European competitors. That membership of the ERM was seen as a staging post to EMU made this essentially monetarist policy more palatable to Mitterrand's left-wing allies; especially as French policy-makers hoped that through new supranational institutions, such as a European Central Bank, they would be able to wrestle control over European economic policy from the Bundesbank (Sandholtz 1993: 27–30; Greico 1996).

As already intimated, the forced devaluation of the French franc in January 1987 and the attempts to reform ERM intervention rules through the Basle–Nyborg accords served to confirm these fears. For sure, measures to strengthen the short-run defence of parties were agreed. Extended credit facilities were provided to central banks that might come under future pressure to intervene in currency markets. At the same time, countries were encouraged to make more use of intra-marginal intervention. However, these initiatives were negotiated by central bankers in the context of a more general recommendation that less reliance be placed on intervention to stabilize exchange rates and more active and flexible use be made of interest rate policy. As Dyson notes, 'In broad terms, the view of central bank governors was that there was no need to consider a radical revision of goals' (Dyson 1994: 123). The Basle–Nyborg reforms certainly did little to provoke the Bundesbank into providing more active support for currencies which came under pressure in the system (Grahl 1997: 73–4).

If Paris was firmly behind initiatives for greater economic and monetary integration, Bonn's initial response was more ambiguous. Put another way, while the related structural shifts noted above led to the eventual creation of a Franco-German axis during this period, achieving this consensus on strengthening the EU's monetary institutions was not an unproblematic process. Faced with Balladur's proposals in January 1988, the German policy-making community was divided. Foreign Minister Genscher came out in immediate support, arguing in a speech to the European Parliament that the European Central Bank was 'essential' and 'logical' for the future development of the EU (Andrews 1993: 111; Sandholtz 1993: 31–4). Not surprisingly, the Bundesbank was much more cautious in its support. It accepted that the creation of such a bank ought to be a long-term goal of the Union, but argued that such an objective could only be realized after substantial convergence between the economies of member states. This initial ambiguity provoked anxiety in Paris, especially when German reunification became an increasing reality. In a move which revived German fears of a renewed Franco-Russian alliance, Mitterrand made speeches in the Soviet Union and East Germany warning of the pace of reunification and the threat to the balance of power in Europe (Baun 1995/6: 614–15). By the end of 1989, talk of a crisis in Franco-German relations could be heard in some European capitals.

Despite German equivocation, eventual support for EMU emerged, largely on foreign policy grounds. Sensitive to the concerns of its European partners, Bonn realized that positive and public support for these proposals would help to allay suspicions that unification would herald a new era of dominant German power. Some authors (Andrews 1993: 112; see also Greico 1996: 302–3) argue that a quid pro quo was reached. German support for rapid progress on EMU was agreed in exchange for a post-summit statement from her European partners endorsing the idea of a single German state, as long as unification was achieved in the context of broader integration. A joint Franco-German letter in December 1990 setting out proposals for political union confirmed that the alliance was back on track. Ominously for British negotiators, these included: calls for greater majority voting in the Council of Ministers; an extension of powers of co-decision enjoyed by the European Parliament; and the eventual adoption of a common defence policy (Baun 1995/6: 618).

Finally, this axis was substantially strengthened by a conscious strategy on the part of the Commission, most notably Delors, to strengthen and broaden the scope of European integration. Driving this strategy was Delors' attachment to the vision of an 'organized European space' through which European citizens and values would develop and flourish. Central to this goal was a long held belief in 'personalism', often associated with European Christian Democracy. In essence, this doctrine viewed society as made up of persons, not individuals: beings who were in essence outgoing and fundamentally sociable and whose development was realized through their insertion and interaction in different types of community. According to personalism, society was more than the sum total of market relations within an economy. Society was something which imbued the individual with moral beliefs and codes. Likewise, capitalism was not an end in itself, but something which should be harnessed for the good of mankind as a whole (Grant 1994: 83–7; Hanley 1994; Ross 1995: 46). After the completion of the SEA, with its commitment to liberalize the Single Market, it should come as no surprise that Delors sought to complement this policy with initiatives attempting to protect the cohesion of the EU.

Moreover, analysts of the role of the Commission during this period credit Delors and his team with a conscious strategy for furthering the process of European integration. For Ross (1995: 39), this approach was known collo-quially as the 'Russian doll strategy', and represented an alternative version of the old functionalist strategy whereby the Commission sought to extend its existing economic mandate through the process of spillover. In pursuing such tactics, Delors was fortunate during the 1980s because he was able to take advantage of a political opportunity structure: the political consensus within national capitals for these ideals, as noted above. However, part of the skill in being able to sustain such momentum was to design EU institutions in a way so that they become evolutive – open to reconfiguration by agents (Ross 1995: 3–6). In this context, the SEA, with its commitment to EMU in its preamble, was an important part of this process, so much so that during the Ninth Jean Monnet Lecture delivered at the European University Institute at Florence in the late 1980s, Delors referred to the SEA as:

> our moment of truth . . . both for the functioning of its institutions and for the direction we wish to give Europe as a whole . . . we have all the trump cards we need if we are to realize Europe's potential and achieve our highest political objective.

European Integration and the Collapse of the Court

How can we explain the collapse of the Court under the leadership of Thatcher in the late 1980s? How were these European developments related to this question? In essence, the external changes and the pressure for European integration that was generated, intensified the debate within the Court over the merits of Europeanizing its statecraft strategy. More particularly, for the Euro-enthusiasts, this pressure confirmed the logic of the argument that further Europeanization represented the only route to the preservation of domestic governing autonomy. At the same time, the case for the European-ization of policy widened. It was only by working at the heart of this European process that the Court stood any chance of frustrating the worst manifestations of this integrationist momentum. Faced with this external context, the Euro-sceptics drew the opposite conclusions. Working at the heart of Europe threatened more than ever to trap the party on a 'Euro-ratchet': a metaphor highlighting how much British negotiators were losing control of the policy-making process at the EU level (Bulpitt 1992). Not surprisingly, the Euro-sceptics increasingly argued that the implications for domestic auton-omy and governing competence threatened to be disastrous.

Before outlining this argument, it is important to note that clear (if contested) thinking concerning the relationship between domestic and exter-nal politics was not always in evidence during this period. More specifically, the Court does not seem to have taken the initial momentum behind European integration particularly seriously in the immediate period after the signing of the SEA. Thatcher's self-confessed misjudgement on this subject emanates from the first sentences of 'Jeux sans Frontières', the chapter in her memoirs devoted to the SEA:

> The wisdom of hindsight, so useful to historians and indeed to authors of memoirs, is sadly denied to practising politicians. Looking back, it is now possible to see the period of my second term as Prime Minister as that in which the European Community subtly shifted its direction away from being a Community of open trade, light regulation and freely co-operating sovereign nation states towards statism and centralism. I can only say that it did not seem like that at the time. (Thatcher 1993: 536, 739; see also Ridley 1992: 142–3)

Whether the momentum towards greater integration could be described as statism or centralism is a contentious question. However, writing in his memoirs, Howe confirms the more general sense of perplexity within White-hall during this period:

> I often found myself wondering why the European agenda seemed always to be unfolding at such breakneck speed. Why this now, when so much earlier business remained to be concluded? In domestic politics one had at least the feeling of being able to control the speed and manner in which policies developed. But in the Community we often seemed to be on a remorselessly moving carpet. (Howe 1994: 533)

As noted in Chapter 1, an element of uncertainty will always be involved when it comes to the process of institutional change. Unpredictable shocks can appear from nowhere, setting off momentum for reform. What is interesting from the point of view of the general thesis being presented here is that senior figures involved in EU policy also understood the issue in these terms. One official closely connected to the negotiations remarked: 'You never know exactly what the implications are going to be when you sign a new treaty. You ask your lawyers and your advisers, and you think it through, and the answer is that you don't actually know.' The official did confirm, however, that the British government suspected there was 'something of a process at work here, and it wasn't going to stop completely with the European Council in Luxembourg in 1985' (non-attributable interview with the author). Howe again confirms this point, suggesting that the SEA had a number of unmeasurable, unforeseeable impacts on the culture of the Community: 'The habit of working together, of sharing sovereignty, of give and take, which we had so strongly urged for the Single Market was not something that could be ruthlessly confined' (Howe 1994: 457–8).

That said, this general air of confusion and misunderstanding seems to be confirmed by the behaviour of the Court during the initial months of the Delors Committee on EMU. Most obviously, the decision to allow the President of the Commission to head this group of central bankers now looks like a misjudgement from the Court's point of view, although this accusation may be too harsh. More serious perhaps is Thompson's (1996: 128) argument that ministers were too slow in communicating negotiating instructions to Leigh-Pemberton. Informal discussions among committee members began as far back as July 1988, yet little consultation went on between Whitehall and the Governor of the Bank of England for a full five months after this debate had begun.

If it was slow to appreciate the initial importance of the Delors Committee, the Court, and Thatcher in particular, continued to misinterpret the conduct of talks as they progressed. Although she was in no position to halt the setting up of the Committee at Hanover in June 1988, attempts to frustrate progress towards a Single Currency again evinced a lack of understanding concerning the dynamics driving the policy. More particularly, while Thatcher succeeded in removing any reference to a future European Central Bank from the remit of the committee, her assertion in the House of Commons shortly afterwards that she had diverted pressure for a Single Currency provoked incredulity among her fellow Cabinet ministers. As Lawson pointed out at the time, the committee's aim of studying and proposing 'concrete stages to the progressive realization of EMU' would almost certainly lead in such a direction (Lawson 1992: 903). By April 1989, the committee had published a three-stage plan for the eventual implementation of a Single Currency. Stage One would establish the free movement of capital within EC borders, as well as closer monetary and macroeconomic cooperation between member states and central banks. Stage Two recommended a new Treaty establishing a European System of Central Banks, while at the same time working for the progressive narrowing of ERM bands. Finally, Stage Three would lead to the creation of 'irrevocably fixed' exchange rate parities, with full authority for economic and monetary policy being transferred to EU institutions.

As this period wore on, the Court became increasingly alive to the importance of these external structural developments, yet more divided over the question of how to respond. Of course, these differences partly reflected the strong personalities of the politicians involved. However, the seriousness of these splits by 1990 reflected more fundamental debates concerning the future of Conservative statecraft. Put another way, the reason why the divisions in the party seem so serious is because these leaders had become hopelessly split over a question that goes to the heart of British Conservatism itself: What is the most appropriate way of preserving governing autonomy and competence in the context of rapidly growing economic and political integration in the 1990s?

The Euro-enthusiasts

To understand the continual and heightened attraction of the Euro-enthusiasts to ERM membership and the increased Europeanization of economic policy, it is worth recalling the pressures and motives behind this original policy switch. After five years of governing within an 'open economy', the Court found that its domestic monetarist strategy was increasingly vulnerable to unpredictable and destabilizing fluctuations in the international financial markets. More particularly, the growth and importance of such markets ensured that sterling behaved in ways totally unrelated to the fundamentals of the British economy, but with important potential knock-on effects. In this increasingly uncertain and perplexing world, ERM member-ship offered comfort for Conservative Party leaders in two senses. It provided grounds for hoping that these destabilizing exchange rate fluctuations could be minimized. Moreover, the system was perceived to place an external discipline on domestic inflationary pressures, thus helping the Court to reassert some governing autonomy from these societal forces.

If these were the motives behind the attraction to ERM membership in 1985, the experience of economic management in the second half of the 1980s served to confirm and strengthen these perceptions. Take, for example, Lawson's failed attempt to shadow the Deutschmark within an unpublished band of DM2.90–3.00. The abandonment of this policy once again confirmed the difficulties of monitoring and predicting movement in the exchange rate from more general developments in the real economy. One could point to the seemingly inexplicable rise of the pound throughout 1987, despite persistent cuts in interest rates. By December, weakness in the level of the dollar induced a temporary lull, and the pound fell back to DM2.96. Thinking wrongly that the markets had finally got the message, Lawson raised interest rates in the face of worries about inflation. Unfortunately, the markets interpreted DM2.96 as the floor of the band for sterling and proceeded to test the ceiling. Despite Lawson cutting interest rates to 7.5 per cent, the pound broke through DM3.00, thus forcing him to eventually abandon the policy of shadowing (Smith 1992: 132–9).

For Lawson, this episode confirmed the need for a public target if his disciplinarian strategy was to achieve credibility in the eyes of the financial markets and thus protect the Court's governing autonomy (Lawson 1992: 660–2). As already noted in Chapter 4, ERM membership provided this public external discipline. However, one additional attraction increasingly articulated by Lawson was the fact that the constitution of the EMS conferred obligations on member states to support a currency which came under sustained pressure. Of course, Lawson understood that a real gap existed between these formal obligations and the actual operation of the system in practice. Lawson supported French negotiators in their attempt to secure greater commitment from the Bundesbank to support intra-marginal intervention (as noted above) (Lawson 1992: 733–4). Moreover, the Court experienced the obstructive behaviour of German central bankers first hand when they made it difficult for the British authorities to buy Deutschmarks in support of sterling in December 1987 (Lawson 1992: 786–91). Unfortunately, while ERM membership was attracting increasing support at the Establishment level in Britain, as already noted, European leaders had already begun to move the debate on towards EMU.

Simultaneously, Lawson's participation in experiments in international currency management served more generally to strengthen his belief that the behaviour of financial markets could be brought under control. For Lawson, both the Plaza Agreement between the major international economies to engineer the decline of the dollar and the subsequent Louvre Accord to stop the dollar from falling too far demonstrated the possibilities of imposing stability in this unsettling and unpredictable environment. By September 1987, at the annual meeting of the IMF/World Bank, he was outlining the blueprint for a more permanent regime. His proposals for a global nominal framework included a series of indicators, such as world commodity prices, which would be collectively monitored for inflation purposes as well as the future publication of target bands for world currencies. The latter should be wide and flexible enough to protect the system from speculators engaging in 'one-way bets' on the currency markets. Lawson puts the failure of these proposals down to a change of personnel at the US Treasury: Baker was replaced by Brady, who had little time for such thinking (Lawson 1992: 738). Smith points to more general tensions within the financial system at this time which would have almost certainly led to the failure of Lawson's proposals. These include an increasing strain between the Bundesbank and the Federal Reserve over interest rate levels and a growing gap in expectations in share and bond markets (Smith 1992: 94–102).

Interestingly, with ERM membership temporarily closed off as a policy option, Lawson did not abandon his search for a rule-based disciplinarian framework as a way of institutionalizing the party's position in power. In his last months in office, the Chancellor circulated proposals for an independent Bank of England. Under this scheme, the government would retain responsibility for determining the exchange rate framework, including any future decision on ERM membership. Within these guidelines, bank officials would hold responsibility for the operation of monetary policy, including the setting of short-term interest rates and monetary targets. At the same time, they would have a statutory duty to protect the value of the currency as determined by ministers. For Lawson, the governing advantages of this policy could be partly understood in terms of the protection it afforded to domestic autonomy. Such independence would help to depoliticize the issue of exchange rate changes, thus removing the conduct of monetary policy from political pressure. At the same time, Lawson expected the policy to 'lock-into the body politic of this country a permanent anti-inflation force' (Lawson 1992: 1059–61).

While ERM membership seemed to offer the best route to protect domestic autonomy in the face of continued international financial pressures, Euro-enthusiasts began to widen the argument for such a policy initiative. Faced with this new momentum towards a Single Currency at the European level, they asserted that sterling's membership of the ERM could become the perfect vehicle for British negotiators to 'work within', slow down and divert this pressure for greater integration. Put another way, this period witnessed the origins of the 'heart of Europe' strategy which was to become the *leitmotif* of the Major period. More accurately, while this diplomatic approach had always existed within the corridors of the Foreign Office, the late 1980s was a period which witnessed the advancement of this policy more generally throughout the Court.

More philosophically, behind this 'heart of Europe' strategy lay a number of assumptions concerning the importance of 'agency' and its more general relationship to institutions and structures. Despite acknowledging the pressure towards greater European integration, in essence this position remained characterized by a belief in the neutral, passive yet malleable character of EU institutions, coupled with a hyper-optimism concerning the power of British agents (policy-makers) to tailor these institutions to their own ends. Howe's resignation speech is an excellent example of this voluntarist ontological approach. For Howe, British negotiators had been most successful at the Union level 'when we have seen the Community not as a static entity to be resisted and contained, but as an active process which we can shape, often decisively, provided we allow ourselves to be fully engaged in it, with confidence' (Howe 1994: 700). In his policy tract, *The Challenge of Europe*, Heseltine concurs, arguing that if we accept the general tenor of Howe's comments, 'then we can help to give it [the EU] form, not just because we have ideas and experience but because our very conviction is a key to the opening of doors' (Heseltine 1991: xiv).

Finally, Euro-enthusiasts also lectured on the importance of 'historical learning' when it came to the successful conduct of EU policy. Another prominent theme in Howe's resignation speech was the importance of understanding the mistakes of British statesmanship in the 1950s. Unfortunately, rather than embrace the momentum towards European integration at this time, policy-makers retreated into a 'ghetto of sentimentality' about the importance of British greatness and national sovereignty. As a result, British politicians missed a crucial opportunity to influence the original design of these European institutions and, embed them with their own interests and objectives (Howe 1994: 699–700). For Heseltine, the importance of learning from these past mistakes is also a common theme of his writing on Europe at this time:

> Have we learnt? I profoundly hope so. We have clung too long to past achievements and failed to anticipate the unfolding of a new Europe and our need to find a place within it. We know now the price we have paid for allowing others to design the mould and to pour into it their own driving self-interest. (Heseltine 1991: xii)

Unfortunately, while the above analysis contains a core element of truth, the voluntarist assumptions behind it seemed to underestimate the possibilities that institutions, once designed, may develop a structural power of their own. As a result, any possible 'path dependencies' of EU institutions and the possibilities for British influence within such trajectories remain unquestioned and largely unexamined.

In specific policy terms, by June 1989 the Euro-enthusiasts had become convinced that constructive diplomacy generally, and a decision to join the ERM more specifically, might allow the Court to detach Stage One of the Delors Plan for EMU from Stages Two and Three. The origins of these tactics appear to lie in discussions at the Council of Finance Ministers meeting at S'Agro in May 1989. At the end of deliberations, the Committee stopped short of fully endorsing the Delors Report. While it asserted the importance of initiating immediate preparations for Stage One, it deferred a decision concerning whether an Intergovernmental Conference was needed for Stages Two and Three. The conclusion drawn in London was that the ERM and measures for liberalizing monetary policy could be decoupled from the separate goal of a Single Currency. Indeed, a month earlier, Howe and Lawson had attempted to convert Thatcher to the merits of this approach by engineering a Chequers meeting with Lubbers, the Dutch Prime Minister. The latter did indeed accept the validity of these tactics, while at the same time admitting that his government was in favour of EMU. For her part, Thatcher was suspicious and largely unimpressed (Lawson 1992: 913–15; Howe 1994: 577).

Despite this setback, the British negotiating strategy at the Madrid European Council (June 1989) demonstrated the main tenets of this 'heart of Europe' approach. Thatcher now agreed to allow sterling to participate in Stage One, subject to the complete elimination of exchange controls within the Union and a convergence of inflation rates. In exchange, she insisted that progress towards Stage Three of a Single Currency be postponed until further preparation had been carried out on the exact implications of this move. Just for good measure, the pound would be subject to the wider 6 per cent fluctuation bands, as opposed to the 2.5 per cent margins which constrained the large majority of other ERM currencies. It is worth noting that this 'heart of Europe' strategy was only operationalized after Howe and Lawson agreed a largely unprecedented formal alliance and 'ambushed' Thatcher on the eve of the summit. Their joint ultimatum insisted that movement by the government on ERM was the only way that British negotiators would be able to head off calls for an Intergovernmental Conference on the subject of EMU. Unfortunately, as we shall see, this strategy failed.

That it did fail was not evidence that this strategy was in itself fatally flawed. For the Euro-enthusiasts, the problem was that negotiations were being handled by an 'agent', who had the effect of consistently undermining this 'heart of Europe' approach. Put another way, the reappearance of Thatcher's awkward style became an increasingly common theme in the criticism of the Euro-enthusiasts at this time. One could point to Howe's 'deep dismay' at the way Thatcher 'caricatured' and 'misunderstood' the EU in her (in)famous Bruges speech in 1988. Alternatively, her insistent cry of 'no, no, no' to any prospect of a Single Currency was understood by the Euro-enthusiasts to completely destroy the credibility of the Hard ECU policy and, with it, the chance of using such a proposal to divert pressure towards EMU (see below). In more general terms, not only did this negotiating style make the possibilities of alliance-building increasingly difficult, it also had the more damaging effect of uniting the other eleven delegations against Britain (Lawson 1992: 898–9; Howe 1994: 535–9, 570–2, 702).

The Euro-sceptics

If the development of these changing external structures had confirmed the Euro-enthusiasts' belief in the importance of Europeanization, by 1990 the Euro-sceptics were increasingly coming to the opposite conclusions. More particularly, the experience of negotiating at the European level during this period led this group increasingly to question the importance of British agency and its ability to work at the heart of Europe to control this integrationist pressure. Far from frustrating momentum towards greater European integration, Euro-sceptics increasingly perceived European institutions as a Euro-ratchet: a regional organization which was capable of continually and explicitly penetrating the British political process. At the core of this analysis was a pessimism concerning the possibilities for British influence in the face of a reunited Franco-German-Commission axis. However, behind these balance of power concerns lay a nascent awareness that British policy-makers were increasingly negotiating on an institutional terrain which undermined their position. Moreover, while resisting the Euro-ratchet became more difficult, the Euro-sceptics became more pessimistic concerning the impact of the Europeanization of policy on domestic statecraft.

If the Euro-sceptics had been slow to appreciate the pressures behind this new drive for European integration, the experience of monitoring negotiations within the Delors Committee soon led them to comprehend the constraints on British diplomacy. Negotiating instructions to Leigh-Pemberton (the Governor of the Bank of England) may have taken time to emerge, but this did not stop Whitehall attempting to engage in the sort of alliance-building strategies noted in Chapter 5. In this context, a partnership frustrating progress on the committee was thought to be possible between Leigh-Pemberton and Pohl, as the President of the Bundesbank was known to be sceptical concerning the possibilities for a Single Currency. Unfortunately, the results were almost identical to those experienced by British diplomats during the negotiation of the SEA. If Pohl had reservations concerning the work of the Delors Committee, as Howe noted, he kept his anxieties to himself (Howe 1994: 576; Ridley 1992: 708). Lawson is more forthright on the failure of this particular 'coalition': Pohl proved to be a 'broken reed' (Lawson 1992: 908–9). After the publication of Delors' three-stage plan for EMU, Lawson suggested the Governor attach a minority statement outlining his own objections. Leigh-Pemberton refused, not wanting to be in a minority of one among his central bank colleagues (see also Thatcher 1993: 708; Dinan 1994: 422; Thompson 1995: 262–3).

Pohl himself now appeared pessimistic concerning his abilities to resist the Single Currency proposals on the Delors Committee. Part of this analysis derives from the allegation that he was deceived by Kohl concerning the committee's intended remit. At a meeting of a German Cabinet Committee shortly before Hanover, Kohl instructed Pohl that the German line on the monetary committee would be to let the central bankers write a report and forget it, or ask the central bankers merely to suggest technical improvements as a step towards EMU. Pohl now judges that it was a mistake to take part: 'if I had boycotted it, *I could not have stopped the process*, but I could have slowed it down. I would have been freer to criticise the Delors Report' (author's emphasis) (quoted in Grant 1994: 119–21). This account is not entirely convincing and fails to explain Pohl's silence throughout the committee's deliberations. However, his admission that the process could not be stopped is of more significance in the context of the argument being pursued here.

It has already been intimated that the Court's decision to accept Delors as head of the committee on EMU was a mistake – a testimony to the lack of attention that Whitehall was paying to this issue at the time. However, on reflection, this decision was probably more difficult to veto in practice. Delors had just secured a second term as President of the Commission and had played an important role in securing the passage of the SEA. Moreover, the extent of Delors' attachment to federalism was not yet apparent during the first half of

1988, although it became increasingly so afterwards (Lawson 1992: 908; Thatcher 1993: 739; see also *The Poisoned Chalice*, BBC2, 30 May 1996). One could add that this decision was announced rather suddenly by the German delegation, with minimal consultation, thus limiting any resistance that the British negotiating team might have wanted to mobilize. In the words of Delors himself, 'Kohl invited me round on a Sunday before the European Council of Hanover. I persuaded him to go for a Committee [of governors] and – what audacity! – to give me its chair, which was not necessarily what the governors would want' (Grant 1994: 119). Such a decision had two advantages for those delegations committed to making a Single Currency project work. With Delors in the chair, he would ensure that momentum behind his three-stage scheme would be kept up. At the same time, a report which was agreed and endorsed by a committee of European central bankers would ensure the credibility of the proposals in the eyes of the international financial markets.

Finally, any doubts concerning the heart of Europe strategy were confirmed after the Rome Summit in October 1990. Despite her acceptance of the need for concessions over EMU at Madrid, and notwithstanding the dividends this strategy had seemed to generate in the light of German calls for a long period of preparations before Stage Two, ultimately these tactics failed. In a decision showing an eerie parallel with five years earlier, the Italian chair pushed through a vote supporting the setting up of an IGC on EMU. To make matters worse, Kohl secured the insertion of provisions into the communiqué calling for a firm date for Stage Two and progress towards Political Union. Thatcher's resignation in the face of this ambush is evident in her memoirs:

> I do not believe that spelling out the Madrid conditions significantly modified the pace, let alone the direction, of the discussions on the Delors report on EMU. Only someone with a peculiarly naive view of the world – the sort cultivated by British Euro-enthusiasts ... could have imagined that it would. (Thatcher 1993: 713; see also Ridley 1992: 159–61)

Indeed, the Euro-enthusiasts seemed to lack an adequate response to this set-back. In his resignation speech in the House of Commons, Howe admitted that the Italian Presidency's management of the Rome IGC ought not to be 'a model of its kind' (Howe 1994: 699). Such understatement was typical, but it did little to dispel the concerns of the Euro-sceptics.

As a result, concerns about the balance of power issue in Europe became an increasingly prominent theme in Euro-sceptical discourse by 1990. Of interest here is the work of Ridley, who was charged by Thatcher to produce a strategy paper in response to this rapidly changing geo-political environment. For Ridley (1990: 13–15; see also Bulpitt 1992: 269–70) the concept of the balance of power was a key foundation for future British thinking on Europe, although (sadly) for him it was a term which had largely been neglected in the debate so far. If the key question was how to balance the power of Germany in a post-Cold War world, increased integration and centralization of the Union's institutions was not the answer. German reunification meant that Germany had become too economically powerful to be just another player in the EU. In terms of British foreign policy, a better solution remained grounded in balance of power thinking, but involved returning to pre-1939 considerations. More specifically, British policy-makers should work for enlargement of the EU as a way of diluting the integration process as soon as possible. For Thatcher, only a solid Anglo-French alliance, backed up by the continued military presence of the USA in Europe, would be a successful strategy to 'balance' German power (Thatcher 1993: 791–5). As already noted, the French government resisted such overtures. Moreover, US support for both German reunification and greater European integration only confirmed the poverty of this particular strategy.

These perceived limits to the opportunities for British diplomacy led the Euro-sceptics not only to question the heart of Europe strategy. At the same time, they became increasingly concerned at how British policy seemed to be increasingly locked into this process of European integration. The experience of introducing alternative policy proposals aimed at frustrating momentum towards a Single Currency exacerbated these fears. At this time, the Court proposed the Competing Currencies and Hard ECU (parallel currencies) plans which promised closer monetary cooperation, while stopping short of publicly backing the Single Currency project. Based on the work of Hayek, the Competing Currencies scheme suggested that central bank monopoly over the issuing of currency should be privatized and opened up to competition. As a result, currencies would compete against each other in the currency markets. Naturally, those that kept their value best would eventually gain a greater share of business. It is worth noting that the paper finally produced by the Treasury differed from Hayek's approach in detail. Currency creation would remain in the hands of central banks which would act within the framework of the ERM. However, the principle of competition remained the same. It would come through the removal of all barriers to the use of any national currency in any other Union country. As Lawson pointed out, one logical conclusion was that, if one currency significantly out-performed all other currencies, this situation could lead, in the long term, to its adoption as a Single Currency. However, in a more sceptical footnote, Lawson added that competition rarely leads to monopoly (Lawson 1992: 939).

Similarly, the central tenet of the Hard ECU plan was to provide an alternative, gradual, scheme for greater monetary cooperation, which might eventually lead to the goal of a Single Currency. Under this proposal, the ECU would circulate alongside the currencies of member states, where it would gradually develop and strengthen. Two particular features of this scheme were designed to help 'harden' the ECU. On the one hand, it would be defined so as to ensure that it was never devalued against the twelve national currencies.

On the other hand, the ECU would be privileged by a new European Monetary Fund (EMF) which would issue financial instruments denominated in ECUs in return for national currencies. Central banks would be obliged to redeem their own currencies for ECUs on demand. Eventually, the EMF could develop into a European Central Bank and the Hard ECU could gradually develop into a Single Currency. The use of the conditional tense in these last two sentences was an important part of the attraction of the plan to Thatcher. There was nothing inevitable about the development of a European Central Bank and a Single Currency (Stephens 1996: 161–2).

The response of Britain's European partners to these proposals confirmed what the Euro-sceptics increasingly feared: any initiatives short of giving explicit endorsement to the goal of EMU would not engage Britain's European partners in serious negotiations. The Bundesbank, perhaps the one actor that might have been interested in these suggestions, found both schemes deficient for various reasons. When it came to the Competing Currencies plan, Lawson should have been able to predict the Bundesbank's negative response. According to his memoirs, as far back as the middle of 1988, the British had worked up a proposal to improve European monetary cooperation, whereby each EU country would be allowed to hold the others' currencies in their own reserves. This was not put forward at the time because Lawson knew that the Bundesbank was opposed to this idea and he was wary of alienating Pohl during the time when the Delors Committee was deliberating. Alternatively, when it came to the Hard ECU plan, it was by no means clear to the Bundesbank why the Hard ECU was more likely to take off as a widely traded EU currency than the Deutschmark. At the same time, German officials worried that the introduction of this parallel currency would boost the supply of money and stimulate inflationary pressures within the EU. The British government replied that the creation of ECUs would only take place in exchange for national currencies, so there would be no increase in the money supply. The Bundesbank retorted that national banks would allow their own currency supply to rise in compensation (Dyson 1994: 142).

Despite their advocacy of the 'heart of Europe' strategy, even the Euro-enthusiasts conceded the futility of introducing these initiatives. Again, of particular interest here are the views of Lawson. He accepts that the Competing Currencies plan was received with 'polite scepticism' when it was first presented at a Council of Finance Ministers meeting in Antibes in September 1989: 'my proposals were, of course, disappointing to those who were interested in European Monetary Union only as a means to political union' (Lawson 1992: 908, 941–2; Ridley 1992: 150; Dyson 1994: 136–7; Grant 1994: 132; Dyson and Featherstone 1996: 14). Similarly, the Hard ECU proposal was never given serious consideration because it failed to give explicit endorsement to the goal of a Single Currency. Again, Lawson describes the Hard ECU plan as 'a highly ingenious but fundamentally unworkable proposal which included an unwise Euro-institutional component. . . . Very few outside the UK showed the slightest interest in it, and John Major quite rightly abandoned it well ahead of negotiations over the Maastricht Treaty' (Lawson 1992: 943–4). When he points to the reasons for this lack of interest, Lawson's conclusions are as damning for the heart of Europe strategy as they are correct:

> Whereas, throughout most of the 1980s, the ERM was seen as an exchange rate system in its own right ... by the end of the 1980s the Euro-politicians, with no thought for the consequences, were encouraging the markets to see it as nothing more than an unstable transitional stage towards EMU and a single European currency. (Lawson 1992: 1010–11)

Put in different terms, European statesmen had 'fatally confused the essentially economic question of the ERM with the fundamentally political argument over EMU' (Lawson 1992: 913). To try to detach the one from the other was to misunderstand the developing nature of European institutions. Indeed, it was to promote the vacuity of trying to confront the Euro-ratchet with a strategy of accommodationism (see also Ridley 1992: 150–1; Dyson and Featherstone 1996: 19).

In short, the possibilities for British influence in this rapidly changing external environment did not just reflect balance of power considerations. In addition, the Euro-sceptics increasingly pointed to the importance of an awareness of the more general institutional context within which they worked. The main claim here was that British policy-makers now found themselves negotiating on institutional terrain which undermined an already weak position. Euro-sceptics counselled on the importance of European treaty language and how it could be appropriated for the purposes of furthering integration. Indeed, the key lesson learnt from negotiating the SEA was to be careful of general and ambiguous clauses which could be used for unintended and unforeseen purposes in other negotiations at a later date. In the light of this new momentum towards a Single Currency, naturally attention focused on the preamble and Article 20, which promised to work for greater economic and monetary 'cooperation', while at the same time holding out the possibilities of EMU. In his memoirs, Howe accepts that the goal of EMU was never explicitly defined. More importantly, he confirms that even at the signing of the SEA, Thatcher's habit of stressing the term 'cooperation' in the title of Article 20 conflicted with more expansive interpretations of other EU actors. Lawson also maintains in his memoirs that he counselled against this risky strategy. Even if one couldn't be sure of the exact legal fall-out, the point was that the Preamble, and the Title of Article 20 (especially the reference to EMU in brackets) sent the wrong political signals to the Union level (Lawson 1992: 888–94). Indeed, the whole episode led to a period of 'finger pointing' within Whitehall, including claims of deliberate deception. Just as important for the Euro-sceptics were the implications of this misjudgement. As Thatcher noted, what was important was that, in the absence of highly defined treaty clauses and in the face of a coalition of member states pushing for a single currency, 'I was bound to be fighting on ground not of my own choosing' (Thatcher 1993: 741–2). In other words, the EU was threatening to become an international organization capable of continually and explicitly penetrating British politics.

If the Euro-sceptics increasingly feared that British policy was being locked into a process of European integration, they also worried that the consequences for the statecraft project built up over the 1980s would be disastrous. If the heart of this strategy was a governing code which stressed domestic autonomy, interestingly criticisms revealed a delicate trade-off between such autonomy and discretion as it came to be understood by Thatcher, Ridley and others. If the key to winning elections and achieving governing competence was domestic autonomy, the logic of the argument seemed to lie with the Euro-enthusiasts. What better way of entrenching the autonomy code than to hive-off the responsibility for imposing this rule-based disciplinarian framework to institutions outside Britain's domestic jurisdiction? However, the Euro-sceptics rejected this logic. Autonomy could be taken too far and an element of discretion should always be retained in the complex business of economic management. As the period wore on, Lawson was criticized for proposing policy instruments which would allow him to run the economy on automatic pilot. It was a mistake to 'hanker after some lodestar, some fixed point, against which to measure progress and to assess the need for policy changes' (Ridley 1992: 189).

For the Euro-sceptics, there was no better example of the danger of self-imposed external constraints in the name of domestic autonomy than the failed attempt at shadowing the Deutschmark noted above. Side-stepping the argument concerning how much Thatcher actually knew,[1] it was the lessons learnt which are of more relevance to the argument here. For the Euro-sceptics, shadowing represented a clear illustration of the perverse effects of an external discipline. It was the reason for the unnecessary high inflation in the late 1980s and the recession in the early 1990s. After all, it was only because of the unpublished Deutschmark target that Lawson felt compelled to lower interest rates at a time when he had just introduced a tax-cutting budget in the middle of a credit boom. This episode encouraged the often repeated arguments of Thatcher and Walters concerning the relationship between monetary policy, interest rates and the exchange rate. As already noted, according to this argument, faced with this three-way relationship, policy-makers have a choice. They can choose to hold/fix the exchange rate to a particular level, while sacrificing domestic policy to that goal. Alternatively, they can pursue a domestic policy using a combination of fiscal and monetary instruments, and leave the exchange rate to float. Interest rates cannot be manipulated to influence both goals simultaneously (Thatcher 1993: 689).

Behind this tension over autonomy lay important questions of self-confidence. For Euro-sceptics, this readiness to seek out European solutions to an increasing number of core governing responsibilities smacked of defeatism. Put in different terms, it risked fuelling an image of governing incompetence. As Thatcher emphasized in her memoirs, during the first two terms the leadership had struggled to build up a reputation for competent economic management, despite the implementation problems noted above. By joining the ERM, the party would in effect be saying that it could not discipline itself and 'wanted to pass the responsibility ... to something – or someone else' (Thatcher 1993: 700, 707; Ridley 1992: 188–9, 193). In response, Lawson accepts there was something to the charge that an image of governing incompetence might be an undesirable side-effect of the Europeanization strategy. However, he denies the accusations of defeatism and allegations of wishing to divest responsibility for policy. Indeed, the core of his defence again rested on the need for entrenchment:

> On the contrary, I was anxious above all to entrench our counter-inflation commitment and policies against the vagaries of future governments, possibly of a different political complexion ... she [Thatcher] seemed quite incapable of accepting the possibility that there might be another government some day ... so far as she was concerned, she really was going to go on and on. (Lawson 1992: 871)

By 1990, the Court had collapsed. Ridley was forced to resign in 1989 after some ill-judged comments alleging that EMU was a 'German racket' designed to take over Europe. Lawson went in the same year, citing Thatcher's increasingly autocratic style and reliance on Alan Walters, her economic adviser, as his main reasons for leaving. By 1990, Howe, having been moved from the Foreign Office to the post of Deputy Leader, also departed. While Thatcher's belligerent style, both at home and abroad, was also an important theme of his resignation speech, Howe maintained that the decision was over policy substance. Although the exact nature of this dispute was never entirely clear, Howe's deep attachment to the philosophy of working within the grain of the European process meant that eventually he would publicly endorse the goal of a Single Currency (even if he had already come to accept this policy in private). As noted above, this was something that Thatcher (and indeed Lawson) could not accept. Ironically, months later, Thatcher agreed to allow Britain to join the ERM in October 1990 at a rate of DM2.95. In November, she was forced to resign from the leadership after a less than unanimous victory over Heseltine in a leadership contest. She was replaced by the then Chancellor of the Exchequer – John Major.

Conclusions

This chapter has attempted to analyse the downfall of the Conservative Party leadership in the late 1980s. More particularly, it has tried to delineate the contribution of the European issue to this process. In doing so, it has generated two main conclusions. First, it began by asserting that the external structural context facing the Court shifted in the late 1980s in a way which impacted adversely on the domestic fortunes of the Court. More particularly, a number of international economic and geo-political movements in the late 1980s set off further momentum for integration within the EU, most notably in the sphere of monetary policy. Second, it was argued that this external pressure served to exacerbate differences within the Court concerning the future of its statecraft strategy in relationship to this regional association. Of course, these differences were partly a matter of personalities; indeed, they reflected divisions over the question of Prime Ministerial style. However, part of the reason why these splits became so intractable was that they reflected disputes over a question which went to the heart of Conservatism itself: what was the appropriate method of preserving domestic governing autonomy and competence within a world of increasing economic and political interdependence.

1.   Thatcher herself admitted to having known about the shadowing to *The Times* in June 1991 (*The Times* 29 June 1991; see also Thompson 1996: 88–9).

CHAPTER SEVEN

Falling Apart over the 'Heart of Europe': Euro-scepticism and the Electoral Decline of the Conservative Party

With the collapse of the Court during the second half of the 1980s having been charted, this final chapter attempts to explain the spread of Euro-scepticism throughout the Conservative Party in the 1990s, with seemingly disastrous electoral consequences. Once again, from a superficial survey of events, the answer to this question is by no means obvious. Although the leadership cull had been a bitter and painful experience for the party, the emergence of Major as the new leader, flanked by Hurd as his Europhile Foreign Secretary, seemed to promise a new, relatively quiescent chapter in Britain's relations with the EU. Through his new consensual heart of Europe strategy, the party now hoped that Major would rebuild Britain's bargaining strength at the Union level, while simultaneously healing the internal wounds which had developed. In this task, the leadership seemed to be helped by the development of more favourable external circumstances. What looked like the inexorable and unstoppable momentum towards further European integration seemed to have been checked by the early 1990s. This process was most graphically illustrated by the European electorate's less than sympathetic endorsement of the Treaty of European Union (TEU) (more commonly known as the Maastricht Treaty), most notably in the French and Danish referendums. Why then did the Conservative Party continue to tear itself apart over the European question? More particularly, how can we explain the recalcitrant behaviour of an increasing band of Euro-sceptics?

The main argument of this final chapter is that many of the nascent concerns which increasingly excited the Euro-sceptics in the 1980s were confirmed by events in the 1990s. More particularly, three claims are advanced in the discussion below. First, the signing and ratification of the TEU fortified the belief that the EU was an external organization capable of continually and explicitly penetrating the British policy process. Second, as they had done before 1990, the Euro-sceptics warned that the

Euro-enthusiasts' quest for heightened governing autonomy through Europeanization would only serve to further constrain the leadership's freedom of manoeuvre. As Black Wednesday showed, the effect on the government's image of competence could be devastating. Finally, the Euro-sceptics feared that this Europeanization of policy could threaten the whole institutional basis on which the Thatcherite statecraft project was built. In making this argument, they highlighted the normative importance of British parliamentary democracy: the 'regime support function' this institution carries out, which made this centralized style of rule possible. Put another way, the search for autonomy could be taken too far. It ran the risk of precipitating an institutional revolution within the British polity.

Before outlining the argument in detail, a couple of qualifications or problems of analysis should be noted. First, attempts at generalizing about the behaviour of the Conservative Euro-sceptics run the risk of grossly simplifying the complex set of differing motives held by this disparate (desperate?) group. As one would expect, the 1990s heralded a burgeoning literature on the Euro-sceptics. However, one common theme of this work has been the compulsion to categorize and classify the plethora of different sub-groups, sects or camps which this generic term would seem to cover. Euro-sceptics have been variously described as 'traditionalists', 'constitutionalists', 'patriots' and 'marketeers' (Spicer 1992). Others have characterized Conservative MPs as 'Thatcherite Nationalists', 'Neo-liberal Integrationists' or 'Interventionist Integrationists' (Sowemimo 1996). The effects of age and career path have been isolated to explain the reasons for this scepticism (Berrington and Hague 1998), while others have measured attitudes according to axis, stressing the importance of sovereignty, interdependence, extended government and minimal government (Baker *et al.* 1993; see also Garry 1995). Of course, disaggregation is an important exercise in political analysis; genuine differences between Euro-sceptical groupings cannot just be glossed over. That said, the student of politics should at least attempt to seek order and establish generalizations out of this empirical 'clutter'.

In fact, despite the emphasis on differentiation, this literature does proffer some general explanations concerning the motivations of the Euro-sceptics during this period. These Conservative backbenchers are often said to be motivated by 'the politics of nationhood'. Present institutional change at the Union level is perceived as a new phase of integration which poses a fundamental threat to the British nation state and national identity. Central to the politics of nationhood is the concept of sovereignty. The TEU is a 'treaty too far' because its irrevocable nature poses a severe threat to British sovereignty, particularly over economic and monetary affairs. Implicit in this explanation is the view that Thatcherism should be viewed as an attempt by the Conservative Party to revive Britain's status as a strong, patriotic nation state, both internally and in its relations with the external world. It should provoke little surprise that the Euro-sceptics are often characterized as former

Thatcherites (Sowemimo 1996). A second question/problem here is how the Statecraft interpretation outlined above relates to this type of argument.

It would be foolish to deny that this emphasis on nationhood does not illuminate our understanding of the motives and behaviour of the Euro-sceptics. Any superficial reading of the Maastricht debates in the House of Commons would reveal a liberal use of the term 'sovereignty' in the discourse of the average MP. However, by and large, this book has avoided employing this term for a number of reasons. To begin with, there is very little agreement concerning what the concept means. In an influential article published in *Political Studies* in 1955, Stanley Benn discovered six ways in which sovereignty had been defined: as the expression of the supremacy of a norm in a legal hierarchy; as the omnicompetence or supreme competence of a legislative organ (i.e. parliament in Britain); as constitutional independence or self-sufficiency; as a particular kind of legal order which may vary between political systems; as the supreme coercive power within a jurisdiction; and as the ability of a sectional interest to influence policy (S. Benn 1955). In short, sovereignty has multiple, contradictory meanings, leading Benn to conclude that a persuasive case can be made for dispensing with the concept altogether. This argument has been countered by suggesting that words have various uses, not correct or fixed meanings, so the call for abandonment is too premature; and anyway, some of these various meanings might be quite useful (James 1986: 16–17).

These arguments aside, when looked at more closely many of the above definitions can be boiled down into two main categories: sovereignty as a power-based concept and sovereignty as an authority-based concept. Even then, both usages still have their problems. Sovereignty as a power-based or centred concept can be defined in a number of ways. However, one influential definition employed in the British debate sees sovereignty as 'a nation's practical capacity to maximise its influence in the world' (Howe 1990: 678). It follows from this definition that sovereignty is not necessarily a unitary or absolute concept. In a world of increasing interdependence, state sovereignty is relative, variable and flexible through time and space. It is something which can be divided and 'pooled' with others both inside and outside institutions, in the hope that it will be increased. Indeed, Howe goes as far as to argue that because of its flexible, uncodified nature, the British constitution provides an excellent base from which Britain has been able to deploy its sovereignty around the globe. Rather than being a formal, abstract constitutional prop-erty, sovereignty is a practical resource to be exploited (Howe 1990: 679–81).

The obvious problem with sovereignty defined in this way is that it is perilously close to a common understanding of power, defined as the capacity of A to get B to do something that he or she would not otherwise do. In the light of this congruity, it is not clear why sovereignty should just be abolished. Such an act might rid the subject of conceptual confusion, thus simplifying our understanding of the relationship between national policy and

European integration. However, to abrogate the concept of sovereignty in favour of power runs the risk of provoking fresh objections. Power is already a concept which is applicable in a large number of contexts that may not involve the nation state at all. It is to be universally found in all kinds of governmental or non-governmental relations. To employ a term which does not have anything exclusively to tell us about the role and importance of nation states is to render null and void explanations of Euro-sceptical behaviour through our understanding of the politics of nationhood.

Second, as James has argued, the relative nature of sovereignty as a power-based concept is also capable of spreading ambiguity and confusion. It is, of course, perfectly possible to contend that one state is more sovereign than another at a particular moment. However, attempting to operationalize and measure increases in relative sovereignty as the result of state action is a notoriously difficult thing to do. Not surprisingly, in practice it is rarely done. Sympathizers with this approach are reduced to falling back on gross generalizations that the 'pooling' of sovereignty necessarily leads to an accumulation of this resource. This is no more true than the Euro-enthusiasts' case for acquiescing in greater European integration. Unfortunately, such arguments have the effect of distracting analysts from the precise institutional characteristics of these changing EU institutions and whether such change is in the interest of Britain or the Conservative Party leadership.

Not surprisingly, some authors have begun to suggest that sovereignty can be more accurately understood as a discourse rather than a concept. As Camilleri and Falk (1992: 11) assert, sovereignty 'is central to the language of politics but also to the politics of language', although they conclude that this language is outdated. Bulpitt agrees, but detects a more pernicious rationale behind this discourse. Sovereignty is a 'cuckoo' concept, 'crowding out' sensible debate concerning the merits of EU membership for the British polity. At the same time, it provides a handy ideological tool with which the Euro-enthusiasts can beat the Euro-sceptics in debates about British policy towards this regional organization. In the British debate, sovereignty is usually defined in terms of power: the capacity of a state to achieve its interest or will. For the Euro-enthusiasts, to the extent that sovereignty ever existed, it has largely disappeared since 1945. A more modern attitude might be for Britain to 'pool' what little it has of this 'resource' in the hope that it might create and join institutions which have much more. In the same rhetorical movement, the Euro-sceptics can be labelled as old-fashioned reactionary nationalists, harking after a bygone age that never was. Bulpitt concludes by arguing that explanations of Britain's relations with the EU would be better served if British political science employed alternative concepts (Bulpitt 1992: 262–3; 1996: 216–19). Surprisingly, one of the main exponents of this 'politics of nationhood' explanation concurs. Lynch admits that the concept of sovereignty is 'hotly disputed' and its use 'has tended to be symbolic and of rhetorical importance rather than a guiding principle of government European policy' (Lynch 1998).

Alternatively, sovereignty can be defined as a concept with authority at its core. For a state to be 'sovereign', it must be constitutionally independent (James 1986; Malcolm 1996). In external terms, one state may depend on another for economic goods or military protection, but as long as it is not legally subordinate, it still enjoys sovereign status. Internally, states must be exclusively competent with respect to their internal affairs. Put in different terms, sovereignty has three distinguishing qualities according to this definition: it is legal, absolute and unitary in its condition (James 1986: 22–5, 39–57).

The problem with this definition is that, outside the formalities of constitutional law, the concept has little meaning. Once it is insisted that sovereignty should be kept distinct from the concept of power, it becomes very difficult to connect it with the real world of politics. More tellingly, as we shall see, when Euro-sceptics focus on the day-to-day practical effect of European integration on 'sovereignty' defined in this way, they slip into talking about the implications for parliamentary democracy. Of course, in the British context, parliamentary democracy is precisely what sovereignty means in practical terms. However, focusing more specifically on this concept of democracy does seem to open up a different set of questions. Take, for example, Malcolm's chapter on sovereignty in *The Euro-sceptical Reader*, edited by Martin Holmes. While the author defines sovereignty as constitutional independence, he concludes somewhat paradoxically that his fears concerning European integration have very little to do with this authority-based concept as he has defined it. Instead, the challenge for Euro-sceptics is to theorize about the possibilities for *democracy* in a world of increasing economic and political interdependence. It is difficult to shake the feeling that the previous discussion of sovereignty has largely been irrelevant to these pressing practical concerns. A treatise on the concept of democracy might have been more useful (Malcolm 1996: 364–5). In short, Bulpitt looks to be right. Concepts such as power, autonomy and democracy may be of more use in understanding the motives and behaviour of the Euro-sceptics (Bulpitt, 1992: 263).

The Limits to European Integration?
Developments in the 1990s

The paradox running through this chapter is that just as the Euro-sceptics became ever more animated concerning the perceived danger of the EU, the threat of European integration appeared to subside in the 1990s. Or at least that was the argument articulated by the Major leadership throughout this period. As noted in Chapter 6, by the early 1990s one of the core concerns of the Euro-sceptics at the Court was the developing threat of European integration to governing autonomy and competence. Moreover, although their discourse did not evince such thinking, it was argued that this integration was underpinned by broader structural movements in international relations. However, as some authors have noted, these broader geo-political developments left a more ambiguous legacy than initially feared by the Euro-sceptics. While German reunification did set off a drive towards greater European integration, it is also worth remembering that the decline of the Cold War had removed many of the certainties which had inhabited the international scene after 1945. More significantly, attempts to consolidate the 'core' of the EU began to provoke difficult and important questions concerning the future political architecture of the EU in this fast-changing environment (Story 1996).

What was particularly encouraging for the new Major government was the nascent disagreement between France and Germany over the future institutional configuration of the EU in this post-Cold War world. In essence, the tensions boiled down to the seemingly incompatible goals of 'deepening' and 'widening'. The German government supported both, but it was its enthusiastic endorsement of enlargement which caused much consternation in Paris at this time. Such support reflected a mixture of philosophical arguments and cruder calculations concerning the national interest. For Kohl, EU integration had played a vital historical role in ensuring the peace and stability of Europe after 1945. What better way of responding to this new security vacuum on its eastern flank than extending the benefits of EU membership to these former Soviet satellites? (Banchoff 1997: 64–6). At the same time, the collapse of the Soviet bloc posed a real threat of mass migration into Germany. In this context, it was hoped that Bonn's support for enlargement would provide leverage in persuading these democracies to institute effective internal security policies (Welfens 1993: 173–5).

Conversely, Paris began to worry that the Union was in danger of over-burdening itself with too many initiatives. More particularly, French policy-makers were concerned that enlargement would trigger further unacceptable moves towards political integration (De La Serre and Lequesne 1993: 156). Having spent the period since the late 1980s advocating greater European integration as a method of controlling German economic power, Paris hardly welcomed the prospect of seeing this strategy undermined by the process of enlargement. Hence, French officials attempted to stall pressures for widening, particularly in the case of Eastern European countries which were perceived to pose a threat to French agricultural interests. In this, they were supported by the 'Club Med' countries, anxious about the effect of enlargement on their respective shares of the Union budget (see also Haywood 1993: 279–80).

This ambiguity over the future institutional shape of the EU could be seen quite starkly during the negotiations and ratification of the Maastricht Treaty. Take, for example, discussions on the architecture of the new treaty in the IGC on Political Union. Having signed the Joint Letter with the German government, French negotiators then played a leading role in securing the 'pillared' approach over the 'tree-trunk' proposals suggested by Dutch diplomats. As a result, the Common Foreign and Security Policy (CFSP) and Justice and Home Affairs (JHA) would remain separate from the competence of the Union. Moreover, attempts by the Dutch Presidency to describe the EU as having a 'federal vocation' in the Common Provisions of the treaty were roundly condemned by most delegations. Eventually the term was replaced by the phrase: 'an ever closer union among the peoples of Europe' (Treaty on European Union 1992: 7).

Arguably, the Major government was able to expose this equivocation to secure changes to the treaty which make it acceptable to domestic political opinion. One example of this successful diplomacy could be seen in the inclusion of a formal definition of subsidiarity. In a House of Commons appearance before travelling to Maastricht, Major insisted that he would press for the inclusion of such a clause. In fact, pressure for such a move did arise, once the unacceptable nature of the Dutch draft text had been agreed. The phrase 'an ever closer union among the peoples of Europe' was immediately followed by the words 'in which decisions are taken as closely as possible to the citizen' (Treaty on European Union 1992: 7). This statement was followed by a more detailed explication of the concept in Article 3b:

> In areas which do not fall within its exclusive competence, the Community shall take action, in accordance with the principle of subsidiarity, only if and in so far as the objectives of the proposed action cannot be sufficiently achieved by the member states and can therefore, by reason of the scale or effects of the proposed action, be better achieved by the Community. (Treaty on European Union 1992: 13–14)

During negotiations, the British delegation was able to block a Belgian proposal for a legal definition of subsidiarity, which gave the European Court of Justice powers to rule whether EU legislation contravened this principle. For British diplomats, such legalism threatened the prerogative of member states to decide when intervention by the EU was justified. Moreover, Major was successful in putting additional 'flesh' on this principle at the Edinburgh Summit in December 1992. Here it was agreed that proposals for further Union legislation in a particular field had to pass a three-stage test before being accepted. First, the EU had to prove it had the requisite powers to act under existing Treaties. Second, it had to show that the proposed objectives could not be achieved through national or local action. Finally, if it was established that EU action was imperative, it had to be the minimum necessary to carry out the agreed objectives (Peterson 1994).

Moreover, in areas where the pressure for European integration proved impossible to resist, the British delegation secured an opt-out from proposals deemed to be too contentious. During the IGC on EMU, Major and Lamont negotiated an opt-out from Stage Three, although attempts to secure a more general provision whereby all member states would be required to opt-into this commitment were defeated. At the same time, Germany's insistence (in contrast with the Commission's proposals) that strict convergence criteria be respected before and after the launch of the Single Currency was in line with British preferences in this area.[1] Of more interest were suggestions that Major would not have insisted on this opt-out had it not been for Thatcher's public attack on the Single Currency just before he left for Maastricht (see George 1993: 183; Seldon 1997: 164).

Similar concessions were achieved in the area of social policy. It is true that the TEU extended Union competence and qualified majority voting beyond health and safety matters, to include such topics as the improvement of working conditions, the rights of workers to information and consultation, and equal opportunities within the workplace. Moreover, the treaty stipulated a new decision-making framework, giving UNICE and the ETUC (the social partners) important rights to initiate policy. The Commission was now required to consult these partners before tabling proposals, and to delay formulation for nine months if the partners believed they could reach agreement among themselves.[2] However, after first allowing them to be watered down, in a last minute concession, Britain's European partners agreed to remove these proposals from the treaty altogether in deference to the opposition of the British delegation. Instead, they were annexed to the Treaty by way of a protocol. Put another way, although the eleven member states could pursue these new treaty objectives in the field of social policy, they would have to do so by 'borrowing' the EU's institutions (Lo Faro 1992: 31–2).

At the same time, the security challenges posed by this new and indeterminate international environment provided British negotiators with arguments to undermine pressure for a common defence policy. On the one hand, the Court could point to the EU's disparate response to American military action in the Gulf in the summer of 1991 (Grant 1994: 144–5). Closer to 'home', however, was the failure to provide a coherent and effective response to Croatia's declaration of independence from the Yugoslavian federation in June. One could note initial European attempts to broker a plan whereby a Croat would take over the federal presidency and the Yugoslavian army would return to barracks. In exchange, the Croatians would agree to suspend their declaration of independence. However, these proposals were widely ignored, as was the subsequent Brioni Agreement, negotiated by the Italians in July. Eventually, in December, EU foreign ministers reluctantly fell in behind Genscher's decision to push for the recognition of Croatia. However, as some delegations feared, this action only served to escalate the conflict. Recognition of Bosnia could not now be avoided and took place in April 1992. A bitter and bloody war with the Bosnian Serbs ensued shortly afterwards (Grant 1994: 191–2; Edwards 1997).

It was within this context that the Court was largely successful in preserving the intergovernmental nature of decision-making in this area. Faced with Franco-German proposals in February 1991 for the Western European Union (WEU) to be folded into the EU to become its fledgling defence arm, the British delegation launched an alternative initiative in alliance with the Italians. This plan conceded that the Union could take on a gradual role in the formulation of a future European Defence Policy. However, it was insisted that any strengthening of the WEU should take place within NATO, not as a development which challenged the primacy of this alliance. While the treaty did make a provision for an eventual Common Defence Policy, assurances about compatibility with existing security arrangements were also explicitly written into the document (Treaty on European Union 1992: 126). Finally, the procedure for adopting joint action guaranteed that member states remained firmly in control of the decision-making machinery for the present (Grant 1994: 193–4; Forster 1999).

Even then, despite the disjointed nature of the TEU, to the great surprise of the Union's leaders it provoked real opposition among Europe's electorate. In the required referendum in June 1992, the Danish public rejected the treaty by a margin of 50.7 per cent to 49.3 per cent (Siune and Svensson 1993: 102). When Mitterrand decided to employ a similar method to ensure popular consent, the French electorate voted to endorse the agreement by only the narrowest of margins. Although the Danes reversed their decision in 1993, this success could not dispel the more general feeling that Europe's elites were significantly out of step with public attitudes on greater European integration. While findings by Franklin *et al.* (1994) caution against this interpretation, it was perhaps these perceptions (mistaken or not) which were just as important.

Moreover, if the future IGC pencilled in for 1996 was supposed to produce a document which tackled the contentious question of EU institutional reform in preparation for enlargement, subsequent negotiations only served to highlight the differences in this area. The Reflection Group which met to prepare the ground throughout the second half of 1995 highlighted the size of the Commission and the weighting of votes in the Council of Ministers as particular issues which needed to be faced. However, the foreign ministers' meeting at Noordwijk in April 1997 only indicated the real obstacles to progress. Smaller member states objected to French plans to scale down the number of Commissioners from twenty to ten, fearing that they would be increasingly vulnerable to the influence of a Franco-German Directorate. Progress over the reweighing of Council votes fared no better. Under the present arrangements, the proportion of the EU population needed to secure a qualified majority stood at 58.3 per cent (set to drop further as enlargement progressed). Anxiety at the prospect of being continually over-ruled by a coalition of small states meant this situation had become increasingly unacceptable to the larger member states. However, initiatives aimed at introducing a double majority, whereby decisions by qualified majority voting in the Council of Ministers would have to meet an additional population threshold, proved equally contentious (*Financial Times* 8 April: 1997). At the signing of the Amsterdam Treaty, the best negotiators could do was to attach a protocol postponing the resolution of the problem to a future date (Langrish 1998: 4).

Finally, in the area of EMU, arguably the core of the momentum towards European integration, tensions between Germany and other member states placed the future of the Single Currency project in jeopardy. The obvious example of this problem lay in the collapse of the ERM in 1993. The main events have been documented elsewhere and need only a brief rehearsal here. As a result of German reunification and the programme of subsidies to the former East German Länder, German inflation began to rise in the early 1990s. Ever sensitive to the historical parallels of the 1920s, the Bundesbank sought to counter this inflation problem by raising interest rates. Throughout 1992, the Deutschmark rose steadily on the foreign exchanges, a development helped by lower US interest rates and a movement of funds out of the dollar into marks. Eventually, the inexorable rise of the German currency, as well as the Bundesbank's unwillingness to support other European currencies which came under pressure, placed uncontainable strains on the ERM. By September 1992, the pound and the lira were ejected from the system. In November the escudo and peseta had devalued, and in February 1993 the punt followed suit. By July, the French franc was forced to leave the ERM, leading to its dissolution and eventual recrystallization around a system of 15 per cent bands. These wide margins led some commentators to question whether the new ERM was really a semi-fixed exchange rate system at all (Dinan 1994: 430–1; Grahl 1997: 87–9).

Even after the re-establishment of the ERM, continual pessimism existed at the EU level concerning whether EMU would go ahead. Worries were expressed about the increasing use of 'creative accounting' techniques by member states as they strained to meet the convergence criteria. The introduction of a special Euro-tax by the Italian government was perhaps to be expected. However, Wagel's failed attempt to implement a revaluation of Germany's gold and currency reserves as a way of meeting the 3 per cent GDP measure provoked a round of speculation that EMU's Third Stage might not go ahead (Davidson 1997; Nolling 1997; Norman 1997; Rattner 1997). Continual Franco-German tensions concerning the future operation of a Single Currency policy did not help confidence. Most notable were increasingly strident French demands for a political counter-weight or Stability Council to counter what it feared would be the European Central Bank's (ECB) excessive concern with inflation at the expense of growth and jobs. Not surprisingly, this provoked cries of political interference from the Bundesbank. Matters were not helped by France's attempt to reopen the decision over the first President of the ECB, proposing its own Claude Trichet as opposed to

Duisenberg, who had the support of Germany (Strauss-Kahn 1997; see also *Financial Times* 18 May 1997, 24 May 1997, 15 September 1997, 6 November 1997).

In short, by the mid-1990s the Major leadership could point to significant successes in rolling back the integrationist/centralist tide within the EU. Its heart of Europe strategy meant that Britain was now winning the argument over the future direction of this organization's institutional development. Central to this discourse was the new concept of 'variable geometry'. According to this approach, future European structures would be able to accommodate different groups of member states wishing to work together at different paces. European cooperation would respect the sanctity of the nation state – the essential unit on which the EU was built. Alongside this new emphasis on flexibility existed a renewed support for enlargement. Any union of twenty or more members would necessarily need more flexible and decentralized institutional arrangements to accommodate the multitude of national interests contained within. Moreover, as the Major government warned, to ignore the pressures for enlargement was to run the risk of creating new divisions within Europe. It should be the EU's priority to consolidate democracy and prosperity across the continent. Of course, this emphasis on variability was in no way intended to detract from the core commitments of existing treaties, particularly the Single Market. It was certainly not intended to give licence to a 'two-speed Europe': 'the door to each area of co-operation should always remain open to all member states' (Hurd 1993: 9–10; see also Garel-Jones 1993: Major 1993; Cm 3181, 1996: 6; Conservative Central Office 1997: 45–6).

Europeanization and the Electoral Suicide of the Euro-sceptics: Towards a Statecraft Explanation

In the light of the above discussion, the problem becomes how to explain the truculent behaviour of the Euro-sceptics over the European question. Why did this group insist on putting this issue before the political fortunes of the party, thus arguably contributing to one of the worst electoral defeats in living memory? Lack of remaining space precludes a detailed answer to this question; indeed, it probably merits a book on its own. Instead, what follows is a preliminary intellectual probe or experiment. The task is to extrapolate the Statecraft interpretation as developed so far and apply it to this present problem.

In essence, it is argued below that the behaviour of the Euro-sceptics reflected their anxiety about the future of Conservative statecraft in the context of Union membership. Put another way, the search for domestic autonomy and governing competence through the process of Europeanization could be, and has been, taken too far. More particularly, three concerns are highlighted. The discussion begins by explicating the Euro-sceptics' disdain for the heart of Europe strategy. For this group, the EU is now an organization capable of explicitly penetrating British politics, with adverse consequences for the Conservative Party in office. It follows that continual close association with these structures risks stretching the party out on a Euro-ratchet. Second, and not surprisingly, the implications for domestic autonomy and governing competence are perceived to be disastrous, not beneficial as the Euro-enthusiasts argue. Euro-sceptics point to Britain's short-lived membership of the ERM as evidence in support of this claim. Finally, the Euro-sceptics became increasingly concerned about the impact of Europeanization on British parliamentary democracy. This anxiety was not just a question of 'misplaced sentimentality' concerning the future of this age-old institution. It was the parliamentary nature of the British polity which made any centralized autonomy strategy possible. To be seen publicly to be abusing Parliament ran the risk of undermining the whole basis of elite autonomy as traditionally enjoyed in Britain.

The Euro-sceptics, the Treaty of European Union and the Increasing Strain of the 'Euro-ratchet'

As noted in Chapter 6, the Euro-sceptics at the Court increasingly perceived the EU as an organization which was capable of penetrating the British policy. Naturally, the existence of a powerful coalition of member states and institutions favouring greater European integration was central to this perception. More important, however, was the ability of EU institutions (in alliance with other member states or on their own) to use ambiguous treaty language to generate such momentum. If anything, developments in the 1990s confirmed Euro-sceptical fears in this area. This was no more so than in the government's decision to sign and ratify the TEU. This experience strengthened the view that any strategy of accommodationism was counterproductive in confronting the Euro-ratchet. Indeed, the Euro-sceptics increasingly began to articulate the dangers of such a response.

There was no better example of this thinking than in the Euro-sceptics' criticisms of the concept of subsidiarity. If the Major government's hopes for a more flexible, decentralized Union rested on this term, Euro-sceptics feared it could provide an 'opportunity structure' for integrationists to strengthen their position. This argument drew attention to two problems with subsidiarity. The first related to the ambiguity and confusion surrounding the meaning and practical policy implications of the concept. The important question here was the exact division of competencies between the Union and member states. As the Euro-sceptics were fond of pointing out, subsidiarity only applied to 'areas which do not fall within its [the European Union's] exclusive competence'. Unfortunately, the Treaty did not set out a clearly defined list of competencies which fell within the scope of the concept. As Wincott (1994: 579) has noted, this practice is common in other federal states from which the principle is derived.

It followed that, in the absence of any clear definition, arguments over the meaning of subsidiarity would ultimately come down to Union politicking. In this sense, the key question for the Euro-sceptics was: who decided whether action could be sufficiently achieved by member states or not? In answering this question, they pointed to the Catholic origins of the concept. Originally a papal doctrine, subsidiarity was designed with the intention of allowing power to flow down to constituent parts of the papal dominions. However, the key factor was that the decisions were made by the central authority. In the context of the EU process, Euro-sceptics increasingly pointed to the European Court of Justice (ECJ) as a body which would make the crucial decisions. The Euro-sceptics expected the Court, as a guardian of EU law, both to protect and to consolidate the power of European institutions, thus contributing to a process of greater European integration (Spearing in *Hansard* (Commons) vol. 201, 19 December 1991: cols 495–6; see also Duncan-Smith, cols 354–5; Knapman, cols 395–6; Gill, col. 414 in *Hansard* (Commons) vol. 208, 20 May 1992). Some academics question this analysis, arguing that European judges will not relish being drawn into the increasingly political process of adjudicating on the diversion of competencies between the Union and member states. However, to the extent that this involvement is inevitable, it seems reasonable from past behaviour to expect the ECJ to protect the integrity of the EU rather than act as a motor for decentralization and intergovernmentalism (Weiler 1993).

Arguably, it was the legal manoeuvring over the Working Time Directive which provided the most blatant example of EU institutions being able to penetrate the British domestic political process. Ironically, this action had nothing to do with the TEU and was brought forward by the Commission under the SEA. This proposal sought to guarantee a maximum 48-hour week for all EU employees under Article 118a, which, as already noted, related to health and safety matters. Although the issue of whether working hours counted as a health and safety issue could be questioned, the advantage for Brussels was that all legislation pertaining to this article was subject to qualified majority voting. As a result, the Commission could by-pass any possibility of a British veto. In June 1993, the Commission's proposals passed into law and, as predicted, the Conservative government challenged this interpretation of Article 118a by taking the Commission to the ECJ. In November 1996, the Court rejected British claims, thus provoking a wave of criticism from Britain's Euro-sceptics (Bale and Buller 1996: 70).

If the Working Time Directive represented something of a *cause célèbre* for the Euro-sceptics, this decision took place against the perceived backdrop of an increasing number of judicial verdicts which seemed to by-pass British politicians altogether. Take, for example, the Factortame Case in 1991, which forced home the principle of the supremacy of Union law. In this judgement, the ECJ overturned the Merchant Shipping Act (1988), which represented a British attempt to respond to the problem of 'quota-hopping' within the Common Fisheries policy. Under this practice, Spanish fishing vessels took advantage of British registration laws in order to fish in waters around the UK. Under the new legislation, the then Thatcher government stipulated that 75 per cent of the directors and shareholders of companies operating vessels off the UK mainland, must be of British nationality. The Court annulled this legislation, arguing that it was incompatible with EU treaty commitments ensuring the freedom of establishment and the freedom to provide services (Dinan 1994: 299; Rice 1995).

Alternatively, one could point to *Francovitch and Boniface* v. *Italy* (1991), which related to the issue of enforcing Union law. In this case, the ECJ held that, in certain circumstances, EU individuals were entitled to sue governments for damages sustained as a result of a failure to implement EU directives within a prescribed period (Dinan 1994: 303). It was under this principle that Nicole Seymour-Smith and Laura Perez successfully challenged the UK's unfair dismissal laws in 1995 (Rice 1995). The Court of Appeal ruled that legislation barring UK employees who had less than two years of service from bringing cases of unfair dismissal discriminated against women. In turn, this decision opened the way for female employees sacked between 1985 and 1991 to claim compensation (*Financial Times* 1 August 1995).

As a result, when the Major government came to finalize its negotiating objectives for the Amsterdam Summit, proposals to restrict the powers of the ECJ were something the party could now unite around. The 1996 White Paper *A Partnership of Nations* now expressed 'concern that the ECJ's interpretation of laws sometimes seems to go beyond what the participating governments intended in framing these laws'. More specific proposals to rectify this situation included: strengthening the ability of the Court to limit retrospective applications of its judgements; the introduction of a principle whereby member states would only be liable for damages in case of a serious breach of its obligations; and streamlined procedures for the rapid amendment of EU legislation which had been interpreted in a way not intended by the Council of Ministers. Euro-sceptics wanted to go further by amending the 1972 European Communities Act so that it unequivocally established the supremacy of Parliamentary statute over EU law. In defence of this proposal, they cited German law, which contained a similar principle (Thatcher 1995: 504–5; see also Cash 1996: 7; Redwood's remarks in the Warwick debate with Leon Brittan, *Financial Times* 16 May 1996).

If the debate around subsidiarity indicated the premature nature of arguments suggesting that the forces of integration had been overcome, Euro-sceptics also pointed to the inability of the government's legal opt-outs to insulate the British polity from the Euro-ratchet. Take, for example, the Works Council Directive, one of the few measures to be negotiated under the Social Chapter during this period. Despite Britain being legally exempt from this directive, in practice it was widely adopted. The ruling required all companies with operations in two or more EU countries to establish representative mechanisms through which employees could be informed and consulted over company strategy. Furthermore, while UK multinationals were legally entitled to exclude British workers from these consultative arrangements, in practice the majority of these firms extended these arrangements to their British operations. Indeed, a survey in the *Financial Times* in 1995 predicted that the directive would affect at least 140 and possibly up to 300 UK companies (Bale and Buller 1996: 70).

More generally, continual Commission warnings of its desire to see social policy formulated under a common legislative framework demonstrated the vulnerability of this opt-out to institutional pressure at the EU level. For example, the Commission's 1994 *White Paper on Social Policy* 'noted the strong desire of all member states to proceed as 12 [thus hoping] that Union social policy will in the future be founded on a single legal framework. This is vital if the integrity of the law and the principle of equal opportunities for all the Union are still to be upheld.' This plea was echoed by both EU President Santer and Commissioner for Social Affairs Padraig Flynn (*The Times* 8 November 1994; *Financial Times* 12 July 1995). While the reality of Britain being forced to end its opt-out in this area was remote, it is significant that such pressure existed throughout the lifetime of the Major government.

Similar Euro-sceptical arguments applied to the opt-out from EMU. The essential point to note here is that British negotiators only secured an opt-out from Stage Three of the process. While the precise degree to which the first two stages limited Britain's economic freedom is contested, Euro-sceptics pointed out that the constraints would be considerable. As well as the UK preparing the Bank of England for independence, all member states were required to treat their economies as a matter of common concern. More particularly, this involved avoiding excessive exchange rate fluctuations and government deficits. Furthermore, the Euro-sceptics argued that the magnetic attraction of a Single Currency after the transition to Stage Three would be significant. Sterling would still come under substantial pressure to maintain an agreed parity against the ECU (now called the Euro).[3] Yet it would have no influence in the setting of Europe-wide interest rates, which would exercise a crucial influence on domestic rate levels. As a result, the chorus of calls for Britain to be influencing policy from inside might well be considerable.

Finally, if a future British government succumbed to this irresistible pressure to join a Single Currency bloc, Euro-sceptics were quick to highlight the enhanced powers enjoyed by EU institutions in this particular policy area. Reference has already been made to the five convergence criteria governing entry into Stage Three of the process. However, when it came to the question of judging whether member states continued to meet these criteria on an annual basis, the Commission enjoyed increased competence. More particularly, it possessed the right to judge and single out member states deemed to be in contravention of these criteria. Furthermore, it had the power to recommend courses of action to the Council of Ministers, who retained the right to make any final decision according to a qualified majority vote (Treaty on European Union 1992: 25, 27). These powers were reinforced during the negotiation of the Stability Pact in December 1996, where the Commission attained the right to adjudicate on new, more stringent, national Stability Programmes (Redwood 1997: 143–6).

Similarly, day-to-day operation of monetary policy in a Single Currency bloc would witness the rise of a new European institution – the European Central Bank. Working through a network of independent national banks, the TEU guaranteed the independence of these European bankers: any attempts by other EU institutions to influence the conduct of monetary policy were expressly forbidden. Of course, the exact shape and nature of the ECB's policy instruments remained to be determined. However, this did not stop Redwood from warning that the implications for national accountability were likely to be dire. Having taken instructions from the Governing Council of the ECB, the Governor of the newly independent Bank of England would be reduced to informing the government and Parliament of the consequent action to be taken. Of course, opportunities for scrutiny of the Governor would exist. However, the stress on statutory independence necessitated that questioning would only be of a limited nature (Redwood 1997: 185). Besides, behind this new framework lay a new 'cult of central bankism' which displayed a paranoia towards the potentially malign impact of politicians on policy of the like not seen since the inter-war period.

Finally, by signing up to the principles of the TEU, irrespective of the opt-outs, British negotiators, the Euro-sceptics argued, faced significant obstacles in persuading other member states of the merits of their alternative vision of EU development. In this sense, replacement of the phrase 'federal vocation' with 'ever closer union amongst the peoples of Europe' represented very little in practice. What it meant was the substitution of one ambiguous and confused expression for another. Of far more importance were the objectives set out in Article B. These committed all member states to work for EMU, including the eventual and 'irrevocable' creation of a Single Currency; a Common Foreign and Security Policy, including the eventual implementation of a common defence policy; and the creation of a European citizenship. Far from promoting a decentralized vision of the EU, founded on the nation state, the TEU represented a new phase of European integration for the Euro-sceptics: it was a treaty too far.

In short, Britain's decision to sign the TEU heightened the fears of the Euro-sceptics that the Major government had inadvertently presided over the tightening of the Euro-ratchet. At the same time, the diplomatic response of Conservative leaders to the EU after Maastricht strengthened Euro-sceptics' fears about the counter-productive nature of the heart of Europe strategy. For

Thatcher and her followers, this 'accommodationism' was both misguided and dangerous. It was misguided because it continued to place a premium on the importance of balance of power politics, while almost completely neglecting the broader institutional terrain on which the negotiating game was being played. Take, for example, the leadership's plea for Europe to be built on the 'bedrock' of the nation state in its 1996 White Paper, *A Partnership of Nations*, prepared for the forthcoming Amsterdam IGC. In his reply, Cash highlighted the contradictions of articulating this discourse of intergovernmentalism, while signing up to the objectives set out in Article B noted above. If the Major government was serious about this intergovernmental rhetoric, it should adopt a two-stage strategy. First, it should invite other delegations to debate the exact constitutional nature of the EU. Once this debate had taken place, it should then seek to have the phrase 'partnership of nations' inscribed unambiguously in the preamble of the treaty. The leadership's failure to ask these more fundamental questions demonstrated the mistaken nature of the heart of Europe strategy. In short, by neglecting these broader institutional questions, Conservatives risked repeating the mistakes of the 1980s (Thatcher 1993: 761–2; Cash 1996: 4–5; see also Marlow, *Hansard* (Commons) vol. 208, 20 May 1992: col. 355).

Faced with the perceived increase in these institutional constraints, the Euro-sceptics also criticized the dangerous nature of this accommodationism. It was dangerous in the sense that the Euro-sceptics questioned the will of the leadership to resist these forces of European integration. In other words, they suspected Major of presiding over the Europeanization of British politics 'by stealth'. One decision of crucial importance to the crystallization of such fears was the refusal of the leadership to use the Danish rejection of the TEU in June 1992 as a pretext for renouncing the treaty and negotiating a looser arrangement. Cash was said to be 'thunderstruck' at Major's resolution to carry on with the treaty (*The Poisoned Chalice*, BBC2, 30 May 1996), while another prominent Euro-sceptic remarked: 'it was this very moment we realised that Major was not one of us' (quoted in Seldon 1997: 294). Other figures at the centre of events concur. For example, Michael Jay, Under-Secretary at the Foreign Office at this time, agrees that there was a real change of mood in the Euro-sceptic camp after this decision.

If the refusal to ditch the TEU after the Danish referendum decision became a defining moment in the development of Euro-scepticism in the Conservative Party, the failure to challenge the legal nature of the treaty after the collapse of ERM fuelled distrust concerning the motives of particular senior party figures. Of particular relevance here was the decision of Britain's partners to replace the discredited 2.5 per cent bands with the broader 15 per cent fluctuation rates, irrespective of the precise legality of this move. Indeed, the new 15 per cent bands were automatically incorporated into the convergence criteria. Euro-sceptics wanted Major to place the failed ERM arrangements on the agenda of the Amsterdam Summit as a way of provoking debate about the relevance of the Single Currency project (Cash 1996, 1997). The leadership's reply reminding them that EMU was not on the agenda at Amsterdam did nothing to alleviate their anxieties. Neither did claims in a 1996 book by two French journalists, alleging that Ken Clarke had intervened at an ECOFIN meeting in 1993 to plead for action from his fellow Finance Ministers to save the ERM.[4]

By the 1997 election, Clarke had become the chief target of Euro-sceptical grievances and concerns. For a party publicly dismissive of the possibilities that a Single Currency would start on time, ruling out membership for the lifetime of the next parliament seemed a logical extension of policy. That this key Euro-sceptical demand failed to make its way into the 1997 election manifesto was due primarily to Clarke: he was perceived to be holding the party to ransom. At key moments, Euro-sceptics could point to his 'malign' influence over fellow Cabinet Ministers who seemed about to join 'the cause'. In alliance with Heseltine, Clarke made great efforts to kill a story which appeared in the *Sunday Telegraph* in December 1996, claiming that Major had now come out against sterling joining EMU during the next parliament. In February 1997, Foreign Secretary Rifkind's remarks that he was 'hostile' to the Single Currency were explained away as a slip of the tongue. Indeed, when Dorrell accidentally ruled out the pound's membership of the first wave on the Jonathan Dimbleby programme, such was Clarke's apparent presence that the Health Secretary immediately phoned to apologize. These interventions aside, it is important not to forget that Clarke also played a leading role in disciplining the rebels during the 1992–7 parliament. This included supporting the unprecedented move of withdrawing the whip from eight Conservative MPs who voted against the 1995 Finance Bill (Seldon 1997: 507–12, 685–6, 702; *Financial Times* 3 March 1997).

The Folly of 'Tying One's Hands': Governing Incompetence and the ERM Crisis

Faced with the seemingly inexorable 'logic' of Europeanization, Euro-sceptics increasingly cautioned against the disastrous implications for Conservative statecraft. A key event in this context was the party's experience with ERM membership from 1990 to 1992. Although the decision for sterling to join had been taken before the TEU had been negotiated, the Euro-sceptics understood the link between the two to be 'inexorable' (Spicer 1992: 1). As already noted, ERM membership was a central part of Stage One of the EMU process and, therefore, a crucial treaty obligation. More particularly, if Lawson's experiment with shadowing had demonstrated the dangers of self-imposed external constraints in the name of domestic autonomy, Britain's experience in this semi-fixed exchange rate system confirmed the folly of this policy instrument. Thatcher's decision to join the ERM in 1990 had locked

Britain into a Deutschmark zone when the economies of both countries were diverging significantly. The Bundesbank, coping with the inflationary consequences of reunification, sought to raise interest rates throughout the early 1990s. The Treasury, seeking to manage the economy slipping into recession, sought every opportunity to cut them. With German monetary policy increasingly restricting Chancellor Lamont's room for manoeuvre, membership of the ERM came to be held responsible for: a balance of payments deficit which topped £1 billion; an unemployment rate which had reached 2.8 billion; increasing levels of 'negative equity', which were reported to have touched £6 billion. It all made rather a mockery of the leadership's pre-election claims that the economy was experiencing the 'green shoots' of recovery.

The fact that ERM membership had now become a 'virility test' for EMU qualification brought home to the party just how tight the constraints of the system had become. In this sense, it was no good John Smith lambasting Major for not seeking an agreement with Britain's partners for a general realignment of ERM parities (*Hansard* vol. 212, 24 September 1992: cols 16–19). As Stephens has made clear, such a general realignment was never really on. It was true that the devaluation of the lira just before sterling's exit raised the possibility of such a move. However, Trichet, Director General of the French Treasury, ruled the option out, choosing not even to call a meeting of ECOFIN to discuss the situation (Stephens 1996: 236–7; Seldon 1997: 311). Ministers were no more successful in persuading their German counterparts to ease interest rates. Kohl and Waigel were said to respond sympathetically, while maintaining there was little they could do to interfere with the Bundesbank's constitutional right to set monetary policy. That little help was forthcoming from that quarter either seemed to confirm Lawson's earlier expressed doubts concerning the system's currency support mechanisms.

At the same time, a number of domestic policy options suggested by commentators faced obstacles which developed out of the party's own historical experience with economic policy. For example, Stephens and Johnson suggest that one of the biggest mistakes made by the Major government in its handling of ERM membership was not to seek a devaluation of the pound. Instead, the leadership 'boxed itself into a corner' by treating sterling as a 'badge of national pride'. This analysis is shared by Sarah Hogg, one of Major's closest advisers at Number Ten. The most notable misjudgements in this context were the declarations that the devaluation of the pound was a 'soft option' and that 'everything possible' would be done to guarantee its position within the band. By making such public pronouncements, the leaders sealed their own fate by 'nailing themselves to the mast of a sinking ship' (Stephens 1996: 212–14, 219).

The problem with this explanation is that it ignores one consistent theme of British economic policy since 1979 – the search for an anchor or discipline.

As already noted, such a policy instrument offered a way of controlling inflationary forces at the domestic level, while simultaneously restoring credibility in the financial markets. The failure of the Medium Term Financial Strategy, a domestic attempt to operationalize this disciplinarian philosophy, led Lawson to switch to an external discipline by shadowing the Deutschmark. Yet, by the Court's own admission, one of the major reasons for the failure of this policy was that it lacked an explicit exchange rate target which the financial markets could take seriously. Now that the leadership had entered the ERM and, through this, achieved a public target which restored credibility to its economic strategy, it was unlikely that ministers were going to devalue at the first sign of trouble. In this sense, there seems little point in complaining that the Court treated the ERM parity as a badge of national pride. The explicit nature of this policy instrument meant that an investment of public support was both necessary and unavoidable (see also Thompson 1996: 191).

Of course, the explicit and public nature of this fixed exchange rate policy also put the leadership in a vulnerable position if the policy instrument was rendered unworkable by events beyond the control of ministers. Indeed, this was the central point of the Euro-sceptics' case. The opposition was easily able to use these assertions that devaluation was a 'soft option' and that the leadership would do 'everything possible' to defend sterling, to expose the complete nature of the policy failure after Black Wednesday. At the same time, because Major was so closely identified with the policy, Labour and the Liberal Democrats were able to personalize the issue of this defeat. Smith, who had replaced Kinnock after Labour's 1992 election defeat, was particularly cutting during a parliamentary debate just after the September debacle:

> In the course of a few weeks, the one policy with which Mr Major was uniquely and personally associated, the contribution to policy of which he appears to have been most proud, has been blown apart, and with it has gone forever any claim by the Prime Minister or the party that he leads to economic competence. He is the devalued Prime Minister of a devalued Government. (*Hansard* (Commons) vol. 212, 24 September 1992: col. 22)

Or, as Peter Tapsell ruefully remarked later on in the same debate, 'another aspect of fixed currencies that I dislike is that they tend to devalue the reputations of the statesmen who must operate them' (*Hansard* (Commons) vol. 212, 24 September 1992, col. 88).

Furthermore, when it comes to charting the deleterious effect of the Europeanization of policy on domestic statecraft, it is worth remarking that 'Black Wednesday' is increasingly held to be an important factor in contributing to the Conservative election defeat in 1997. For Seldon, this crisis and its aftermath represented a critical juncture at which the support of the Tory press for Major began to decline. Of particular importance to these editors seemed to be the absence of any government apology for 'wasting' billions of taxpayers' money in defending the pound (Seldon 1997: 288–9; 707–13). More generally, 'Black Wednesday' and the detrimental effect it had on the government's reputation for governing competence is now increasingly held to be an important factor in explaining why the 'feelgood factor' failed to materialize for the Conservatives before the election. Research undertaken by Kleinwort Benson and the University of Strathclyde in August 1994 pointed to the problem of 'competence', arguing that what the Conservatives needed was a political and not an economic recovery (*Financial Times* 3 August 1994). More recently, these conclusions have been confirmed by Sanders's attempt to apply aggregative voting models to the 1997 election result (Sanders 1997: 67–8; see also Crewe 1996: 428).

Statecraft, the Parliamentary State and the Limits to Governing Autonomy

If the heart of Europe strategy demonstrated the real dangers of inadvertently (or deliberately) encouraging the Europeanization of British policy in the name of domestic autonomy, Euro-sceptics finally cautioned that this autonomy strategy could be taken too far. The increasingly obvious attempts to hive off responsibility for governance to European institutions would create the effect of an increasingly arrogant, isolated and rather defeatist political class, insensitive to any kind of popular pressure. The reverse side of this process represented the increased emasculation of British parliamentary democracy. Euro-sceptics have always bemoaned the erosion of Parliament's authority as a disastrous development in itself. However, they also intimated that it is the parliamentary nature of the British state which gives any centralized autonomy strategy its legitimacy. To preside over the debilitation of Parliament's authority is to undermine the institutional basis of this traditional mode of British governance.

While it is sometimes argued that Euro-sceptics have become preoccupied with Britain's gradual loss of sovereignty or control over policy, on closer inspection their more detailed arguments often rest squarely on the importance of democracy. Both Spicer (1992) and Portillo (1998) attempt explicit definitions of this concept before discussing its relationship to the increasingly interdependent world they see around them. For both authors, democracy consists of more than the election process. Central to the concept is the notion of accountability. For democracy to exist, the people must feel properly represented in the institutions which govern their lives. Spicer highlights two elements within this notion of accountability: representatives of the people must genuinely be in *authority*, even if they are not in total *control* over policy – ultimately the responsibility is theirs; and the electorate must have the effective sanctions to impose their will if they become unsatisfied with their representatives, i.e. by voting them out of office (Spicer 1992: 105–6; Portillo

1998: 14–15). In operational terms, when Euro-sceptics discuss democracy in the British context, it is Parliament they refer to. Likewise, it is the erosion of parliamentary accountability which most exercises them.

As already suggested, the loss of domestic control (power) over policy which the Europeanization process has compelled is an important concern for Euro-sceptics. However, the above discussion of democracy suggests that the exact relationship with statecraft (governing autonomy) is more subtle. The Euro-sceptics understand that the British Parliament has never played an important policy-influencing role in British politics. That said, it does carry out other important functions. By investigating, discovering and publicizing what the executive is doing, Parliament undertakes an important scrutiny role. At the same time, by providing an important source of information about politics, it helps to concentrate the minds of the electorate on the important issues of the day: it plays a vital educative role. In short, by carrying out these tasks, many people still think that Parliament is or ought to be important. Parliament plays a vital regime support function which helps to legitimize the centralized and autonomous style of government which British politicians have tradition-ally preferred. To undermine Parliament is to threaten the institutional basis of this governing style. Domestic autonomy through the Europeanization of policy can have counter-productive results.

During the Major government, events served to confirm Euro-sceptics' fears on this subject. Take, for example, the ERM crisis described above. What was notable about the debate that followed in the House of Commons was the ill-disguised distaste for the leadership's attempt to off-load responsibility for this failure on to the 'fault-lines' of the system. For example, Budgen wanted to know why, bearing in mind the fact that ERM membership had been discussed exhaustively since the mid-1980s, it had taken Major until Sep-tember 1992 to discover these fault-lines (*Hansard* (Commons) vol. 212, 24 September 1992: col. 6; Spicer 1992: 88–93). A number of other Euro-sceptics refused to condemn Germany for Britain's plight, saying that policy-makers in Bonn were only following their own legitimate national interests (see contributions by Biffen, col. 34; Watts, col. 40; Baker, col. 57; Townend, col. 73). Indeed, this was one of the more interesting aspects of the debate and seemed to cast doubt on the view that Euro-sceptics are little more than narrow-minded chauvinists. In short, Spicer's comments in *A Treaty Too Far* summed up the mood:

> The decision in 1990 by Britain to rejoin the ERM was, indeed not the first time this century that she had tried to defend herself from the possible consequences of wrong decisions by her own politicians by linking herself to those made in another country, through the mecha-nism of a fixed or managed exchange rate. (Spicer 1992: 96)

The previous occasion was, of course, the Gold Standard in 1925.

In this sense, the increasingly authoritarian style of party management experienced by the Euro-sceptics served to underline the leadership's apparent contempt for Westminster. One could point to the growing practice of turning difficult votes into confidence motions. During the November 1992 paving motion on the EC (Amendment) Bill (drawn up to enshrine the TEU in domestic law), this strategy represented little more than carefully planted rumours which eventually had to be withdrawn when the story found its way into the newspapers (Seldon 1997: 339–40). By the Third Reading of the Bill, the threat of a confidence motion became a reality in order for the leadership to escape from a lost vote on its own motion merely to 'note' the Social Chapter. Similar pressures were exerted at the local constituency level by the National Union, with Sir Basil Feldman playing a key role in operations (Baker *et al.* 1993). More generally, there was last minute pleading, cajoling and bullying by whips, which some Euro-sceptics claimed was as tough as anything they had experienced since 1979. Finally, there was the 'unprecedented' action of withdrawing the whip from eight MPs who voted against the government during the passage of the 1995 European Finance Bill (Alderman 1996). As Seldon concludes, 'Never in the twentieth century had as many Conservative MPs received this, the most severe punishment open to the party's discipline machine' (Seldon 1997: 511).

In their more melodramatic moments some Euro-sceptics went further, questioning the future of representative party politics in this environment of ever increasing European integration. As Heathcoat-Amory put it in an article just before the 1997 election:

> If a loss of autonomous monetary policy is followed by a loss of autonomous fiscal policy, what is the function of nationally elected politicians? These powers go to the root of what a parliament is for and their loss must call into question whether such a country is in any real sense self-governing. (Heathcoat-Amory 1996)

Portillo (1998: 17–18) makes the same point in his discussion of the relationship between the Single Currency and democratic values:

> If people feel that in elections they are unable to give their view of economic management through their vote, they will rightly feel that their democracy no longer counts for much. What will be the point of voting for political parties if they are powerless to change policy?

Indeed, far from successfully preserving domestic autonomy and governing competence, Euro-sceptics suggest, further encouraging the Europeanization of British politics will fuel nationalist and xenophobic tendencies in the electorate. National politicians will become little more than 'lightning conductors' for popular frustration and discontent at the remoteness of decision-making. For Chris Gill:

> Stripped of power to influence or decide matters of state, we shall have created the classic recipe for failure: responsibility resting with a body of

people who do not have the authority to discharge that responsibility in full measure. This will result in public disillusionment with politicians and with people's capacity to obtain satisfaction through their elected representatives. In the fullness of time that disillusionment will turn to frustration and anger, which will lead ultimately to the rejection of established political leadership, traditional party loyalties and the whole body politic. (*Hansard* (Commons) vol. 201, 18 December 1991: col. 415)

In the same debate, Toby Jessel had similar concerns:

I recognise that some economic functions have to be pooled, but beyond that, most of the British people do not want any power over, say, Italy or Spain. They certainly do not want the Italians or the Spanish, for example, to share in ruling Britain. . . . I feel that I have no sense of duty, owe no loyalty and have no sense of belonging to any of them. I believe that I speak for the majority of my constituents. (*Hansard* (Commons) vol. 201, 18 December 1991: col. 384)

For Redwood, writing six years later,

the electorates will want to make their views known. In this system [Economic and Monetary Union] there will be no way of letting the pressure out. The valve in the pressure cooker will have been soldered over, and as the temperature rises, as people become more disenchanted with the economic and monetary policy being pursued, the pressure will build up. (Redwood 1997: 187)

On the malign effect of EMU, the last and most apocalyptic word goes to Tebbit:

It would both bring about the resentments which are already fuelling the march of the Nazis and neo-Nazis in Germany, the National Front in France, the Lombardy Front, the Ulaams Blok and others. These forces will be unleashed and will destroy the European Community. (*Hansard* (Commons) vol. 201, 18 December 1991: cols 326–7)

Conclusions

To explain the behaviour of the Conservative Euro-sceptics in these terms does not mean having to gloss over the glaring gaps and contradictions in their arguments. In a new global era of powerful multinationals and financial speculative flows, such concern for the much derided institution of Parliament might seem abstruse, even frivolous. Arguably, it borders on the hypocritical if one remembers that these 'born again' Euro-sceptics were once Cabinet ministers in the Thatcher government and happily presided over the executive domination of British Parliament with few qualms. That said, the above discussion suggests that Euro-sceptics still have important points to make. Despite being much maligned, parliamentarianism has historically existed as the bedrock of the British political tradition. Primarily, it is this institution which has served to integrate different regions, groups and classes into the British polity, thus legitimizing this institutional set-up (for better or worse). If parliamentarianism is of little consequence, or is perceived to be of little consequence, in these new global conditions of the 1990s, then the disruptive effects on the present British political system are likely to be serious. Those who work for the increased Europeanization of British politics must acknowledge and face up to this fact. Assuming that popular representation, participation and accountability are still deemed to be desirable principles on which our system of government should rest, Euro-enthusiasts should pay more attention to the question of how they are going to fill this democratic deficit. The solutions are by no means simple or straightforward.

Notes

1. The Treaty on European Union contained five criteria for convergence: a country's planned or actual government deficit to GDP should not exceed 3 per cent at market prices; the ratio of a government's debt to GDP should not exceed 60 per cent at market prices; a country or member state should have an average rate of inflation which does not exceed by more than 1.5 per cent that of the three best performing countries; a member state should respect the normal fluctuation margins of the ERM for at least two years without severe 'tensions' and should not devalue its currency's bilateral central rate during that period; and member states should have an average nominal long-term interest rate which does not exceed by more than two percentage points that of the three best performing countries (TEU 1992: 185–6).
2. If this method was deemed unworkable, decision-making would revert to the normal procedures stipulated by the Treaty of Rome.
3. The details of ERM2, agreed at the Dublin European Council in December 1996, and governing relations between those countries joining the Single Currency and those remaining outside, would seem to confirm this view. For outsiders, membership of the ERM would not be compulsory, although countries would be expected to join. Indeed, Britain's membership of ERM as a prerequisite for Single Currency membership has become a matter of some debate at present (see, for example, the *Financial Times*).
4. See E. Aeschimann and P. Riche, *La Guerre de Sept Ans*, quoted in the *Sunday Telegraph*, 22 October 1996.

CHAPTER EIGHT

Conclusions

This book began by highlighting a number of questions surrounding Britain's relations with the European Union. In signing the Single European Act, why were the Conservatives content to give away partial control over many aspects of supply-side policy by accepting the extension of qualified majority voting on issues pertaining to the completion of the Single Market? In shadowing the Deutschmark and then joining the Exchange Rate Mechanism in 1990, why did the party accept further constraints on the formulation of macroeconomic policy? Indeed, why after the disaster of Black Wednesday did the Major government ratify the Treaty on European Union, including a commitment to complete Stages One and Two of the Single Currency? Finally, why did the Conservatives, one of the most successful political parties in the twentieth century, eventually tear itself apart over the European question? In short, how can we explain the Conservatives' acceptance of the Europeanization of economic policy in the 1980s, yet at the same time account for the party's electoral suicide over this issue in the 1990s?

Applied to these questions, the Statecraft approach has generated the following conclusions. Chapter 2 began by charting the historical development of the Court's governing code before 1961. It concluded that British public policy-makers have always understood the governing advantages of placing external constraints on their own control over economic policy. Neo-classical economics proved attractive to the Court, partly because of the perceived verities of these ideas and partly because the stress on sound money, free markets and the external discipline of the Gold Standard yielded a relatively neutral and automatic economic policy framework which minimized relations with societal groups. As a result, the Court's autonomy and governing competence was preserved. At the same time, it was noted that this 'governing orientation' was heavily influenced by structural constraints surrounding these policy-makers. The international orientation of British capital, the open nature of the British economy and the tradition of voluntarism in industrial relations meant that the Court often saw itself as having few alternative governing choices.

Understood in this way, the role of external policy before EU membership was to complement or 'support' these domestic governing principles. In general, this meant constantly promoting the link between any problems in the supply side of the British economy and external market solutions. In specific policy terms, the Empire had always represented an external market 'solution' to domestic problems of unemployment. However, on occasions, usually after the impact of 'shocks' from the international system (either real or perceived), the Court found itself having to appropriate external structures to support its domestic concerns. During the inter-war period, it attempted to reinforce British access to imperial markets by creating the Overseas Sterling Area. However, in the 1960s, with the shock of Britain's relative economic decline and the politicization of more discretionary methods of economic management, EU membership came to be perceived as an alternative: one external support structure for another. Indeed, it sometimes seemed that the EU represented less of an external support and more of an external 'escape route' to domestic autonomy and governing competence. Evidence suggests that part of the attraction of membership for the Court was that this 'Common Market' offered a sort of automatic, neutral 'invisible hand' which would 'sift through' and solve Britain's economic problems.

If the Court had continually understood that its autonomy concerns could be supported by external structures before 1979, it was not clear that these lessons were passed on to the Thatcher government. As Chapter 3 showed, 'New Conservatism', with its emphasis on sound money and free markets, could certainly be interpreted as a return to the old governing code of the inter-war period, particularly after the party's unsatisfactory experience with 'Tripartite' policy instruments in the 1970s. Ministers were attracted to these economic ideas because they reasserted the importance of a neutral, automatic, economic framework for economic management. However, this was to be a domestic-based experiment, designed with little thought paid to the potential impact of international economic forces. Certainly, there was no notion of the EU playing a supporting role to these domestic concerns: Europeans, like other 'foreigners', were there to be 'handbagged', as the protracted dispute over Britain's budgetary contributions indicated.

However, by 1984, international economic forces were increasingly perceived to be undermining monetarism in one country, leading the Court to cast around for alternative policy instruments as a route to domestic autonomy and governing competence. In the light of these implementation problems, Chapter 4 charted the Court's gradual acceptance of the Europeanization of economic policy. The SEA, with its commitment to complete the Single Market by 1992, offered a solution to the concerns of some in the leadership about the need to entrench its free-market supply-side strategy in the face of persistent unemployment problems. Just as important was the fact that this initiative helped to maintain the unity of the Court in the face of tensions over the future of its European strategy. The source of such strain could be found in the fact that increased numbers within the Conservative leadership were also becoming attracted to the Europeanization of monetary policy: ERM membership represented a possible external disciplinarian framework which could replace the discredited Medium Term Financial Strategy as a route to domestic governing autonomy.

Chapter 5 charted the Court's experience of negotiating the SEA in the mid-1980s. Despite beginning from an isolated and unpopular position, the discussion showed, the Court was willing to introduce initiatives, build alliances with other member states and accept concessions where circumstances dictated. Moreover, a superficial survey of the Act's contents indicated the relative success of this strategy. The Single Market programme became the centrepiece of the negotiations, while proposals for European Political Cooperation were heavily influenced by Howe's earlier plan on the subject. Despite this success, the main message of this chapter was to highlight the real constraints facing the Court at the EU level. Actual attempts at alliance-building were unsuccessful, while the importance of supranationality as a principle underlying the creation of the Union meant that some semblance of institutional reform would have to be accepted. Of course, such reform could generate unintended consequences for those involved in the redesign of these institutions.

Chapter 6 began by describing how these institutional constraints tightened considerably during the late 1980s. Economic and geo-political movements in the international system combined to set off and lock in pressure for further integration at the EU level. At the heart of this changed external context was a new agreement to work for EMU as a way of containing the new Germany which had been reunited after the fall of the Berlin Wall. The discussion then moved to the question of why the Court, under Thatcher's leadership, collapsed in the late 1980s, and how these European developments were related. It concluded that differing perceptions about the implications of these structural movements fed into and crystallized the already nascent divisions within the leadership concerning the desirability of Europeanizing its statecraft strategy. For Euro-enthusiasts, this pressure for further European integration confirmed the logic of Europeanization: only by working at the heart of Europe would British diplomats stand any realistic chance of frustrating the worst manifestations of this momentum. Euro-sceptics reached the opposite conclusions. The possibilities for creative diplomacy within these tight constraints were increasingly disappearing. The heart of Europe strategy led to only one destination: increasing governing pain on the Euro-ratchet.

Chapter 7 concluded by analysing the electoral suicide of the Conservative Party. More particularly, it focused on the recalcitrant behaviour of the Euro-sceptics in the 1990s. The central argument here was that this group became the self-appointed guardians of Thatcher's statecraft legacy in the context of what they perceived to be the inexorable threat of Europeanization. To persist with an autonomy strategy through the self-imposition of these European constraints held potentially disastrous consequences. The EU was not just another international organization like NATO or GATT, whose membership entailed obligations but whose penetrative capacities were largely *ad hoc* and discrete. It was increasingly a super-state in the making. It had its own body of law and institutions with the power to protect these legislative achievements. The supremacy of EU regulations and directives over national statute law meant that its penetrative capacities were continual and explicit. The Europeanization of policy risked creating a governing class that would be viewed as even more arrogant, isolated and defeatist than it already was. Respect for national institutions would decline even further from their already low point. Autonomy could be taken too far.

What insights has the Statecraft approach provided when it comes to understanding Britain's relations with the EU? In conclusion, six can be stated briefly. First, in a book concerned to investigate the domestic sources of Europeanization, Statecraft has highlighted the fact that this process can partly be explained as the product of a conscious governing strategy. This is not to suggest that Europeanization represents the outcome of a premeditated choice by an elite group, largely in control of its domestic and external environment. Instead, the origins of this strategy are better viewed as a reactive series of manoeuvres in response to a growing sense of crisis within British politics in the 1960s. Moreover, the intensification of this process in the 1980s was largely the result of a number of tensions within the Court and perceived problems with its statecraft strategy. In other words, while Europeanization has taken place, it has not been accompanied by the grand pro-European rhetoric sometimes observed in other European countries. The British style has been to 'back into the process by stealth', sometimes presenting the decision as an inevitable *fait accompli*.

Second, if the Europeanization of British economic policy reflects the outcome of an elite governing strategy, this interpretation throws up interesting questions concerning the extent of change represented by this process. Not surprisingly, it confirms Bulmer and Burch's (1998) observation that a significant shift has taken place in terms of policy. However, from this Statecraft perspective, the issue of change is more complicated. As already noted, change at the policy level can often play a supporting role to cruder governing objectives. Put in different terms, while Conservative ministers presided over the Europeanization of economic policy in the 1980s and the 1990s, motives for this action show a continuity of thinking which can be traced back to the inter-war period, if not before. Perhaps the key theme here is the perceived governing advantages of neo-liberal economics. The promotion of the verities of 'sound' money, stable inflation and free markets has historically helped to preserve the Court's autonomy by minimizing responsibility for economic management. Historically, by stressing the importance of imperial markets and the external value of sterling in maintaining this policy framework, these same decision-makers were able to further embed these ideas within the structure of the British Polity. In this context, membership of the EU after 1960, with its stress on the economic advantages of the Common Market, played a similar role. Moreover, the goal of the Single Market, and eventual membership of the ERM, was supposed to further entrench a return to neo-liberalism and the old governing benefits that this doctrine conferred. This point demonstrates the real conservatism of the Conservative regime after 1979.

Third, if Europeanization can be partly explained as a conscious governing strategy, this book has helped to show that Statecraft need not neglect the ontological importance of structures, even if analytical primacy is given to the question of how politicians govern within them. Indeed, this study has highlighted how certain aspects of Britain's *economic* institutions have *facilitated* this process of Europeanization. This point is significant, if only because the continuity of Britain's *political* structures is often viewed as *constraining* the possibilities for policy change in this area. We have already noted how, historically, the openness of the British economy and the voluntarist tradition in industrial relations helped to complicate the task of designing domestic policy instruments for dealing with supply-side problems. However, developments in the international economy in the 1970s and the 1980s increased the burden on macroeconomic management; most notably the difficulty of finding a reliable relationship between the level of money supply and inflation. Two were particularly important from the perspective of Whitehall: the increased importance of capital flows, as evidenced by the growth of the Eurodollar market; and the spread of ('dirty') floating exchange rate regimes after the collapse of Bretton Woods. Of course, it is important not to exaggerate the causal power of these structural factors. Moreover, as Chapter 3 noted, the Conservatives contributed significantly to this problem through their programme of deregulating British financial markets. That said, these developments still provided a powerful contribution to momentum behind the Europeanization of economic policy.

Fourth, this book has helped to develop an understanding of 'governing culture' in this particular area. More specifically, it has helped to clarify the role of autonomy, by showing how this quality is related to a number of other principles in the area of British political economy. Historically, such space and freedom has been predicated on an economic framework which has promoted the importance of published rules. Examples covered in this book include the Gold Standard in the early years of the twentieth century, the Medium Term Financial Strategy and the ERM. These rule-based frameworks provided a discipline or anchor which helped to ensure that economic policy was not blown off course by the arbitrary demands of societal groups. In addition, two other principles seemed to have been important in protecting this rule-based autonomy. First, any economic framework should be *neutral*: that is, it should appear to apply equally to as many groups as possible. Second, in the event of adjustments to policy, these should take place as *automatically* as possible, with little need for political interference. Hence the attraction of a policy which stressed the importance of free markets. Automatism and neutrality guard against the impression of a governing regime which is arbitrary and discriminatory. Such perceptions could lead to the politicization of governance and a loss of domestic autonomy and competence.

As already noted, the role of external policy was to support these governing principles. Indeed, it was divisions within the party concerning whether the EU should play such a support role which contributed to the electoral decline of the Conservatives in the 1990s. However, one issue that needs further attention is the attitude of Thatcher and her Euro-sceptical followers. As a champion of monetarism, she certainly presided over the resurrection of an autonomy code, which stressed the importance of domestic rules in economic policy. Moreover, she would have understood the argument, often put to her, that the ERM and the Single Currency provided even better rule-based frameworks for autonomy because they were further removed from British politics. Of course, part of her opposition lay in arguments about the economic consequences of the policy. But, as already noted, there were never any clear-cut answers to this question. Economic reasoning could be found to justify almost any course of action.

In this context, it was concerns about the governing consequences of Europeanization, as much as anything else, which went to the heart of the Euro-sceptic case. Europeanization threatened the institutional (indeed, the normative) basis of elite rule in Britain. Abolishing sterling would further expose the impotence of Westminster, exacerbating the air of cynicism that surrounded the activities of those who worked there. To the extent that this political class retained a function, it would be as a 'lightning conductor' for all manner of criticism, without the requisite powers of defence against this disquiet. Of course, an underlying theme running through this book is how Thatcher and her followers lost the argument to those who were rather more pessimistic concerning the possibilities for governance in the UK. For this group, statecraft was best practised when politics as well as economics was run on 'auto-pilot'.

Fifth, if this interpretation contains any plausibility, future accounts of Britain's relations with the EU need to guard against the sort of 'false particularism' which sometimes informs our understanding of this topic. As noted at the start of Chapter 1, Britain is popularly viewed as an 'awkward' or 'semi-detached' partner in Europe. Yet the argument presented here casts doubt on the wisdom of treating Britain as a 'special case' in this context. One of the most interesting features of British politics in recent decades is how national politicians seem to have lost confidence in their own abilities to govern Britain. Perhaps this trend is partly the result of Britain's national obsession with its own record of relative economic decline. As noted above, it certainly reflects a feeling of uncertainty and perplexity concerning the possibilities for national action in this new era of globalization. In response, British policy-makers are reacting in similar ways to their European colleagues. They accept the logic of 'tying one's hands' with European binds (Giavazzi and Pagano 1988): not with as much rhetorical enthusiasm and gusto, but it is acceptance all the same. Whitehall increasingly worships the 'cult of the central banker' (for an interesting discussion, see Luttwak, 1997). With its decision to give operational independence to the Bank of England to set interest rates, New Labour represents the most recent convert to this cause (see, for example, George and Rosamond 1992: 181–2; Radice 1992: Chapter 7; Anderson and Mann 1997: 70; Buller 2000b). Only those who remain fixated with the dominant personality and impact of Mrs Thatcher could have failed to notice this trend.

The sixth conclusion concerns the issue of practising political science. As noted, this book represents an interpretation of one aspect of Britain's relations with the EU and nothing more. It was certainly intended to be a theoretically informed narrative: indeed, many of the assumptions underlying the Statecraft thesis were laid out explicitly in Chapter 1. Moreover, like many academics, this author brought a number of normative biases to the study of this subject. While every effort was made to account for these, no doubt their influence can be detected in the analysis above. Put in different terms, when it comes to studying Britain's relations with the EU, scholars cannot pretend to insulate themselves from the broader discursive battles going on in the real world over this issue. Nor should they try to. There is, of course, nothing novel or surprising in this statement.

What this point does highlight is the limits of empiricism as an epistemological position. If what is to count as knowledge is empirical and based on sensory, observable experience, and theory is something which explains this empirical material when tested against it, it follows that it must always be possible to make a distinction between theory and observable facts. Yet 'experience' refers not only to the 'end product' which we recognize, but also to the actual *process* of the experiencing. To describe what we see, we must apply concepts to order the information we receive. This process involves an *a priori* choice, with different concepts deemed appropriate for different sensory experiences. Likewise, theories in political science will always be informed by a number of untestable assumptions and underlying positions which will guide their users down particular avenues of inquiry, thus helping them to cope with the mass of contradictory and *ad hoc* material they are likely to uncover (Bulpitt 1986: 20; Hollis 1994: 70–1). This issue becomes even more important when we recognize that researchers are often observing agents whose own perceptions of reality will influence political outcomes. This 'double hermeneutic' shows up the poverty of empiricism, while highlighting the acute difficulties in doing political science (see Clegg 1989: 129–48). In short, 'the facts' never speak for themselves. Theory will always be relevant to good stories about Britain's relations with the EU, or any other subject for that matter.

To highlight this issue is not to sanction a slide into relativism. While academics should not be unduly preoccupied about empiricism, this does not mean they should be able to get away with saying anything about anything. The problem remains: if we reject empiricism as a valid test of a theory, how can we subject rival interpretations to critical scrutiny? On what grounds can we talk about some narratives being better or more useful for ordering our knowledge about a particular subject area? Bevir (1994) and Rhodes (1997: 7–8) suggest a number of ways in which knowledge claims of theories can be confirmed. First, the concepts and assumptions underpinning an interpretation should be meaningful to the practitioners engaged in translating them for the purposes of fieldwork. Second, the interpretation must be logical and consistent with the data uncovered. Finally, the interpretation should be open and subject to serious criticism. It should create new lines of inquiry rather than blocking off existing avenues of investigation. Although these criteria pose problems (see Buller 2000a), they provide an important start in establishing how we might go about evaluating differing theories in a post-positivist world. Hopefully, the interpretation provided in this book will be deemed satisfactory when judged against these benchmarks.

Bibliography

Government and Parliamentary Publications

Cmnd 9725 (1956) *The Economic Implications of Full Employment*. London: HMSO.

HMG (1962) *Britain and the European Communities: Background the Negotiations*. London: HMSO.

Cmnd 3301 (1967) *Legal and Constitutional Implications of UK Membership of the European Communities*. London: HMSO.

Cmnd 3345 (1967) *The United Kingdom and the European Communities*. London: HMSO.

Cmnd 4289 (1970) *Britain and the European Communities: An Economic Assessment*. London: HMSO.

Cmnd 4715 (1971) *The United Kingdom and the European Communities*. London: HMSO.

HL 39 (1983) *Select Committee on the European Communities, Fifth Report on the European Monetary System*. London: HMSO.

HL 226 (1985) *Fourteenth Report of the House of Lords Select Committee on the European Communities: European Union*. London: HMSO.

HC 21 (1983) *International Monetary Arrangements. Treasury and Civil Service Select Committee, Fourth Report* (4 vols). London: HMSO.

HC 57II (1985) *Thirteenth Report from the Treasury and Civil Service Select Committee, the Financial and Economic Consequences of UK Membership of the European Communities: the European Monetary System, Vol. One*. London: HMSO.

Cm. 3181 (1996) *A Partnership of Nations: The British Approach to the European Union Intergovernmental Conference 1996*. London: HMSO.

Books and Articles

Abercrombie, N., Hill, S. and Turner, B. S. (1994) *The Penguin Dictionary of Sociology*. London: Penguin.

Alderman, K. (1996) 'The passage of the European Communities (Finance) Act (1995) and its aftermath'. *Contemporary Record*, 10(3), 1–20.

Almond, G. (1988) 'The return to the state'. *American Political Science Review*, 82(3), 853–73.

Alt, J. (1987) 'Crude politics: oil and the political economy of unemployment in Britain and Norway, 1970–85'. *British Journal of Political Science*, 17(2), 149–99.

Anderson, P. and Mann, N. (1997) *Safety First: The Making of New Labour*. London: Fontana.

Andrews, D. (1993) 'The global origins of the Maastricht Treaty on EMU: closing the window of opportunity'. In A. W. Cafruny and G. G. Rosenthal (eds), *The State of the European Community Vol. Two: Maastricht Debates and Beyond*. Harlow: Longman.

Archer, M. S. (1995) *Realist Social Theory: The Morphogenetic Approach*. Cambridge: Cambridge University Press.

Ardagh, J. (1984) 'Europe's soured ideal'. *The Times*, 25 March.

Armstrong, K. and Bulmer, S. (1996) 'United Kingdom'. In D. Rometsch and W. Wessels (eds), *The European Union and Member States: Towards Institutional Fusion*. Manchester: Manchester University Press.

Ashford, N. (1980) 'The European Economic Community'. In Z. Layton-Henry (ed.), *Conservative Party Politics*. Basingstoke: Macmillan.

Ashford, N. (1992) 'The political parties'. In S. George (ed.), *Britain and the European Community*. Oxford: Clarendon Press.

Aughey, A. (1978) *Conservative Party Attitudes towards the Common Market*. Hull: Hull Papers in Politics.

Baker, D., Gamble, A. and Ludlam, S. (1993) 'Whips or scorpions? Conservative MPs and the Maastricht Paving Motion vote'. *Parliamentary Affairs*, 46(2), 151–66.

Baker, D., Gamble, A. and Ludlam, S. (1994) 'The parliamentary siege of Maastricht 1993: Conservative divisions and British ratification'. *Parliamentary Affairs*, 47(1), 37–60.

Baker, D., Fountain, I., Gamble, A. and Ludlam, S. (1995) 'Backbench Conservative attitudes to Europe'. *Political Quarterly*, 66(2), 221–33.

Baldwin-Edwards, M. (1991) 'Immigration after 1992'. *Policy and Politics*, 19(3), 199–212.

Bale, T. and Buller, J. (1996) 'Casting doubt on the new consensus; Conservatives, Labour and the Social Chapter'. *Review of Policy Issues*, 2(1), 59–80.

Banchoff, T. (1997) 'German policy towards the European Union: the effects of historical memory'. *German Politics*, 6(1), 60–76.

Baun, M. J. (1995/6) 'The Maastricht Treaty as high politics: Germany, France and European integration'. *Political Science Quarterly*, 110(4), 605–24.

Behrens, R. (1980) *The Conservative Party from Heath to Thatcher*. Farnborough: Saxon.

Benn, S. I. (1955) 'The uses of sovereignty'. *Political Studies*, 3(2), 109–22.

Benn, T. (1974) 'The Common Market: loss of self-government'. In M. Holmes (ed.), *The Euro-sceptical Reader*. Basingstoke: Macmillan.

Benn, T. (1989) *Against the Tide: Diaries, 1973–76*. London: Hutchinson.

Berrington, H. and Hague, R. (1998) 'Europe, Thatcherism and traditionalism: opinion, rebellion and the Maastricht Treaty in the backbench Conservative Party, 1992–1994'. *West European Politics*, 21(1), 44–71.

Bevir, M. (1994) 'Objectivity in history'. *History and Theory*, 33, 328–44.

Bilski, R. (1977) 'The Common Market and the growing strength of Labour's Left Wing'. *Government and Opposition*, 12, 306–31.

Bruges Group (1990) *Shared Thoughts, Shared Values: Occasional Paper 11*. London: The Bruges Group.

Buchan, D. and Colchester, N. (1990) *Europe Relaunched: Truths and Illusions on the Way to 1992*. London: Hutchinson.

Budd, A. (1978) *The Politics of Economic Planning*. London: Fontana.

Buller, J. (1995) 'Britain as an awkward partner: reassessing Britain's relations with the EU'. *Politics*, 15(1), 33–42.

Buller, J. (1996) 'Foreign and defence policy'. In S. Ludlam and M. J. Smith (eds), *Contemporary British Conservatism*. London: Macmillan.

Buller, J. (1998) 'Britain as an awkward partner in the European Union (EU): a critical assessment of new institutionalism'. Paper presented to the Political Studies Association, University of Keele, April.

Buller, J. (2000a) 'A critical appraisal of the statecraft interpretation'. *Public Administration*, 77(4), 691–712.

Buller, J. (2000b) 'External support structures and domestic politics: New Labour's foreign and defence policy'. In S. Ludlam and M. J. Smith (eds), *New Labour in Office: New Ideology, New Party, New Policies?* London: Macmillan.

Bulmer, S. (1992) 'Britain and European integration: of sovereignty, slow adaptation and semi-detachment'. In S. George (ed.), *Britain and the European Community*. Oxford: Clarendon Press.

Bulmer, S. and Burch, M. (1998) 'Organising for Europe: Whitehall, the British State and the European Union'. *Public Administration*, 76 (Winter).

Bulmer, S., Jeffrey, C. and Paterson, W. (1996) 'Germany's European diplomacy: shaping the regional milieu'. Paper for the Forschungsgruppe Europa of the Centrum für Angewandte Politikforschung, Munich.

Bulmer, S. and Paterson, W. (1987) *The Federal Republic of Germany and the European Community*. London: Allen and Unwin.

Bulpitt, J. (1982) 'Conservatism, Unionism and the problem of territorial management'. In P. Madgwick and R. Rose (eds), *The Territorial Dimension in United Kingdom Politics*. Basingstoke: Macmillan.

Bulpitt, J. (1983) *Territory and Power in the United Kingdom*. Manchester: Manchester University Press.

Bulpitt, J. (1986) 'The discipline of the new democracy: Mrs Thatcher's domestic statecraft'. *Political Studies*, 34(1), 19–39.

Bulpitt, J. (1988) 'Rational politicians and Conservative statecraft in the open polity'. In P. Byrd (ed.), *British Foreign Policy Under Thatcher*. Deddington: Philip Allan.

Bulpitt, J. (1992) 'Conservative leaders and the Euro-ratchet: five doses of scepticism'. *Political Quarterly*, 63(3), 258–75.

Bulpitt, J. (1995) 'Historical politics: macro, in-time, governing regime analysis'. In J. Lovenduski and J. Stanyer (eds), *Contemporary Political Studies 1995, Vol. Two*. Belfast: Political Studies Association.

Bulpitt, J. (1996) 'The European question'. In D. Marquand and A. Seldon (eds), *The Ideas that Shaped Post-war Britain*. London: Fontana.

Burgess, M. (1989) *Federalism and European Union*. London: Routledge.

Butler, D. and Kavanagh, D. (1984) *The British General Election of 1983*. Basingstoke: Macmillan.

Cafruny, A. W. and Rosenthal, G. G. (eds) (1993) *The State of the European Community, Vol. 2: Maastricht Debates and Beyond*. Harlow: Longman.

Cain, P. and Hopkins, A. (1993) *British Imperialism: Crisis and Deconstruction, 1914–1990*. London: Longman.

Camilleri, J. A. and Falk, J. (1992) *The End of Sovereignty?* Aldershot: Edward Elgar.

Campbell, J. (1993) *Edward Heath: A Biography*. London: Pimlico.

Camps, M. (1963) *Britain and the European Community*. Oxford: Oxford University Press.

Capie, F. (1983) *Depression and Protectionism: Britain between the Wars*. London: George Allen and Unwin.

Carmichael, P. (1996) 'The changing territorial operating code of the United Kingdom: evidence from Northern Ireland'. *Public Administration*, 74(Autumn), 413–33.

Cash, B. (1997) 'Renegotiation is the only answer', *European Journal*, April, 2.

Cash, W. (1986) 'Warding off the EEC steamroller'. *The Times*, 16 June.

Cash, W. (1991) *Against a Federal Europe*. London: Duckworth.

Cash, W. (1996) 'A response to the government's White Paper'. *European Journal*, 3(6), 3–10.

Castle, B. (1980) *The Castle Diaries, 1974–76*. London: Weidenfeld and Nicolson.

Castle, B. (1983) 'Figuring out the facts'. *The Times*, 6 June.

Castle, B. (1984) *The Castle Diaries, 1964–70*. London: Weidenfeld and Nicolson.

Cerny, P. (1996) 'Globalisation and other stories: the search for a new paradigm for international relations'. *International Journal*, 4(Autumn), 617–37.

Clegg, S. (1989) *Frameworks of Power*. London: Sage.

Cockfield, Lord (1994) *The European Union: Creating the Single Market*. London: Wiley Chancery Law.

Cohen, C. D. (1983) 'Growth, stability and employment'. In C.D. Cohen (ed.), *The Common Market: Ten Years After*. Deddington: Philip Allan.

Cole, A. (1994) *François Mitterrand: A Study in Political Leadership*. London: Routledge.

Conservative Central Office (1977) *The Right Approach to the Economy*. London: CCO.

Conservative Central Office (1989) *Leading Europe into the 1990s: The Conservative Manifesto for Europe 1989*. London: CCO.

Conservative Central Office (1997) *You Can Only Be Sure with the Conservatives*. London: CCO.

Conservative Research Department (1979) *Campaign Guide for Europe 1979*. London: Conservative Central Office.

Conservative Research Department/European Democratic Group Secretariat (1984) *Handbook for Europe 1984*. London: Conservative Central Office.

Contemporary Record (1990) Symposium: Conservative Party Policy-Making, 1965–70. 3(4).

Corbett, R. (1987) 'The 1985 Intergovernmental Conference and the Single European Act'. In R. Pryce (ed.), *The Dynamics of European Union*. London: Croom Helm.

Cosgrave, P. (1989) *The Lives of Enoch Powell*. London: The Bodley Head.

Crewe, I. (1996) '1979–96'. In A. Seldon (ed.), *How Tory Governments Fall: The Tory Party in Power Since 1783*. London: Fontana.

Crossman, R. H. S. (1963) 'British Labour Looks at Europe'. *Foreign Affairs* 41(4), 732–43.

Crossman, R. H. S. (1975) *The Diaries of a Cabinet Minister: Vol. 1, Minister of Housing, 1964–66*. London: Hamish Hamilton.

Crossman, R. H. S. (1976) *The Diaries of a Cabinet Minister: Vol. 2, Lord President of the Council and Leader of the House of Commons, 1966–68*. London: Hamish Hamilton.

Crouch, C. and Marquand, D. (1989) *The New Centralism: Britain out of Step in Europe?* Oxford: Basil Blackwell.

Cutler, T., Haslam, C., Williams, J. and Williams, K. (1989) *1992: The Struggle for Europe*. Oxford: Berg.

Davis, E., Geroski, P. A. and Kay, J. A. (1989) *1992: Myths and Realities*. London: London Business School.

Davidson, I. (1997) 'Lunatic instability'. *Financial Times*, 11 June.

De La Serre, F. and Lequesne, C. (1993) 'France and the European Union'. In A. W. Cafruny and G. G. Rosenthal (eds), *The State of the European Community, Vol. 2: Maastricht Debates and Beyond*. Harlow: Longman.

Denman, R. (1996) *Missed Chances: Britain and Europe in the Twentieth Century*. London: Cassell.

Dessler, D. (1989) 'What's at stake in the agent–structure debate?' *International Organisation*, 43(3), 441–73.

Dinan, D. (1994) *Ever Closer Union?* Basingstoke: Macmillan.

Donoughue, B. (1987) *Prime Minister*. London: Jonathan Cape.

Drucker, P. (1986) 'The changed world economy'. *Foreign Affairs*, 64(4), 768–91.

Dudley, J. (1990) *1992: Strategies for the Single Market*, 2nd edn. London: Kogan Page.

Dunleavy, P. and O'Leary, B. (1987) *Theories of the State*. Basingstoke: Macmillan.

Dyson, K. (1994) *Elusive Union: The Process of Economic and Monetary Union*. London: Longman.

Dyson, K. and Featherstone, K. (1996) '*Britain and the re-launch of EMU: just say no?*' Paper delivered to the Political Studies Association Conference, University of Glasgow, 10–12 April.

Edwards, G. (1992) 'Central government'. In S. George (ed.), *Britain and the European Community: The Politics of Semi-Detachment*. Oxford: Clarendon Press.

Edwards, G. (1997) 'The potential and limits of the CFSP: the Yugoslav example'. In E. Regelsberger, P. de Schoutheete de Tervarent and W. Wessels (eds), *Foreign Policy of the European Union*. London: Lynne Rienner.

Emerson, M. *et al.* (1988) *The Economics of 1992: the EC Commission's Assessment of the Economic Effects of Completing the Internal Market*. Oxford: Oxford University Press.

European Foundation (1994) *The Bournemouth Speeches*. London: The European Foundation.

Franklin, M., Marsh, M. and McLaren, L. (1994) 'Uncorking the bottle: popular opposition to European unification in the wake of Maastricht'. *Journal of Common Market Studies*, 32(4), 455–72.

Frey, F. (1985) 'The problem of actor designation in political analysis'. *Comparative Politics*, 17(2), 127–52.

Friedman, M. (1953) *Essays in Positive Economics*. Chicago: University of Chicago Press.

Forster, A. (1999) *Britain and the Maastricht Negotiations*. Basingstoke: Macmillan.

Gamble, A. (1994) *Britain in Decline*, 4th edn. London: Macmillan.

Garel-Jones, T. (1993) 'The UK presidency: an inside view'. *Journal of Common Market Studies*, 31(2), 261–7.

Garry, J. (1995) 'The British Conservative Party: divisions over European policy'. *West European Politics*, 18(4), 170–189.

Gaventa, J. P. (1980) *Power and Powerlessness: Quiescence and Rebellion in an Appalachian Valley*. Urbana: University of Illinois Press.

George, A. (1969) 'The operational code: a neglected approach to the study of political leaders and decision-making'. *International Studies Quarterly*, 13(2), 190–221.

George, S. (ed.) (1992) *Britain and the European Community*. Oxford: Clarendon Press.

George, S. (1993) 'The British government and the Maastricht Agreements'. In A. W. Cafruny and G. G. Rosenthal (eds), *The State of the European Community, Vol. 2: Maastricht Debates and Beyond*. Harlow: Longman.

George, S. (1994) *An Awkward Partner*. Oxford: Oxford University Press.

George, S. (1995) 'A reply to Buller'. *Politics*, 15(1), 43–7.

George, S. and Rosamond, B. (1992) 'The European Community'. In M. J. Smith and J. Spear (eds), *The Changing Labour Party*. London: Routledge.

George, S. and Sowemimo, M. (1995) 'Conservative foreign policy towards the European Union'. In S. Ludlam and M. J. Smith (eds), *Contemporary British Conservatism*. London: Macmillan.

Giavazzi, F. and Pagano, M. (1988) 'The advantage of tying one's hands: EMS discipline and central bank credibility'. *European Economic Review*, 32, 1055–82.

Giddens, A. (1979) *Central Problems in Social Theory*. Basingstoke: Macmillan.

Gilmour, I. (1977) *Inside Right: A Study of Conservatism*. London: Hutchinson.

Gilmour, I. (1992) *Dancing with Dogma*. London: Simon and Schuster.

Gilpin, R. (1987) *The Political Economy of International Relations*. Princeton: Princeton University Press.

Grahl, J. (1997) *After Maastricht: A Guide to European Monetary Union*. London: Lawrence and Wishart.

Grahl, J. and Teague, P. (1990) *1992: The Big Market. The Future of the European Community*. London: Lawrence and Wishart.

Grant, C. (1994) *Delors: Inside the House that Jacques Built*. London: Nicholas Brearley.

Grant, W. (1997) 'BSE and the politics of food'. In P. Dunleavy *et al.* (eds), *Developments in British Politics 5*. Basingstoke: Macmillan.

Gregory, F. E. C. (1983) *Dilemmas of Government: Britain and the EC*. Oxford: Robertson.

Greico, J. M. (1996) 'State interests and institutional rule trajectories: a neorealist interpretation of the Maastricht Treaty and European Economic and Monetary Union'. *Security Studies*, 5(3), 261–308.

Gross, D. and Thygesen, N. (1998) *European Monetary Integration*, 2nd edn. London: Longman.

Guzzini, S. (1993) 'Structural power: the limits of neorealist power analysis'. *International Organisation*, 47(3), 443–78.

Hall, P. A. (1986) *Governing the Economy*. Cambridge: Polity Press.

Hall, P. A. (1989) 'Introduction'. In P. A. Hall (ed.), *The Political Power of Economic Ideas: Keynesianism Across Nations*. Princeton, NJ: Princeton University Press.

Hall, P. A. and Taylor, R. C. A. (1996) 'Political science and the three new institutionalisms'. *Political Studies*, 44(5), 936-57.

Ham, C. and Hill, M. (1984) *The Policy Process in the Modern Capitalist State*. Brighton: Wheatsheaf.

Hanley, D. (1994) 'Introduction: Christian Democracy as a political phenomenon'. In

D. Hanley (ed.), *Christian Democracy in Europe: A Comparative Perspective*. London: Pinter.

Hart, J. (1976) 'Three approaches to the measurement of power in international relations'. *International Organisation*, 30(2), 289–305.

Hay, C. (1996) 'Structure and agency'. In D. Marsh and G. Stoker (eds), *Theories and Methods in Political Science*. Basingstoke: Macmillan.

Haywood, E. (1993) 'The European policy of François Mitterrand'. *Journal of Common Market Studies*, 31(2), 269–82.

Heathcoat-Amory, D. (1996) 'A Single European Currency: why the United Kingdom must say no'. *European Journal*, September, 6–9.

Heclo, H. (1974) *Modern Social Policies in Britain and Sweden*. New Haven, CT: Yale University Press.

HMG (1984) 'Europe – the Future'. *Journal of Common Market Studies*, 23(1), 73–81.

Heseltine, M. (1987) *Where There's a Will*. London: Arrow.

Heseltine, M. (1991) *The Challenge of Europe: Can Britain Win*. London: Pan.

Hirst, P. and Thompson, G. (1996) *Globalization in Question: The International Economy and the Possibilities of Governance*. Cambridge: Polity.

Hobsbawm, E. J. (1969) *Industry and Empire*. Harmondsworth: Penguin.

Hoffman, S. (1989) 'The European Community and 1992'. *Foreign Affairs*, 68(4), 27-47.

Holland, R. (1991) *The Pursuit of Greatness: Britain and the World Role, 1900–1970*. London: Fontana.

Hollis, M. (1994) *The Philosophy of Social Science*. Cambridge: Cambridge University Press.

Holmes, M. (1982) *Political Pressure and Economic Policy*. London: Butterworth.

Holmes, M. (1985) *The Labour Government, 1974–79*. Basingstoke: Macmillan.

Holmes, M. (ed.), (1996) *The Euro-sceptical Reader*. Basingstoke: Macmillan.

Horne, A. (1989) *Macmillan 1957–1986*. Basingstoke: Macmillan.

Howe, G. (1982) *Conservatism in the Eighties*. London: Conservative Political Centre.

Howe, G. (1988) *The Conservative Revival of Britain*. London: Conservative Political Centre.

Howe, G. (1990) 'Sovereignty and interdependence: Britain's place in the world'. *International Affairs*, 66(4), 675–95.

Howe, G. (1994) *Conflict of Loyalty*. London: Macmillan.

Hurd, D. (1981) 'Political co-operation'. *International Affairs*, 57(3), 383–93.

Hurd, D. (1993) *Our Future in Europe*. London: Conservative Political Centre.

Jacobs, F. (1990) *The European Parliament*. Boulder, CO: Westview.

Jacquemin, A. and Sapir, A. (eds) (1989) *The European Internal Market: Trade and Competition*. Oxford: Oxford University Press.

James, A. (1986) *Sovereign Statehood*. London: Allen and Unwin.

Jay, D. (1980) *Change and Fortune*. London: Hutchinson.

Jessop, B., Bonnet, K., Bromley, S. and Ling, T. (1988) *Thatcherism: A Tale of Two Nations*. Cambridge: Polity.

Johnson, P. (1986) 'EEC trickery that Thatcher must halt'. *The Times*, 23 June.

Jones, M. (1992) 'The Major mess'. *Sunday Times*, 27 September.

Jordan, A. (1999) National ministries: managers or cyphers of European integration? Paper presented to the European Consortium of Political Research, Mannheim, Germany, 26–31 March.

Judge, D. (1988) 'Incomplete sovereignty: the British House of Commons and the internal market'. *Parliamentary Affairs*, 57(3), 321–8.

Judge, D. (1993) *The Parliamentary State*. London: Sage.

Kavanagh, D. (1990) *Thatcherism and British Politics*, 2nd edn. Oxford: Oxford University Press.

Kavanagh, D. and Morris, P. (1994) *Consensus Politics from Attlee to Major*, 2nd edn. Oxford: Blackwell.

Kennedy, P. (1981) *The Realities Behind Diplomacy*. London: Fontana.

King, A. (1975) 'Overload: problems of governing in the 1970s'. *Political Studies*, 23, 284–96.

Kirchner, E. J. (1989) 'The Federal Republic of Germany in the European Community'. In P. Merkl (ed.), *The Federal Republic of Germany at Forty*. Cambridge: Cambridge University Press.

Kitzinger, U. (1973) *Diplomacy and Persuasion*. London: Thames and Hudson.

Kramer, H. (1993) 'The European Community's response to the "New Eastern Europe"'. *Journal of Common Market Studies*, 31(2), 213–44.

Krasner, S. (ed.) (1983) *International Regimes*. Ithaca, NY: Cornell University Press.

Langrish, S. (1998) 'The Treaty of Amsterdam: selected highlights'. *European Law Review*, 23 (February), 3–19.

Lawson, N. (1992) *The View from Number Eleven*. London: Bantam.

Leach, S. and Stewart, J. (1982) *Approaches to Public Policy*. London: Allen and Unwin.

Levy, D. A. L. (1987) 'Foreign Policy: Business as Usual?' In S. Mazey and M. Newman (eds), *Mitterrand's France*. London: Croom Helm.

Lieber, R. J. (1970) *British Politics and European Unity*. Berkeley: University of California Press.

Lindblom, C. E. (1959) 'The science of "muddling through"'. *Public Administration Review*, 19, 79–88.

Lindblom, C. E. (1979) 'Still muddling, not yet through'. *Public Administration Review*, 39, 517–26.

Lodge, J. (1986) 'The Single European Act: towards a new European dynamism?' *Journal of Common Market Studies*, 24(3), 203–23.

Lo Faro, A. (1992) 'EC social policy and 1993: the dark side of European integration?' *Comparative Labour Law Journal*, 14(1), 1–32.

Lord, C. (1993) *British Entry to the European Community under the Heath Government, 1970–74*. Aldershot: Dartmouth.

Ludlam, S. (1996) 'The spectre haunting Conservatism: Europe and backbench rebellion'. In S. Ludlam and M. J. Smith (eds), *Contemporary British Conservatism*. Basingstoke: Macmillan.

Luttwak, E. (1997) 'Central bankism'. In P. Gowan and P. Anderson (eds), *The Question of Europe*. London: Verso.

Lynch, P. (1998) 'Conservative statecraft, European integration and the politics of nationhood'. Paper presented to the Political Studies Association Annual Conference, University of Keele.

McCarthy, P. (1993) 'Condemned to partnership: the Franco-German relationship, 1944–83'. In P. McCarthy (ed.), *France–Germany, 1983–93: The Struggle to Cooperate*. Basingstoke: Macmillan.

Macmillan, H. (1972) *Pointing the Way, 1959–61*. Basingstoke: Macmillan.

Madge, J. (1953) *The Tools of Social Science*. London: Longman.

Major, J. (1993) 'Raise your eyes, there is a land beyond'. *Economist*, 25 September.

Malcolm, N. (1996) 'Sense on sovereignty'. In M. Holmes (ed.), *The Euro-sceptical Reader*. Basingstoke: Macmillan.

March, J. and Olson, J. (1989) *Rediscovering Institutions: The Organizational Basis of Politics*. New York: The Free Press.

Marquand, D. (1988) *The Unprincipled Society*. London: Fontana.

Marsh, D. (1992) *The New Politics of British Trade Unionism*. Ithaca, NY: ILR Press.

Marsh D. (1995) 'Explaining "Thatcherite" policies: beyond uni-dimensional explanation'. *Political Studies*, 43(4), 595–613.

Marsh, D. and Rhodes, R. (eds) (1992) *Implementing Thatcherite Policies*. Buckingham: Open University Press.

Marsh, D. and Stoker, G. (eds) (1995) *Theories and Methods in Political Science*. Basingstoke: Macmillan.

Middlemas, K. (1994) 'The party, industry, and the city'. In A. Seldon and S. Ball (eds), *Conservative Century: The Conservative Party Since 1900*. Oxford: Oxford University Press.

Middleton, R. (1985) *Towards a Managed Economy: Keynes, the Treasury and the Fiscal Debate of the 1930s*. London: Methuen.

Milward, A. S. (1994) *The European Rescue of the Nation State*. London: Routledge.

Minford, P. (ed.) (1992) *The Cost Of Europe*. Manchester: Manchester University Press.

Moravcsik, A. (1991) 'Negotiating the Single European Act'. In R. Keohane and S. Hoffman (ed.), *The New European Community*. Oxford: Westview Press.

Moravcsik, A. (1993) 'Preferences and power in the European Community: a liberal intergovernmentalist approach'. *Journal of Common Market Studies*, 31(4), 473–524.

Morgan, K. O. (1984) *Labour In Power, 1945–51*. Oxford: Clarendon Press.

Murray, I. (1984) 'Britain remains a Euro-outsider'. *The Times*, 20 March.

Nicoll, W. and Salmon, T. C. (1994) *Understanding the New European Community*. London: Harvester Wheatsheaf.

Nolling, W. (1997) 'The test-tube currency'. *Financial Times*, 19 May.

Nordlinger, E. (1981) *On the Autonomy of the Democratic State*. Cambridge, MA: Harvard University Press.

Nordlinger, E. (1988) 'The return to the state: critiques'. *American Political Science Review*, 82(3), 875–85.

Norman, P. (1997) 'In storm-tossed waters'. *Financial Times*, 30 May.

Northedge, F. S. (1983) 'Britain and the EEC: past and present'. In R. Jenkins (ed.), *Britain and the EEC*. London: Macmillan.

Nuttall, S. J. (1992) *European Political Co-operation*. Oxford: Clarendon Press.

Owen, R. and Dynes, M. (1990) *The Times Guide to 1992*. London: Times Books.

Palmer, J. (1982) 'Britain and the EEC: the withdrawal option'. *International Affairs*, 58(4), 638–47.

Panic, M. (1982) 'Monetarism in an open economy'. *Lloyds Bank Review*, 145 (July), 36–47.

Pepper, G. (1998) *Inside Thatcher's Monetarist Revolution*. Basingstoke: Macmillan/IEA.

Peterson, J. (1992) 'The European Community'. In D. Marsh and R. A. W. Rhodes (eds), *Implementing Thatcherite Policies*. Buckingham: Open University Press.

Peterson, J. (1994) 'Subsidiarity: a definition to suit any vision?' *Parliamentary Affairs*, 47(1), 116–32.

Pierson, P. (1996) 'The path to European integration: a historical institutionalist analysis'. *Comparative Political Studies*, 29(2), 123–63.

Ponting, C. (1989) *Breach of Promise*. London: Hamish Hamilton.

Portillo, M. (1998) *Democratic Values and the Currency: Occasional Paper 103*. London: Institute for Economic Affairs.

Powell, E. (1971) *The Common Market: The Case Against*. Kingswood: Elliot Right Way/ Paperfront.

Preston, J. (1992) 'Local government and the European Community'. In S. George (ed.), *Britain and the European Community*. Oxford: Clarendon Press.

Radice, G. (1992) *Offshore: Britain and the European Idea*. London: Tauris.

Rattner, S. (1997) 'Midsummer madness'. *Financial Times*, 18 June.

Redwood, J. (1997) *Our Currency, Our Country: The Dangers of European Monetary Union*. Harmondsworth: Penguin.

Rhodes, R. A. W. (1995) 'The Institutional Approach'. in D. Marsh and G. Stoker (eds), *Theory and Methods in Political Science*. Basingstoke: Macmillan.

Rhodes, R. (1997) 'Organising perspectives on British government'. Paper to the ESRC Whitehall Conference on Whitehall in the 1950s and 1960s, Public Records Office. Kew, 17–19 April.

Rice, R. (1995) 'Europe casts a long shadow over British domestic law'. *Financial Times*, 3 August.

Ridley, N. (1990) Speech to the Bruges Group, reproduced in *Shared Thoughts, Shared Values: Occasional Paper 11*. London: The Bruges Group.

Ridley, N. (1992) *My Style of Government*. London: Fontana.

Roll, E. (1985) *Crowded Hours*. London: Faber.

Rometsch, D. (1996) 'The Federal Republic of Germany'. In D. Rometsch and W. Wessels (eds), *The European Union and Member States*. Manchester: Manchester University Press.

Ross, G. (1995) *Jacques Delors and European Integration*. Cambridge: Polity.

Sanders, D. (1990) *Losing an Empire, Finding a Role*. Basingstoke: Macmillan.

Sanders, D. (1997) 'Voting and the electorate'. In P. Dunleavy, A. Gamble, I. Holliday and G. Peele (eds), *Developments in British Politics 5*. Basingstoke: Macmillan.

Sandholtz, W. (1993) 'Choosing union: monetary politics and Maastricht'. *International Organisation*, 47(1), 1–39.

Sandholtz, W. and Zysman, J. (1989) '1992 – re-casting the European bargain'. *World Politics*, 42(1), 95–128.

Sayer, A. (1992) *Method in Social Science: A Realist Approach*, 2nd edn. London: Routledge.

Scharpf, F. W. (1988) 'The joint-decision trap: lessons from German federalism and European integration'. *Public Administration*, 66 (Autumn), 239–78.

Schmuck, O. (1987) 'The European Parliament's Draft Treaty Establishing the European Union'. In R. Pryce (ed.), *The Dynamics of European Union*. London: Croom Helm.

Schott, K. (1982) 'The rise of Keynsian economics: Britain 1940–64'. *Economy and Society*, 11(3), 292–316.

Scott, A. (1986) 'Britain and the EMS: an Appraisal of the Report of the Treasury and Civil Service Select Committee'. *Journal of Common Market Studies*, 24(3), 187–201.

Seldon, A. (1997) *Major: A Political Life*. London: Weidenfeld & Nicolson.

Shanks, M. (1977) *Planning and Politics: The British Experience 1960–76*. London: George Allen and Unwin/Political and Economic Planning.

Shore, P. (1983) 'Ignore the scare stories: its time to get out'. *The Times*, 4 January.

Singer, J. D. (1961) 'The level of analysis problem in international relations'. In K. Knorr and S. Verba (eds), *The International System: Theoretical Essays*. Princeton, NJ: Princeton University Press.

Siune, K. and Svensson, P. (1993) 'The Danes and the Maastricht Treaty: the Danish EC Referendum of June 1992'. *Electoral Studies*, 12(2), 99–111.

Sjoblom, G. (1982) 'Some problems with the operational code approach'. In C. Jonsson (ed.), *Cognitive Dynamics and International Politics*. London: Pinter.

Skocpol, T. (1979) *States and Social Revolutions*. Cambridge, MA: Harvard University Press.

Skocpol, T. (1985) 'Bringing the state back in; strategies of analysis in current research'. In P. Evans *et al.* (eds), *Bringing the State Back In*. Cambridge: Cambridge University Press.

Smith, D. (1987) *The Rise and Fall of Monetarism*. Harmondsworth: Penguin.

Smith, D. (1992) *From Boom to Bust*. Harmondsworth: Penguin.

Smith, M. J. (1993) *Pressure, Power and Policy*. London: Harvester Wheatsheaf.

Sowemimo, M. (1996) 'The Conservative Party and European integration'. *Party Politics*, 2(1), 77–97.

Spicer, M. (1992) *A Treaty Too Far*. London: Fourth Estate.

Steinmo, S., Thelen, K. and Longstreth, F. (1992) *Structuring Politics: Historical Institutionalism in Comparative Analysis*. Cambridge: Cambridge University Press.

Stephens, P. (1996) *Politics and the Pound*. Basingstoke: Macmillan.

Story, D. and Taylor, T. (1982) *The Conservative Party and the Common Market*. London: Monday Club.

Story, J. (1997) 'The idea of the core: the dialectics of history and space'. In G. Edwards and A. Pijpers (eds), *The Politics of European Treaty Reform: The 1996 Intergovernmental Conference and Beyond*. London: Pinter.

Strauss-Kahn, D. (1997) 'We're in this together'. *Financial Times*, 27 November.

Swann, D. (1996) *European Economic Integration: The Common Market, European Union and Beyond*. Cheltenham: Edward Elgar.

Taylor, A. (1994) 'The party and the trade unions'. In A. Seldon and S. Ball (eds), *Conservative Century: The Conservative Party Since 1900*. Oxford: Oxford University Press.

Taylor, R. (1993) *The Trade Union Question in British Politics*. Oxford: Blackwell.

Taylor, T. (1982) 'Enough of this EEC socialism'. *The Times*, 21 July.

Tebbit, N. (1989) *Upwardly Mobile*. London: Futura.

Tebbit, N. (1994) 'Concern for identity'. *European Journal*, 1(4), 3–4.

Thatcher, M. (1977) *Let Our Children Grow Tall: Selected Speeches, 1975–77*. London: Centre For Policy Studies.

Thatcher, M. (1993) *The Downing Street Years*. London: HarperCollins.

Thatcher, M. (1995) *The Path to Power*. London: HarperCollins.

Thompson, H. (1995) 'Joining the ERM: analysing a core-executive policy disaster'. In R. Rhodes and P. Dunleavy (eds), *Prime Minister, Cabinet and the Core Executive*. Basingstoke: Macmillan.

Thompson, H. (1996) *The British Conservative Government and the European Exchange Rate Mechanism*. London: Pinter.

Tindale, S. (1992) 'Learning to love the market: Labour and the European Community'. *Political Quarterly*, 63(3), 276–300.

Tomlinson, J. (1994) *Government and the Enterprise Since 1900: The Changing Problem of Efficiency*. Oxford: Clarendon Press.

Tsoukalis, L. (1993) *The New European Economy*, 2nd edn. Oxford: Oxford University Press.

Van Kersbergen, K. and Verbeek, B. (1994) 'The politics of subsidiarity in the European Union'. *Journal of Common Market Studies*, 32(2), 215–36.

Walker, P. (1991) *Staying Power*. London: Bloomsbury.

Wallace, H. (1986) 'The British Presidency of the European Community's Council of Ministers: the opportunity to persuade'. *International Affairs*, 62(4), 583–94.

Wallace, H. (1996) 'Britain out on a limb'. *Political Quarterly*, 66(1), 46–58.

Wallace, H. (1997) 'At odds with Europe'. *Political Studies*, 45(4), 677–88.

Wallace, W. (1986) 'What price independence? Sovereignty and interdependence in British politics'. *International Affairs*, 62(3), 367–90.

Wallace, W. and Wallace, H. (1990) 'Strong state or weak state in foreign policy? The contradictions of Conservative liberalism, 1979–87'. *Public Administration*, 68(1), 83–101.

Walters, A. (1990) *Sterling in Danger*. London: Fontana.

Weiler, J. H. H. (1993) 'Journey to an unknown destination: a retrospective and prospective view of the European Court of Justice in the arena of political integration'. *Journal of Common Market Studies*, 31(4), 417–46.

Weiner, M. J. (1981) *English Culture and the Decline of the Industrial Spirit, 1850–1980*. Harmondsworth: Penguin.

Weir, M. (1989) 'Ideas and politics: the acceptance of Keynesianism in Britain and the United States'. In P. Hall (ed.), *The Political Power of Economic Ideas*. Princeton, NJ: Princeton University Press.

Weir, M. and Skocpol, T. (1985) 'State structures and the possibilities for 'Keynesian' responses to the great depression in Sweden, Britain and the United States'. In P. Evans *et al.* (eds), *Bringing the State Back In*. Cambridge: Cambridge University Press.

Welfens, Paul J. J. (1993) 'The New Germany in the EC'. In A. W. Cafruny and G. G. Rosenthal (eds), *The State of the European Community, Vol. 2: Maastricht Debates and Beyond*. Harlow: Longman.

Wendt, A. (1987) 'The agent–structure problem in international relations theory'. *International Organisation*, 41(3), 335–70.

Wilks, S. (1996) 'Britain and Europe: an awkward partner or an awkward state?' *Politics*, 16(3), 159–65.

Winch, D. (1969) *Economics and Policy*. London: Fontana.

Wincott, D. (1994) 'Is the Treaty of Maastricht an adequate "constitution" for the European Union?' *Public Administration*, 72 (Winter), 573–90.

Wood, D. (1981) 'An anti-EEC political portent'. *The Times*, 27 April.

Young, H. (1989) *One of Us*. London: Pan.

Young, J. W. (1993) *Britain and European Unity: 1945–92*. London: Macmillan.

Index

Afghanistan
  invasion by Soviet Union   99–100
alliance building   17, 57, 100, 134
Amsterdam Summit   153, 156–7
Amsterdam Treaty   149
Andreotti, Guilio   115
appeasement, policy of   27
Ardagh, John   89–90
Athens Summit (1983)   65
Attlee government   29–31
automatism
  centrality of to governing policy   22–3, 29,
    48, 170
  EU membership and re-establishment of
    principles of   37, 41–2
  and New Conservatism   48, 51
  qualities of   27
  replacement of by more discretionary style of
    economic management   32
autonomy strategy   85, 165
  core of governing code   10, 29, 48
  criticism and limits of Europeanization in
    furthering   86, 125, 137, 141, 144–5,
    150–1, 160–3, 168
  defined   10
  Europeanization of economic policy as route
    to   23, 37, 41–2, 45, 46, 47, 68, 77–9, 82,
    87, 124, 127, 128, 129, 166, 167, 169
  and gold standard   26, 28
  loss of   37
  and New Conservatism   49–55, 166
  and Parliament   161
  principles that have been important in
    protecting   169–70
  support of by external policy 31, 48, 166

balance of power issue   133–4

Bank of England   50, 126, 132, 155
  and independence   128–9, 154, 171
banks 50, 58–9
  see also European Central Bank
Basle-Nyborg accords   122–3
Benn, S.   142
Benn, Tony   44–5, 55
Berlin Wall, fall of   121, 167
Biffen, John   54, 73
Black Wednesday   4, 5, 141, 159–60
Bosnia   147
'bounded rationality' model   13
Bretton Woods   33, 60, 169
Brioni Agreement   147
British Leyland   35, 44–5
Brown, George   33
Bulpitt, Jim   6–7, 9, 10–11, 12–13, 14, 15–16,
    17, 19, 26, 143
Bundesbank   74, 120–1, 122, 122- 3, 128, 135,
    149, 158
Butler, Sir Michael   66, 101, 104

Cabinet Office Legal Advisers (COLA)   3
  European Secretariat   3, 100, 108, 109, 110,
    112, 113
Callaghan government   35, 40, 44
Campaigning for a Fairer Britain   84
Castle, Barbara   40, 44
Cecchini Report   71, 83
central banks   134, 135
  see also European Central Bank
Christian Democratic parties   57
Clarke, Kenneth   157
Cockfield, Lord   92, 94–5, 95–6, 111
'cold shower' thesis   42
Cold War   145
Common Agricultural Policy (CAP)   57–8, 64,
    66, 114

185

Common Fisheries Policy   153
Common Foreign and Security (CFSP)   146, 155
Communism
  collapse of in Eastern Europe   121–2
Competing Currencies plan   135
Conservative Party
  discourse on EU   55–8
  divisions over Europe   72–3, 76, 80, 126–7, 139
convergence criteria *see* EMU
Council of Ministers   2, 90, 97–8, 155
  and European Parliament   85, 105–6, 107–8
  and qualified majority voting   4, 85, 91, 97, 148–9
Court   6–7
  European integration and collapse of   119–20, 124–7, 167
Croatia   147
Crossman, Richard   42, 43–4

de Gaulle, Charles   41
deficit-financing   26
Delors, Jacques   95, 115–16, 123, 124, 126, 132–3, 133
Delors Report   130, 132
democracy   160–1
Denmark
  and Maastricht Treaty   148, 156
Denning, Lord   36
Department of Economic Affairs (DEA)   33
Deutschmark, shadowing of   4, 127–8, 137, 157, 159, 165
Development Councils   30
discretionary economic management
  attempt to replace   50–1, 52
  rise of   31–7, 47
Dondelinger Committee   107, 110–11
Dooge Committee   92, 97, 98, 106
'Draft Treaty on European Union'   102, 108–10, 113
'Dual Polity'   26–31

Eastern Europe   121–2, 145
Economic Development Councils (EDCs)   34
economic policy, Europeanization of
  acceptance of and reasons for   4–5, 10–12, 15, 20, 68, 69–82
economy
  decline   31–2, 166
  non-interventionist role   24–5
ECU 134–5, 135–6, 154
Edinburgh Summit (1992)   146
EEC Treaty   2
elections
  (1983)   84
  (1997)   159, 160
Elysee Treaty (1963)   114
Emerson Report   71
Empire   27–8, 29, 32, 43, 166

empiricism   171–2
EMS   56, 66, 120
EMU (Economic and Monetary Union)   5, 120, 155, 167
  concerns over   149
  convergence criteria   2, 5, 147, 149, 154–5, 156
  criticism of by Euro-sceptics   163
  and Delors Committee   126, 130, 132
  and ERM *see* ERM
  and Germany   123
  and Major   157
  opt-out from Stage Three by Britain   5, 154
  and SEA   115–16, 122, 124, 136
  setting up of IGC on   133
  and Thatcher   130–1, 133
ERM (Exchange Rate Mechanism)   4, 130, 131, 136, 151, 157
  arguments against entry by Euro-sceptics   76–7
  asymmetrical nature of   120–1
  attractions and benefits of membership   8, 73–4, 87, 121, 127, 128
  and Basle-Nyborg accords   122–3
  and bolstering of domestic autonomy   68, 77–9, 87, 127, 128, 129, 167, 169
  collapse of   5, 149, 156
  disputes within Conservative Party over membership   72–3, 76, 80
  and France   121, 122
  German influence   120, 121
  governing incompetence and crisis of   157–60, 161
  insulating of Court from domestic pressure   20, 68, 87
  joining of by Britain (1990)   138, 157–8, 165
  main features   120–1
  shift from marginal intervention to intra-marginal intervention within   120–1
  tensions within   121
  widening of fluctuation bands   5
EU (European Union)   37–47
  advantages and attractions of   23, 37, 38, 41–2, 56, 64–5, 166
  battle over budget contributions   17, 63–4, 65, 80–1, 89, 95
  Conservative Party's discourse on   55–8
  criticisms of advantages to economy   38–9
  effect on 'discretionary' regional policy   42
  enlargement   134, 145, 150
  gives opportunity to return to governing principles of autonomy and competence   23, 37, 41–2, 45, 46, 47, 166
  and Heath government   45–6
  and Labour Party   55, 64, 134
  seen as form of escapism for domestic problems by opposition   42–4
  and unemployment   64

and Wilson government   39–40
EU institutions   18–19, 129, 130, 154
    impact on SEA negotiations   89, 113–17
EU law   46, 47
Euro-enthusiasts   127–31, 135, 143
Euro-sceptics   66, 85, 85–6, 125, 131–8, 140–2,
    150–63, 167–8, 170
'Europe: The Future' (White Paper)   69–70, 82
European Central Bank   121, 122, 132, 135,
    149, 155
European, Commission   85–6, 95, 110, 148
    and fiscal harmonization   111–12
    furthering of European integration under
        Delors   115–16, 123, 124
    reports on Single Market   71, 75
    and social policy   154
    and trade policy   2
European Communities Act (1972)   46, 153
European Communities (Amendment) Bill   80,
    106, 162
European Court of Justice (ECJ)   108, 146,
    152–3
European Finance Bill (1995)   162
European integration
    limits to and subsiding of   144–50
European Monetary Fund (EMF)   135
European Parliament   4, 57, 85–6
    increase in powers issue   90–1, 92, 99, 104–8
    and Spinelli Treaty   90, 91, 92, 99, 105–6
European Political Cooperation (EPC)   82, 91,
    94, 99–103, 108–10, 167
European Union see EU
Evans, John   75–6
Exchange Equalisation Account   28
exchange rate 54, 58, 59–61, 73
    see also ERM
Exchange Rate Mechanism see ERM
excise duties   111, 112
exports   26, 53

Factortame Case (1991)   152–3
federalism   57
Feldman, Sir Basil   162
Fergusson, Adam   72, 80–2, 93, 113
financial markets, liberalization of   50, 169
fiscal harmonization   111–17
Fontainbleu Summit   63, 66, 69, 70, 71
Foot, Michael   80
Foreign Office
    divisions over EU between No. 10 and
        80–2, 101
foreign policy   2, 12, 17
France
    and completion of Single Market   91–2
    and ERM   121, 122
    on EU enlargement   145
    and increase in powers of European Parliament
        issue   105–7
    referendum on Maastricht Treaty   148

    tensions between Germany and   145, 149–50
Franco-German alliance   17, 100, 108–10,
    112–15, 120, 123
Francovitch and Boniface v. Italy (1991)   153

GATT   2, 168
Genscher-Colombo plan (1981)   90, 91
Germany   18, 74
    attempt at building alliance with by
        Britain   100
    balancing of power of   134
    and EMU   123
    on EU enlargement   145
    and increase in powers of European Parliament
        issue   106
    influence of on ERM   120, 121
    relationship with France 145, 149–50
        see also Franco-German alliance
    reunification   134, 145
Gill, Chris   162–3
globalization   60
gold standard   25, 26, 28, 161, 165, 169
governing code (definition)   6, 8, 19
Graham, Philip Lloyd   24–5

Hall, Peter A.   10
Hard ECU plan   134–5, 135–6
Hattersley, Roy   84
'heart of Europe' strategy   129, 130–1, 133,
    134, 140, 150, 156, 167
Heath government   35, 36, 45–6, 55, 65
Heathcoat-Amory, D.   162
Henderson, Nicholas   65
Heseltine, Michael   60, 79, 129, 130, 157
Hogg, Sarah   158
Howe, Geoffrey   58, 62, 67, 79–80, 83, 101–2,
    108, 125
    and EMU   136
    and EU development   70–1
    and Milan European Council   101–3
    Plan on Political Cooperation see European
        Political Cooperation
    resignation speech   129–30, 133, 138
    and Rome Treaty   92–3
    and SEA   97, 106, 126
    on sovereignty   142
Howell, David   65
Hurd, Douglas   57, 140

IGC (Intergovernmental Conference)   93, 102–3,
    113
Imperial Preference   28–9, 32, 43
In Place of Strife (White Paper)   36
incomes policy   35, 36, 51, 53
indirect institutional power   18
industrial relations   24, 35, 36, 50, 166, 169
Industrial Relations Act (1971)   36
Industrial Reorganization Corporation (IRC)   34
industrial subsidies   54–5

industry
  and EU membership 38, 39
Industry Act 34–5
inflation 49–50, 51, 58–9, 73, 74, 77, 78
Ingham, Bernard 61, 102–3
Institute of Directors (IoD) 83
institutions 2–4 *see also* EU institutions
Intergovernmental Conference *see* IGC
Internal Market Council 92
Iron and Steel Act (1967) 44
Italy 106, 112–13, 121, 149

Jay, Douglas 39–40, 42
Jay, Michael 156
Jenkins, Roy 40, 55, 66
Jessel, Toby 163
Justice and Home Affairs (JHA) 146

Keynesianism 29
Kinnock, Neil 84
Kohl, Helmut, Chancellor 90, 100, 108–10,
  113–14, 116, 132, 133, 145, 158

Labour Party
  and EU 55, 64, 80, 84, 134
Lamont, Norman, Chancellor 158
Lawson, Nigel 54, 67, 95, 112, 126, 132
  and Bundesbank 135
  and Competing Currencies plan 135
  and ERM 73, 74, 78–9, 127–8, 134
  and exchange rates 59–60, 60–1
  on Hard ECU plan 135–6
  and inflation 58, 59
  Mais lecture (1984) 62
  on MTFS 50–1
  and New Conservatism 49
  proposals for independent Bank of
    England 128–9
  resignation 138
  and shadowing of Deutschmark 4, 127–8,
    137, 157, 159, 165
  Sterling Crisis analysis 61
  on what makes a good politician 61–2
Leighton, Ron 86
Lever, Harold 45
limited responsibility 22–3, 26, 49–50
Lloyd George, David 25
London Passenger Transport Board 30
Lord President's Committee 30
Louvre Accord 128
Lubbers 130
Luxembourg Compromise 63, 64, 91, 96–9,
  105, 106
Luxembourg European Council 89, 103,
  115–16
Lynch, P. 143–4

Maastricht Treaty 4, 5, 140, 141, 145–8,
  151–2, 152–3, 155–6, 165
Macmillan, Harold 25, 33, 39, 41, 43, 44, 55

Madrid European Council (1989) 130–1, 133
Major government 129, 136, 138, 140, 150
  and ERM crisis 157–60
Major government (contd)
  and Maastricht Treaty 4, 146, 147
majority voting, extension of 4, 94, 91, 97,
  98–9, 111, 112, 116, 147, 165
Maudling, Reginald 42
Medium Term Financial Strategy *see* MTFS
MEPs 4, 85, 104–7
Merchant Shipping Act (1988) 153
mergers 34, 35
Milan European Council (1985) 79, 89, 96,
  101–3, 108–9, 112–14
miners' strike (1974) 36
miners' strike (1984/5) 62
Mitterand, François 90, 100, 105–6, 107, 108,
  109, 112–14, 116, 123, 148
monetarism 49–50, 52
  and challenge of international economic
    forces 20, 58–63, 68, 86, 166
'Morrison model' 30
mortgages 59
MTFS (Medium Term Financial Strategy) 50–1,
  54, 73, 77–8, 87, 159, 167, 169

National Economic Development Council
  (NEDC) 33
National Enterprise Board (NEB) 34, 35, 54
National Industrial Relations Court (NIRC) 36
National Mineworkers Union 35
National Prices and Incomes Board 35
National Union of Railwaymen 36
nationalization 29–30, 34–5, 44
nationhood 141–2, 143–4
NATO (North Atlantic Treaty
  Organization) 92, 148, 168
neutrality 22–3, 26, 32, 37, 42, 49, 50–1, 52,
  170
New Conservatism
  problems with 53–4
  and quest for governing competence 49–55,
    166
New Labour 171
Nissan 65
non-tariff barriers 71, 75, 85, 96, 98, 110
Noordwijk meeting (1997) 148
Nuttall, S.J. 100, 108, 109

oil prices, rise of 60, 61
Overseas Sterling Area (OSA) 23, 26, 28–9, 31,
  37, 166

Padraig, Flynn 154
Paris Summit (1960) 41
Paris Treaty 44
Parliament 46, 52, 85, 86
  see also European Parliament
parliamentary democracy 144, 151, 160–1

Partnership of Nations (White
    Paper) 153, 156
Perez, Laura 153
'personalism' 123–4
Plaza Agreement (1986) 121, 128
'political actor designation' 7–8
Political Argument Hegemony 6, 8, 10–11,
    63–5, 77, 82–4
Political Cooperation *see* European Political
    Cooperation
politicians
    qualities needed for success 61–2
Portillo, M. 162
Powell, Enoch 42–3
Prentice, Reg 45
Prior, Jim 51
Public Sector Borrowing Requirement
    (PSBR) 50
Pym, Francis 56, 65, 85, 98, 101

rationality 12–13, 14
Reaganomics 60
realism 15–16, 18
Redwood, J. 73, 155, 163
Reflection Group 148
Ridley, N. 55, 57, 73, 133–4, 138
Rifkind, Malcolm 83, 97, 98, 99, 106, 112,
    157
Right Approach to the Economy 54
Rippon, Geoffrey 66
Rome Summit (1990) 133
Rome, Treaty of 1, 45, 66, 89, 91, 93, 96, 98,
    102, 109, 116
'Russian doll strategy' 124

Schuman Plan 79
Scottish National Party (SNP) 16
SEA (Single European Act) 166–7
    Article (20) 136
    Delors on 124
    entrenchment of free-market supply-side
        strategy and maintaining unity of
        Court 20, 68, 79, 81–2, 84–5, 166–7
    impact on culture of the Community 126
    strengthening of cooperation procedure 4, 85
    and trade unions 116–17
    and Working Time Directive 152–3
SEA negotiations 5, 17, 77, 88–117, 119, 136,
    167
    achievement of aims by British
        negotiators 88, 103, 109, 167
    altering negotiating strategy from a cooperative
        to reactive approach 104–13, 116
    and Article 118a 116–17, 152
    attempt at building alliances with France and
        Germany 89, 94, 100, 103, 167
    attempt at frustrating institutional
        reform 94, 96–9, 103

attempt to develop pro-Community
    discourse 99, 101–3
building up of momentum behind Single
    Market project 94–6, 103
and Cockfield 95–6
and EMU 115–16, 122, 124, 136
and European Political Cooperation 82, 91,
    94, 99–101, 102, 103, 108–11, 167
fiscal harmonization negotiations at
    Luxembourg 111–14
and Franco-German alliance 109–10,
    113–14
impact of EU institutions on 89, 113,
    114–17
increase in powers of European Parliament
    issue 104–8
pursual of positive negotiating strategy 94
setbacks at Milan European Council 89,
    101–3, 113
unpopularity and isolation of British
    negotiators over completion of Single
    Market 89–94
Seamen's Strike (1966) 35
Seldon, A. 159, 162
Seymour-Smith, Nicole 153
Single Currency 1, 4, 126, 130, 131, 134, 154–5,
    155
    see also EMU
Single European Act *see* SEA
Single Market 82–3
    attempt to build up momentum behind 94–
        6, 103
    and business 83
    criticism of Commission's reports on benefits of
        completion 75
    enthusiasm for by the Court 69, 71–2
    entrenchment of free-market strategy through
        promotion of 68, 69, 77, 79–80, 87,
        166–7, 169
    governing advantages 77, 79–81
    ignoring of sceptical arguments against
        completion by Court 75–6
    lack of priority for by other countries 91–2
    link between unemployment and 70, 71,
        72
    obstacles hindering completion of 71
    unpopularity and isolation of British
        negotiators in promoting completion of
        89–94
    see also SEA negotiations
Smith, Adam 24
Smith, John 158, 159
Social Chapter 1, 154, 162
Social Charter 117
sovereignty 2, 141–4, 160
Soviet Union 99–100
Spinelli Treaty 90, 91, 92, 99, 105–6, 107
Stability Pact (1996) 155

statecraft   5–8
  advantages for examination of Europeanization
    on economic policy   6–7, 8, 11, 13, 14,
    16–17
  and foreign policy   17
  insights provided by   168–71
  limitations and concerns of   14, 19
  and realism   13, 15–16
  resting on assumptions   12–15
Sterling Bloc *see* Overseas
  Sterling Area
Sterling Crisis (1984–85)   61
Sterling Crisis (1986)   74
Stock Exchange   50
structural power, concept of   18
Stuttgart European Council (1983)   92
Stuttgart Declaration   90, 91
subsidiarity, concept of   5, 146, 151–2, 153
subsidies, industrial   54–5
Supplementary Special Deposits Scheme   50
supranationality   114, 167

Tapsell, Peter   159
Taylor, Teddy   66, 84
Tebbit, Norman   73, 163
territorial politics   16
Thatcher, Magaret   1, 51, 53, 54, 125, 136–7
  belligerent style towards Europe   66, 89–90,
    138
  and Delors Committee   126
  and EMU   130–1, 133
  and ERM   72–3, 76, 77, 138, 157
  and EU budget   63–4, 65–6, 80
  on extension of majority voting   98

and Madrid Summit   130–1, 133
and Milan European Council   102
resignation   138
speech to Institute of Directors (1976)   53
on tripartism   52
trade unions   32, 36–7, 45, 51, 116–17
  see also names of individual unions
Transport and General Workers Union   36
Treaty of Rome   90
Treaty on European Union *see* Maastricht Treaty
Tripartism   32, 33, 47, 49, 52, 53, 166
Tugendhat, Christopher   102

UK Permanent Representative (UK REP)   3
unanimity rule   93, 97–8, 111–12
unemployment   53, 61, 62–3
  and ERM membership   158
  and EU membership   64
  in inter-war years   25
  link with completion of Single Market   70,
    71, 72, 85
  rise of   58
unions *see* trade unions
United States   2, 27, 41, 134

'variable geometry', concept of 150
VAT   96, 111–12
voluntarism   22, 24–5, 29, 47, 166, 169

Walters, Alan   76, 77, 138
Western European Union (WEU)   2, 148
Wilson government   33, 34, 36, 39–40, 42, 43,
  44
Working Time Directive   152–3
Works Council Directive   153–4